IPHIGENIAS AT AULIS

Iphigenias at Aulis

TEXTUAL MULTIPLICITY, RADICAL PHILOLOGY

Sean Alexander Gurd

CORNELL UNIVERSITY PRESS

Ithaca and London

Frontispiece: Iphigenia at Aulis, from the "House of the Tragic Poet," Pompeii. By permission of the Fratelli Alinari Istituto di Edizioni Artistiche.

First published 2005 by Cornell University Press

Printed in the United States of America

Library of Congress Cataloging-in-Publication Data

Gurd, Sean Alexander, 1973–
Iphigenias at Aulis : textual multiplicity, radical philology / Sean Alexander Gurd.
p. cm.
Includes bibliographical references and index.
ISBN 0-8014-4329-6 (cloth : alk. paper)
1. Euripides. Iphigenia in Aulis. 2. Iphigenia (Greek mythology) in literature.
3. Euripides. Iphigenia in Aulis—Criticism, Textual. I. Title.
PA3973.I7G87 2005
882′.01—dc22 2004023505

Cornell University Press strives to use environmentally responsible suppliers and materials to the fullest extent possible in the publishing of its books. Such materials include vegetable-based, low-VOC inks and acid-free papers that are recycled, totally chlorine-free, or partly composed of nonwood fibers. For further information, visit our website at www.cornellpress.cornell.edu.

Cloth printing 10 9 8 7 6 5 4 3 2 1

For Julija,
and
for all who love

The unity of a world is not one: it is made of a diversity, and even disparity and opposition. It is in fact, which is to say that it does not add or subtract anything. The unity of a world is nothing other than its diversity, and this, in turn, is a diversity of worlds. A world is a multiplicity of worlds; the world is a multiplicity of worlds, and its unity is the mutual sharing and exposition of all its worlds—within this world.

JEAN-LUC NANCY (2000)

Contents

Preface

This book discusses thirteen different versions of Euripides' *Iphigenia at Aulis* as they were printed, hypothesized, or imagined by ten textual critics between 1762 and 2003. It contains an attempt to characterize textual criticism as a field defined by multiplicity and variation. It also contains a series of attempts to attend carefully and heedfully to each of its objects. Thus it shares its ambition with every other philological project. But if philology consists for some in training the vision "to see a whole landscape in a bean,"[1] I have tried to see each critical version pulsing with the rich plurality of many others: "the universe in a grain of sand."

My work on this project was sustained by a belief that every literary study of classical literature must be infused with knowledge of how it is produced. This does not simply mean studying authorial processes and publishing structures in antiquity; it also means studying the intellectual technology used in the production of those texts available to us—critical editions. Only a clear picture of how textual criticism produces and disseminates classical texts can provide a basis for their well-grounded literary study.

This work also arose out of simple curiosity about Euripides' *Iphigenia at Aulis*, a play that has changed considerably in the course of the last

1. Barthes 1975, 4.

250 years, as different textual critics developed different hypotheses about its form. I wanted to know more about this fascinating story of textual flux, and I wanted to know what kind of literary practice could continue in the face of texts that were perpetually changing. That is the goal of this book: to come to grips with the critical variation of Euripides' *Iphigenia at Aulis.* My intent is not to criticize textual criticism, which I believe is a necessary and unavoidable cultural practice, even one of considerable sophistication. Rather, my goal is to assess the realities involved in the multiple productions of a classical text so as to facilitate a literary philology alive to the fact of plurality. I call this a *radical philology.*

Part 1 outlines the case for a radical philology by emphasizing the important fact, clearly legible in the stacks of every university library, that critical editions vary, which is to say that classical texts continue to change. I conclude with three hypotheses intended to establish a philology intent on critical variability. My central proposition is that critical texts are *singular plural*—that every *single* edition models and reflects a *plurality* of other versions and variants—and that this singular plurality of the critical edition constitutes its *sense.*

Part 2 is a reading of Euripides' *Iphigenia at Aulis* through some of its texts. It is not a complete history of textual criticism on the play or an extended bibliographical essay; it is a limited discussion of some critical approaches to the play that I find particularly interesting, and an experiment aimed at developing and illustrating the radical philology proposed in part 1.

I do not know if I have succeeded in constructing a sustained or coherent argument. Writing, for me, means struggling to include within a single document a large number of specific encounters with texts, early-morning flashes of inspiration, chains of reasoning, and poetic images, each of which occurred at a different time and under different conditions. The book endured so many drafts and versions that I now think of it as a dense manifold, complexly related to the vicissitudes of my own emotional, intellectual, and scholarly life. From this perspective, however, I think the book could be a model for my idea of what the *Iphigenia at Aulis* became during the epoch of textual criticism: a richly faceted and inherently multiple text that reflects the history of modern scholarship as a convex mirror reflects the contents of an entire room, or as a cubist painting shows a complex plurality of spatial and temporal planes in artificial simultaneity. Whether and how this book is legible is related, I suppose, to the question it poses: whether and how *Iphigenias at Aulis* are legible.

During the research phase of this project I referred frequently to the usual manuals in the history of classical scholarship,[2] which proved indispensable for bibliographical purposes. If I do not cite them frequently, it is because they have pointed me to other works that I discuss in further depth. More recent work by Anthony Grafton, Leonard Barkan, James Porter, and David Ferris[3] was a great inspiration to me, but because our subjects are different I was unable to draw on them as much as they deserve.

Before going on, the reader unfamiliar with Euripides' *Iphigenia at Aulis* should get to know it, but a Greekless reader should be aware that translations, like critical editions, are not all the same. David Kovacs's recent Loeb is an excellent choice.[4] A reader who knows Greek would do well to use the Oxford edition of James Diggle;[5] for reasons I explain in chapter 5, Diggle's text is the basis for this book. Where reference to the play outside of specific editions is made, I cite the line numbers in Diggle's edition as follows: "xxx–yyy Diggle." Translations of Greek and Latin, unless otherwise noted, are my own. For all other languages I cite from readily available English translations.

I owe my thanks first and foremost to Julija Šukys, who continues to teach and inspire me; but also to Ahuvia Kahane, Robert Wallace, and Dan Garrison at Northwestern University, to the Mellon Foundation for the postdoctoral fellowship that allowed me to write this book at Northwestern, to the Alice Berline Kaplan Center for the Humanities, which helped in the conduct of the research, and to the Classical Traditions Initiative, both at Northwestern. Without libraries and archivists nothing is possible, and I owe much to Russell Maylone at Northwestern's Charles Deering McCormick Library of Special Collections, which contains a superb and underutilized collection in the history of philology; to the staff at Trinity College Library, Cambridge, and at the Cambridge University Library; to those who helped me negotiate the catalogue systems at the Bodleian Library at Oxford; to Joan Mertens and the Metropolitan Museum of Art; and to Richard Ratajczak and the Rare Books and Special Collections Library, University of Sydney. Oxford University Press graciously provided permission to reprint images from several works of textual criticism, as did the Alinari Picture Library: thanks to Alessandra Corti there. For the help and encouragement without which I would very quickly have abandoned the task, I owe thanks to Wojtek Fundamenski

2. Particularly Sandys 1967; Pfeiffer 1968; Kenney 1974; Wilamowitz-Moellendorff 1982; Brink 1986; Reynolds and Wilson 1991; and the work of Momigliano.
3. Grafton 1983, 1991; Barkan 1999 ; Ferris 2000; Porter 2000.
4. Euripides 2003 (ed. Kovacs).
5. Euripides 1994 (ed. Diggle) 3:357–425.

and Oriel College; to David Kovacs, James Porter and David Ferris, Chris Collard, Frances Muecke, and Rick Benitez; and to Bernhard Kendler, Marta Steele, Karen Hwa, and others at Cornell University Press, who all labored selflessly to ensure the completion of this work. Finally, I am most grateful to Brian Stock, who taught me and guides me, and whose scholarship is a model I will continue to strive to emulate.

Editions and Essays Discussed

This list includes only those editions and essays discussed at length. A fuller list of editions and commentaries is in the Works Cited.

Boeckh, A. 1808. *Graecae tragoediae principum, Aeschyli, Sophoclis, Euripidis, num ea, quae supersunt, et genuina omnia sint, et forma primitiva servata, an eorum familiis aliquid debeat ex iis tribui.* Heidelberg: Mohrii and Zimmeri.

Euripides (R. Porson, ed.). 1802. *Hekabe.* Cambridge: J. Burges.

—— (A. H. Matthiae, ed.). 1813–1837. *Tragoediae et Fragmenta.* 10 vols. Leipzig: I. A. G. Weigel.

—— (G. Hermann, ed.). 1831. *Tragoediae.* Leipzig: Weidmann.

—— (J. A. Hartung, ed.). 1837. *Iphigenia in Aulide.* Erlangen: J. J. Palmii and E. Enkii.

—— (E. B. England, ed.). 1891. *The Iphigenia at Aulis.* London: Macmillan.

—— (J. Diggle, ed.). 1994. *Fabulae.* 3 vols. Oxford: Clarendon.

—— (D. Kovacs, ed. and trans.). 2003. *Bacchae, Iphigenia at Aulis, Rhesus.* Cambridge: Harvard University Press.

Hermann, G. 1816. *Elementa doctrinae metricae.* Leipzig: Fleischer.

—— 1877. "De interpolationibus Euripideae *Iphigeniae in Aulide* dissertatio (1847–1848)." In *Opuscula,* edited by T. Fritzsche, 218–242. Leipzig: Fleischer.

Musgrave, S. 1762. *Exercitationum in Euripidem.* Leiden: Dammeanus.

Page, D. 1934. *Actors' Interpolations in Greek Tragedy.* Oxford: Clarendon.

Porson, R. 1812. "Praelectio in Euripidem." In *Adversaria,* edited by J. H. Monk. Cambridge: Joannes Smith.

PART 1

Introduction to Part 1

The monumental histories of philology by August Boeckh, John Edwin Sandys, Ulrich von Wilamowitz-Moellendorff, and Rudolf Pfeiffer presented themselves as grand *summae* of self-definition:[1] as Pascale Hummel showed, these authors aimed to stake out an epistemological and ontological terrain where, for the most part, orthodox practitioners have continued to reside.[2] Once this had been done, the study of the history of philology migrated to other disciplines, such as the cultural history of early modern Europe,[3] while professional classicists for the most part acquiesced to the old master-narratives. Times, however, have changed, and today, as James Porter puts it, "There is no single vantage point from which the totality of classical studies can be viewed, let alone controlled";[4] we might add that the borders of classical studies have become porous as well. To the hybrid formations of modern scholarship the old narratives of disciplinary purity have lost much of their attraction.

This is not to say that writing the history of philology has faltered. Some recent scholars, steeped in poststructuralist discourse, approach

1. Boeckh 1886; Sandys 1967; Pfeiffer 1968; Wilamowitz-Moellendorff 1982.

2. Hummel 2000.

3. One thinks immediately of Anthony Grafton, but also of a host of others working in the underappreciated regions of "neo-Latin."

4. Porter 2000.

the history of the discipline and its aspirations in the light of postcolonial identities, gender theory, and interdisciplinarity[5] or use nineteenth-century philology as a foil for the corporatization of the modern university (though here the figures of Alexander von Humboldt, Friedrich August Wolf, and Boeckh are sometimes held up slightly uncritically as counterexamples).[6] These studies emphasize the contingency of the field of classical studies and its involvement in broader cultural trends. Far from being an autonomous "science," they imply, the field of classical studies is in a complex relationship of mutual feedback with greater contexts. As a counter to old orthodoxies, this work has great value, but its liminal position vis-à-vis the mainstream of classical studies mutes its effect. For critical work of this ilk to play a decisive role in the creation of a new charter for the practice of philology, there is needed a vision more at home with the technical procedures of classics, where the quasi-autonomous functioning of subdisciplines like textual criticism play an influential role in the proliferation of subjects and trajectories.

Here a second source of contemporary work in the history of philology is relevant. For technical subdisciplines like textual criticism never rest from constant and pervasive investigation into the history of scholarship. It would be inconceivable for a critical edition to emerge if its producer had not made a serious effort to achieve a critical understanding of the centuries of work that came before; indeed, the apparatus of a modern critical edition, like the notes in *variorum* editions, is a condensed history of philology. Hardly an ancillary discourse, the history of philology is an integral part of the fabric of textual study. It would be a misreading of a contemporary critical edition to believe that it presents *the* text of a classical author in a pristine condition devoid of history, and (notwithstanding the protests of some of its practitioners) it would be a misapprehension of the project of textual criticism in general to believe that it aims simply to negate history, to defy it in a return to some chronological origin. The close complication of the history of scholarship and the project of textual criticism is exemplified by Reynolds and Wilson's *Scribes and Scholars*, a history of scholarship that presents itself in recognizably text-critical terms as a "guide to the transmission of Greek and Latin literature."[7] In the very bowels of classical philology, in other words, lies the material for an immanent critique missing from the more critical histories of philology mentioned above.

It is a crossbreeding of these two kinds of history—the exoteric and

5. Marchand 1996; Stray 1998; Prins 1999; Morris 2000; Goldhill 2002.
6. I am thinking here in particular of Readings 1996 and Asensi and Miller 1999.
7. Reynolds and Wilson 1991.

the esoteric—that I propose under the name of radical philology. My starting point is the fact of plurality. Critical texts differ, and this difference is fundamental. I am not the first to have turned a critical eye on the history of textual criticism; Jean Bollack's *Oedipus Rex* is a significant forerunner (and much more exhaustive than my small offering), as is the work done by Hummel on the Pindaric epithet from a diachronic and synchronic perspective.[8] I differ from these scholars, however, in my aim; Bollack focused on the history of textual criticism to challenge and problematize that history, and to remind his readers of the contingency and historicity of the text-critical project. I do not believe that this is necessary; the historicity of textual scholarship is as well known to textual critics as it is to everyone else.[9] What is needed instead is a means of *performing* this knowledge, of transforming contingency from an embarrassing fact into the basic core (or the fundamental abyss) of a new critico-interpretive practice. Radical philology will attempt this by heeding the complex histories condensed in every critical edition. This will, as I hope to show, empower a literary practice that can move within the pluralities of textual experience, actualize their promise, and avoid the pitfalls of naive historicism. I begin, however, with an argument for the necessity of such an approach based on the empirical datum that critical texts differ.

8. Bollack 1990; Hummel 1999.

9. Hugh Lloyd-Jones's unfortunate reaction to this edition ("I have struggled through it without finding that the deadly boredom of the task and the fury occasioned by the unspeakable pretentiousness of the monstrous work were compensated by the discovery of one thing that increased my understanding" [Lloyd-Jones 1992]), while unjust, nevertheless points to an important fact: *merely* reciting the historicity of classical scholarship has the effect of telling people what they already knew, only in more detail.

1

On Critical Variation and a Sacrifice

Like thumbprints, every critical edition of Euripides' *Iphigenia at Aulis* is unique. Editions differ from each other in small details like punctuation, capitalization, and the attribution of speakers:

> Αγ. τίς ποτ' ἄρ' ἀστὴρ ὅδε πορθμεύει
> σείριος ἐγγὺς τῆς ἑπταπόρου
> Πλειάδος ᾄσσων ἔτι μεσσήρης;

AGAMEMNON. What is that baleful star traveling there, still darting in the middle of the sky near the sevenfold route of the Pleiades?[1]

> Αγ. τίς ποτ' ἄρ' ἀστὴρ ὅδε πορθμεύει;
> Πρ. Σείριος ἐγγὺς τῆς ἑπταπόρου
> Πλειάδος ᾄσσων ἔτι μεσσήρης.

AGAMEMNON. What is that star traveling there?
OLD SLAVE. It is Sirius, still darting in the middle of the sky near the sevenfold route of the Pleiades.[2]

They differ in the individual words they print:

> Αγ. τίς ποτ' ἄρ' ἀστὴρ ὅδε πορθμεύει;
> Πρ. Σείριος ἐγγὺς τῆς ἑπταπόρου
> Ἑλίκης ᾄσσων ἔτι μεσσήρης.

1. Euripides 1994 (ed. Diggle), vv. 6–8.
2. Euripides 1899 (ed. Wecklein and Prinz), vv. 6–8.

AGAMEMNON. What is that star traveling there?
OLD SLAVE. It is Sirius, still darting in the middle of the sky near the sevenfold route of Helike.[3]

Different lines are printed in different orders in different editions:

Αγ. πέμπω σοι πρὸς ταῖς πρόσθεν
δέλτους, ὦ Λήδας ἔρνος ...
Πρ. λέγε καὶ σήμαιν', ἵνα καὶ γλώσσῃ
σύντονα τοῖς σοῖς γράμμασιν αὐδῶ.
Αγ. μὴ στέλλειν τὰν σὰν ἶνιν πρὸς
τὰν κολπώδη πτέρυγ' Εὐβοίας
Αὖλιν ἀκλύσταν.

AGAMEMNON. Oh daughter of Leda, I send to you this letter in addition to my earlier one—
OLD SLAVE. Tell me and signify, so that with my tongue I may speak things in harmony with your letters.
AGAMEMNON. Do not send your daughter to the waveless bay of Aulis, the wing of Euboea.[4]

Πρ. λέγε καὶ σήμαιν', ἵνα καὶ γλώσσῃ
σύντονα τοῖς σοῖς γράμμασιν αὐδῶ.
Αγ. πέμπω σοι πρὸς ταῖς πρόσθεν
δέλτοις, ὦ Λήδας ἔρνος,
μὴ στέλλειν τὰν σὰν ἶνιν πρὸς
τὰν κολπώδη πτέρυγ' Εὐβοίας
Αὖλιν ἀκλύσταν.

OLD SLAVE. Tell me and signify, so that with my tongue I may speak things in harmony with your letters.
AGAMEMNON. In addition to my earlier letter, oh daughter of Leda, I send to you this: Do not send your daughter to the waveless bay of Aulis, the wing of Euboea.[5]

Different lines are evaluated as genuine or spurious differently in different editions, their status attributed to different processes of interpolation or deformation:

- †ἔμολες, ὦ Πάρις, ᾗτε σύ γε† (epode)
  βουκόλος ἀργενναῖς ἐτράφης
  Ἰδαίαις παρὰ μόσχοις,
  βάρβαρα συρίζων, Φρυγίων

3. Euripides 1837 (ed. Hartung), vv. 67–69.
4. Euripides 1913 (ed. Murray), vv. 115–121. δέλτους in 116 is for δέλτοις in L and P.
5. Euripides 1771 (ed. Markland), vv. 115–121.

αὐλῶν Οὐλύμπου καλάμοις
μιμήματα †πνέων†.
εὔθηλοι δὲ τρέφοντο βόες,
†ὅτι σε κρίσις ἔμενε† θεᾶν,
ἅ σ' ἐς Ἑλλάδα πέμπει·
ἐλεφαντοδέτων πάροι-
    θεν θρόνων ὃς στὰς Ἑλένας
ἐν ἀντωποῖς βλεφάροις
ἔρωτά τ' ἔδωκας ἔρωτί τ'
αὐτὸς ἐπτοήθης.
ὅθεν ἔριν ἔριν
Ἑλλάδα σὺν δορὶ ναυσί τ' ἄγεις
†ἐς Τροίας πέργαμα.†

[Perhaps not by Euripides:]
†You came, oh Paris, there where† you were raised, a shepherd among the white Idean calves, piping alien melodies on your syrinx, †breathing† imitations of the Phrygian aulos of Olympus on your reed pipe. And the cows with full udders were grazing, †when the judgment of the Goddesses awaited you,† the one that sent you to Hellas. Standing before the ivory inlaid throne, your gaze entwined with Helen's, you gave love and were yourself set aflutter with love—whence you bring strife, strife—Greece with spear and ships †to the citadel of Troy.†[6]

[μή μοι φῶς πότ' ἐς ἁμέρας]
ἔμολες, ὦ Πάρι, μηδὲ σύ γε (strophe)
βουκόλος ἀγραύλοις ἐτράφης
    Ἰδαίαις παρὰ μόσχοις,
βάρβαρα συρίζων, Φρυγίων
αὐλῶν Οὐλύμπου καλάμοις
[πολυπλόκον] μίμημα πνέων.
* * * * * * *
εὔθηλοι δὲ [πλανώμεναι (antistrophe)
κατὰ νάπας] τρέφοντο βόες,
εὖτε κρίσις σ' ἔμηνε θεᾶν,
    ἅ σ' [εἰς] Ἑλλάδα πέμπει.
* * * * * * * *
* * * * * * * *
* * * * * * * *
* * * * * * *
* * * * * * (epode)
ἐλεφαντοδέτων πάροιθε θρόνων,
Ἑλένας [ἵν'] ἐν ἀντωποῖς βλεφάροις
ἐρωτά τ' ἔδωκας, ἔρωτι δ' αὐτὸς ἐπτοάθης·
ὅθεν ἔρις, ἔρις
Ἑλλάδα σὺν δορὶ ναυσί τ' ἄγει
πρὸς πέργαμα Τροίας.

6. Euripides 1994 (ed. Diggle), vv. 573–589.

> [I wish you never came to the light of day,] oh Paris, nor were raised a cowherd among the rural Idaean calves, piping alien melodies on your syrinx, blowing [complex] imitations of the Phrygian aulos of Olympus. (*hiatus of one line*)
>
> and cows with full udders were [ranging through the dells and] grazing, when the judgment of the Goddesses made you mad and sent you [to] Hellas. (*hiatus of four lines*)
>
> (*hiatus of one line*) before the thrones inlaid with ivory, [where,] your gaze entwined with Helen's, you gave love and were yourself set aflutter with love; whence strife, strife led Hellas with spears and ships to the citadel of Troy.[7]

Faced with these differences, I am compelled to say that in dealing with Euripides' last play we should speak not of a single, unique text, but of a differential set, a multiplicity or plurality of texts. There is not one *Iphigenia at Aulis*; there are many *Iphigenias at Aulis*—at least thirty-four, in fact, excluding several manuscripts, a few papyrus fragments, and a host of essays, dissertations, commentaries, and articles touching on questions of text.[8]

Perhaps we should feel no surprise at this, for "textual instability," as James McLaverty remarks, "is not a feature that shows the strangeness of literary texts but their ordinariness; and if we have been in the habit of thinking differently, it must have been from some last Romantic longing for simplicity and foundation—or from the desire to maintain the power of editors."[9] Indeed, a study of the fact that classical texts fluctuate through successive editions might seem overdue.[10] As long ago as 1983, Jerome McGann noted, in a well-known discussion of the textual criticism of modern literature, that textual variability was an important datum in the study of modern English authors;[11] Jack Stillinger has completed a major study on multiplicities of authorship, form, and meaning in English Romantic poetry;[12] and recent work on poets like Hölderlin emphasizes the extreme difficulty of ever speaking of one, final, authorized, or "established" version of a text.[13] Indeed, it seems necessary to

7. Hermann 1877, 230.

8. Euripides 1988 (ed. Günther) counts thirty-one separate editors (some of whom produced multiple editions), excluding itself; since 1988 have appeared Euripides 1994 (ed. Diggle), Euripides 2003 (ed. Kovacs), and Euripides 1992 (ed. Stockert). The significant MSS are Laurentianus pl. 32, 2 (L); Palatinus gr. 287 (P). Several papyrus witnesses are now known: P Leiden inv. 510, P Köln II 67; POxy 3719.

9. McLaverty 1991, 136.

10. A call for such a study was voiced by Tarrant 1991, 99.

11. McGann 1983.

12. Stillinger 1991, 1994, 1999.

13. Zeller 1975, 1995; Hurlebusch 2000.

conclude that Joseph Grigely was correct when he said in 1991 what several generations of medieval philologists after Joseph Bédier[14] have been saying:

> A literary work... is an assemblage of texts, a polytext. This formulation can be expressed by the equation
>
> $W \rightarrow T_1, T_2, T_3, \ldots T_n$
>
> Where W = work and T = text. It is important to note that the work is not equivalent to the *sum* of its texts (which would create some kind of hybridized eclectic text), but instead is an ongoing—and infinite—manifestation of textual appearances, *whether those texts are authorized or not.*[15]

And yet no one has attempted to theorize the long history of textual criticism in classics, even though many works were multiply re-edited and each edition differs from all others. This is surprising, not only because this is a time rich in sophisticated literary and philosophical discussions of difference,[16] or because the contemporary intellectual apparatus is at a stage where it has become possible to think of a literary work as a "polytext" and to conceive of the singularity of literature as constituted by its own essential plurality.[17] It is also surprising because the continuing fluctuation of the form of ancient literary work even now, and even in scholarly critical editions, speaks against some of our most basic assumptions about scholarship and textual criticism. Printing and the mechanical replication of texts are often supposed to have made the wide and accurate dissemination of literature possible for the first time, and the scholarly structures that grew up beside the printing press and oversaw the production of ancient literature in printed form were supposed to negate the variations presumed to be caused by medieval scribes. The observable result, however, of the growth of modern printing and an increasingly sophisticated scholarly apparatus seems to be exactly opposite to this. Indeed the heterogeneous and seemingly endlessly variable field of editions of a single classical text argue against Marshall McLuhan's axiomatic proposition that "the interface of the Renaissance was the meeting of medieval pluralism and modern homogeneity and mechanism."[18] Plurality survived the printing press and the

14. See most recently Zumthor 1992; Cerquiglini 1999.
15. Grigely 1991, 176.
16. One could not begin to exhaust the bibliography on difference. Crucial are Derrida 1978, 1981, 1982; Deleuze 1994; Nancy 2000.
17. See in particular Deleuze and Guattari 1986.
18. McLuhan 1962, 141.

technologization of the word. Gutenberg, Aldus, and Erasmus did not end the variation usually blamed on scribes, monks, and interpolators; they merely restructured the millennia-old process of compositional, scribal, and scholarly alteration that begins moments after an author puts down the pen.[19]

But despite the fact that the modern period of textual editing represents a field of textual variation, and despite powerful literary and philosophical tools to approach textual variation in general, literary scholars of antiquity have not approached it. Why?

Partly, I suspect, because doing so means reconsidering a well-established division of scholarly labor. It is usually assumed that work on ancient literature proceeds as follows: first, the textual critics establish the texts; next, the literary scholars "read" them. Textual criticism remains, in this model, "preliminary matter," as René Wellek and Austin Warren dismissed it in 1954.[20] From it literary scholars get a text to read; this text is only the ground on which the literary scholar stands, the base on which higher orders of intellectual work are supposed to be constructed. J. Grigely writes:

> Traditionally, textual studies has involved an objective of stability, a way of organizing, stabilizing, or "framing" a work of literature as an ordered set of texts. . . . Order, in short, seems to make things easier: it allows us to move beyond the act of ordering to other issues that build upon the distinctions we make. This is both tempting and beguiling, since it promises a certain good: it promises to deliver us from the chaos of reality—textual entrammelment—and answers our desire for such deliverance.[21]

Thus is born a situation in which the textual critic supplies the ground for everything the literary scholar does. This division of labor seems peaceful and productive, though there may often be misunderstanding and even mistrust between the two labor forces:

> The angels of hermeneutics . . . have long feared to tread in the fields of textual/bibliographical studies, which are widely regarded, in fact, as a world well lost. Reciprocally, the bibliographers, editors, and textual critics have largely agreed to the bad eminence they have achieved, whence they may hurl defiance at the heavens of the interpreters.[22]

19. See Eisenstein 1979, 1993.

20. "It must be recognized that these types of study only lay the foundation for an actual analysis and interpretation as well as causal explanation of literature. They are justified by the uses to which their results are put" (Wellek and Warren 1954, 62).

21. Grigely 1991, 168.

22. McGann 1985, 181.

Despite this Miltonic geography, the literary scholar depends absolutely on the work of the textual critic; to emphasize the historicity and contingency of critical texts, to be aware of the variations between critical editions, will not embarrass a textual critic anywhere near as much as it might an "angel of hermeneutics." It may suit the latter to assume that the text has been finally and correctly established by McGann's devils (or perhaps by Cyclopes, toiling in subterranean foundries). But scholars who ignore the fact that critical editions vary may link their readings too closely to the individual style and temperament of a particular editor.[23] Literary treatments must be close to the text, and where the text is liable to fluctuate, the literary scholar's objects—and with it, his or her truth—can vanish with the flick of an editorial pencil.

Allow me an example.

It comes at the beginning of Aeschylus's *Oresteia*, from a portion of the text printed in 1972 by Denys Page. This version prompts reflections on questions of memory and amnesia, speech and silence, trauma, and the use of the self-consciously artistic to shield us from harsh realities. But some aspects of Page's text that support such a reading are absent from other important critical editions of the play, in particular a delicate balance between sound and sense and a surprising synctactic twist that turns a simile into a moment in the narrative.

The Greeks have been away from home for ten years, fighting on Trojan soil, and the house of Agamemnon awaits their return. It is just before dawn, and from the roof of the royal house a watchman waits, singing against sleep. A light breaks in the east, not the sun but a letter in light, a signal fire, the last in a long relay of beacons that runs north from Troy then west and south to Argos; and it signifies that in that night the Trojan citadel has fallen. The watchman shouts for joy and sends word to Clytemnestra. The fire streams down on Argos, and a thousand altars burn with incense and sacrifices, though we do not yet know what prayers accompanied the rituals. Clytemnestra commanded all this; no announcement has been made to the public yet, and a crowd of curious elders gathers in the predawn light. They are the only men left in the city, already too old ten years ago to fight, and now they are ancient and infirm, leaning on canes and no stronger than children.

23. A student of classical literature could prefer no extant critical text but instead base her analyses on her own text-critical judgments. In this case she reads a text that, though it has not been printed as a critical edition, belongs in the general set of critical texts. It may not satisfy other readers; such a scholar stands on the same shifting ground as others.

In the confused melee of this gathering crowd, a collective memory surfaces. Ten years ago the Greek fleet mustered at Aulis. But an ill wind started to blow against the bay and they found themselves shore bound. Quickly their supplies began to deplete, and there was the danger of famine. The winds brought omens, too: a pair of eagles, the birds of Zeus, circling overhead and to the right, dived and killed a pregnant hare. The omen was ambiguous. Calchas disseminated its meaning slowly, and with reluctance. *The Greeks will take Troy and all that is within it—only let the other, darker meanings remain unfulfilled.* But the winds grew worse, the army sickened, and Calchas was forced to reveal the rest: *Artemis, protectress of the unborn, hates the eagles' feast and demands another horrible sacrifice to atone for the death of the hare's unborn children.* Calchas did not name it. But Agamemnon understood and summoned his daughter to the island, his mind set on an unholy course. Iphigenia was brought, and as they prepared for the sacrifice, she began to appeal to the Greeks to spare her life. The old men speak this part of their memory in beautiful but terrifying poetry:

λιτὰς δὲ καὶ κληδόνας πατρῴους (antistrophe)
παρ' οὐδὲν αἰῶνα παρθένειόν τ'
230 ἔθεντο φιλόμαχοι βραβῆς·
φράσεν δ' ἀόζοις πατὴρ μετ' εὐχὰν
δίκαν χιμαίρας ὕπερθε βωμοῦ
πέπλοισι περιπετῆ παντὶ θυμῷ
προνωπῆ λαβεῖν ἀέρ-
235 δην στόματός τε καλλιπρῴ-
ρου φυλακᾷ κατασχεῖν
φθόγγον ἀραῖον οἴκοις,

βίᾳ χαλινῶν τ' ἀναύδῳ μένει· (strophe)
κρόκου βαφὰς δ' ἐς πέδον χέουσα
240 ἔβαλλ' ἕκαστον θυτή-
ρων ἀπ' ὄμματος βέλει φιλοίκτῳ,
πρέπουσά θ' ὡς ἐν γραφαῖς, προσεννέπειν
θέλουσ', ἐπεὶ πολλάκις
πατρὸς κατ' ἀνδρῶνας εὐτραπέζους
245 ἔμελψεν, ἁγνᾷ δ' ἀταύρωτος αὐδᾷ πατρὸς
φίλου τριτόσπονδον εὔποτμον παι-
ῶνα φίλως ἐτίμα.[24]

This is how their words are spoken in the text of Denys Page, but not in the editions of Martin West or Eduard Fraenkel, where there are

24. Aeschylus 1972 (ed. Page), *Agamemnon* 228–247.

some significant differences.[25] Page's version might be translated as follows:

> But the war-loving arbitrators set at naught her prayers, her ominous cries of "father,"[26] and her youth, and Agamemnon, after a prayer, signaled to his ministers to take heart and lift her prone above the altar like a she-goat, her robes falling around her, and to restrain any utterance baleful to the house with a guard on her beautiful mouth, with the strength of a bridle, a force causing voicelessness; and pouring her saffron robe to the ground and standing out as though in a painting she shot at each of her slaughterers with pitiable bolts from her eyes, wanting to address them—since she had often sung at her father's well-laid table among the men and had loved to honor the final libation of her beloved father with an auspicious paean, from the holy voice of a virgin.[27]

The two stanzas belong to different units in the broader composition and have different metrical structures, and the fact that they are syntactically joined makes them unusual, as though the old men who speak them are having trouble keeping the utterance of their memory within prescribed bounds. But even though this single long sentence is plotted in counterpoint to the metrical structure of the old men's song, it has a tightly constructed form which increases the pathos of the scene and makes us see more vividly how terrible Agamemnon's resolution really was.

The second stanza is a mirror image of the first, and the whole unit is made in the form of a series of concentric rings that can be represented schematically as follows:

(A) speech of Iphigenia (228–230)
(B) simile (231–232)
(C) robes of Iphigenia (233–234)
(D) silence of Iphigenia (234–237)

25. Aeschylus 1950 (ed. Fraenkel); Aeschylus 1972 (ed. Page); Aeschylus 1990 (ed. West). On the differences between the texts, see below.

26. The translation of κληδόνας πατρῴους is difficult. Aeschylus 1950 (ed. Fraenkel) and Aeschylus 1957 (ed. Page and Denniston) translate "her cries of father," but note that the use of κληδών in the sense of "cry, appeal" is very rare, occurring only here and at *Eumenides* 397. *LSJ* gives Sophocles' *Ichneutai* 232 for an example of the sense "shouting." My translation tries to take into account the word's connotation that the utterance is ominous; see *Odyssey* 18.117, 20.120; Herodotus 5.72, 9.91–92; Aeschylus *Agamemnon* 1652, *Prometheus Bound* 486; Pausanias 9.11.7. Agamemnon's response to Iphigenia's entreaties—gagging her—is explicitly motivated by his worry that her utterances may turn out to be inauspicious.

27. Aeschylus 1972 (ed. Page), *Agamemnon* 228–247.

(D) silence of Iphigenia (238)
(C) robes of Iphigenia (239)
(B) simile (240–242)
(A) speech of Iphigenia (243–247)

Progressing toward the center of the composition, the old men move from a description of Iphigenia's speech in the moments leading up to her sacrifice, through a simile that compares her to a mute animal, and into a description of her silence. Traveling outward from the center to the end, they describe her silence, compare her to a mute object (this time a painting), and finish with another description of her speech, this time in the past, in peacetime, at Agamemnon's court. The outer rings, presenting descriptions of her speech, contrast with the inner rings, which describe the nature of her silence: and in doing so they contrast her humanity, her right to life, with the attempt to dehumanize her, to reduce her to a sacrificial animal or to an image, which is how she will remain.

The outer rings (A) display the terrible and tragic trap in which Agamemnon finds himself. Forms of *φίλος* (love, friendship) are used in both places: in the first stanza we find it compounded with the word for "battle" to characterize the generals' motivation for the sacrifice, a love of war (230): in the second stanza it is used twice to describe Iphigenia's affection for her father and her willingness to honor his feasts with her voice (246–247). The repetition of *φίλος* in the outer edges of the ring establishes a contrast between the two motivations that crucify Agamemnon on the shores of Aulis: love of war and love of his daughter.

Another piece of sound symbolism in the old men's song reinforces Agamemnon's dilemma: the Greek word used to name Iphigenia's youth in line 229 (*αἰῶνα*) finds a perfect echo in the word used to describe the song she had sung at Agamemnon's court in lines 246–247 (*παιῶνα*): then she had honored her father with a song; now they set her age at naught. The two most eloquent arguments against Iphigenia's sacrifice, her youth and her voice, disregarded by the generals intent on fulfilling Artemis's demands and beginning the expedition against Troy, are reinforced in the outer rings by a sonic echo.

If the outer rings, their unity enforced by sound-symbolism, tell of forgetting, the inner rings tell a story of effacement. Just as he disregards her youth (*αἰῶνα*) and forgets about her voice (*παιῶνα*), and just as he lets his love of war eclipse his love of his daughter, Agamemnon tries to efface the human being before him by taking away her voice. She is bridled, silenced, held above the altar like a she-goat.

Agamemnon is not the only one who tries to ease the shock of the atrocity. The old men will not narrate the final moment. "What came next," they say, "I neither saw, nor do I tell" (248). Why not? Were they not there when Iphigenia was killed? Then how could they describe with such exquisite and compelling detail the heartbreaking scene before the sacrificial altar, as Iphigenia, gagged and desperate, is lifted up to meet the blade? Perhaps they are inspired—for persuasion breathes over them from the gods, they say when they commence their story (105–106). Then why should the inspiration stop at just this moment? Perhaps they were there, but turned their eyes away at the critical moment, unable to bear the sight of such a terrible act. Perhaps their memory erased that last scene, some part of their collective mind closed off the final traumatic death from recollection. Memory itself, the ability to describe this founding moment in the future of the ills of the house of Argos, is beginning to strain and crumble under the terrible weight of the past. The focus on silence and speech in the two stanzas we have been listening to sets up the aposiopesis that follows, as though these old men knew already that the end would have to be left out, unspeakable and unspoken. It is as though, recalling in words the terrible scene at Aulis, they are also inaugurating a meditation on the impossibility of continuing the story; as if, faced with the agonizing clarity of the tableau they are describing, they are already dimly aware that their speech will be unable to show the whole picture, that they will have to leave it fragmented, leave us with an image that will have to serve as synecdoche for the whole narrative. Her death is effaced even as it is described.

This happens not only through silence, but through transformation as well. Agamemnon, bridling the girl and holding her aloft, treats her like a sacrificial beast. When he does this, the old men resort to similes that transform her into an image. She "stands out, as though in a painting" (242). This simile does not refer specifically to her silence but to her position in the scene: πρέπουσα here means "standing out,"[28] being at the focal point of the image. Fraenkel visualized the scene with striking vividness: "At this moment, the great complex group of men, chieftains and ministrants at the sacrifice, is in the foreground; away behind them the mass of the army; both alike appear as a mere foil against which stands out the central figure of Iphigenia."[29]

But this figure marks a *literal* transformation of the human victim into an aesthetic object. A τε (and) in 242 includes her "standing out

28. See Aeschylus 1950 (ed. Fraenkel), *ad* 242.
29. *Ibid.*

as though in a painting" in the narrative sequence. As the old men in this version of the text tell it, Iphigenia casts bolts from her eyes at her slaughterers while pouring her robes to the ground *and* standing out, as though in a painting; that is, her silence, her nakedness, and her being transformed into the kind of visual object that can be vividly described are all part of the narrative: in this story, *Iphigenia turns into an image.* At the moment of her death, she is transformed, not into an animal but into a mimetic representation, a painting. All this is done by the placement of a single particle.

In a curious way this memory of Agamemnon's attempt to transform his daughter into a mute sacrificial beast tells us something about the impossibility of remembering the atrocity. Iphigenia's death begins to disappear behind a cloud of occluding language and gestures, and it is clear speech, memory itself, that is being killed. Faced with the task of uttering what we cannot, we resort to literary language. We speak in figures that, we hope, will conceal the unspeakable while leaving it legible at the same time. Thus the task of remembering and narrating the sacrifice of Iphigenia has something in common with undertaking the sacrifice: in both cases we must proceed toward the impossible, hoping that at the final moment the thing will be elided or replaced in some salvific transfiguration. Just as the old men leave off their story before the critical moment, so would Agamemnon hope that something will transform or translate Iphigenia, so that the impossible act would itself be transformed into something possible, as Isaac was replaced at the last moment beneath the blade of Abraham. Agamemnon tries to do this for himself twice, first by silencing Iphigenia, an attempt to make her mute and bestial, and second by forgetting ("setting at naught") her former status in the house. These are attempts, in the absence of divine intervention, to make Iphigenia into something she is not, into an empty simulation of the thing that would have made his murder atrocious.

So the story has always been, in a sense, about representations. Both Agamemnon's representation of Iphigenia and that of the old men are made out of equal measures of memory and forgetting, or, which might be the same thing, of reproduction and transformation. This little passage in the *Oresteia* points us toward representations of the past in general, since at every level we witness the same dialectic between memory and forgetting and between what may be represented and what must not. And just as Agamemnon's act was repeated in the recollection of the old men at Argos, so other representations spin off this one. A painting on the wall of the "house of the tragic poet" at Pompeii, itself possibly a reproduction and transformation of a lost original by

Timanthes, gives another glimpse of the events at Aulis (see frontispiece). In the center of the image two men hold Iphigenia, whose robes have fallen from her torso, aloft. To her right Calchas strikes a dignified but sorrowful pose. But in this depiction Iphigenia's form is strangely disproportional: her torso twists up and out, and her legs are barely visible, concealed behind the men who restrain her. Iphigenia's strange contorted form seems to emerge out of the painting (she literally "stands out"), her naked upper body more vivid, more present than the rest of the scene. Because of her strange proportions, which defy physical possibility, this hyper-vivid Iphigenia makes us painfully aware that we are looking at a painting. It almost seems as though the painter wanted to use Iphigenia's form to mask the reality of what is being represented, purposefully distorting his Iphigenia to emphasize the materiality of the image at its emotional center; as though her transfiguration—into a phantom or a beast, a goddess or a corpse—were signified by the painting's becoming painterly at its focal point. The painting abandons realist technique just as Page's old men in Aeschylus insert an *and* that actually transforms Iphigenia into an image. Figuration conceals. The drama of effacement that begins at Aulis and continues in the old men's failed recollection continues here, surprisingly and far away, on the walls of Pompei.

To the left of this scene in which Iphigenia becomes an image of herself, a drama of unrepresentability is taking place. Agamemnon is there, his head in his hands, his face veiled. The easiest way to understand this image is to say that he cannot bear to watch the terrible atrocity that is about to take place, and so he turns away and covers his head in grief. But to this representation of Agamemnon's unwillingness to witness, his desire to efface the impossible, we must add a story of the impossibility of representation in general, for that was how this detail was read in antiquity. Cicero praises the original of which this may be a copy in the following way: "That painter, portraying the sacrifice of Iphigenia, made Calchas sad, Ulysses more sorrowful, Menelaus grief-stricken, but saw that Agamemnon had to have his head covered, since that highest degree of grief could not be imitated with his brush."[30] There is a sense in which this Agamemnon, veiled because he refuses to behold and because he cannot be depicted—both blind and blinding—is a figure for all the versions of the events at Aulis; Iphigenia's death can only be told in a narrative that defaces the tale at the same time as it tells it. It can only be seen via an occluding and transformative prism that reveals

30. Cicero, *Orator* 74.

as much about our inability to see as it does about our need to do so. And to the degree that they also try to forget as well as to remember, the old men in our passage from Aeschylus are also like this Agamemnon, turning away from the memory that afflicts them.

THUS not only is Page's text a powerful poem about forgetting and effacement; it also organizes other material in the Iphigenia dossier. But many of these observations can only be made of Page's edition of the *Agamemnon.* The remarkable piece of sound symbolism that pairs Iphigenia's voice with her youth at the outer edges of Aeschylus's composition and sets it in stark contrast with her dehumanized silence in the center is not in Fraenkel's text of 1950, and it is gone again in Martin West's 1990 Teubner edition.[31] Where Page prints αἰῶνα παρθένειον τ' (and her maidenly age) at 229, Fraenkel and West both print αἰῶ τε παρθένειον. The meaning is the same: all that has changed is that the word meaning "and" has been moved in front of the word meaning "maidenly" or "young," and an alternative form of the accusative singular for αἰών, "age," has been used.[32] Also gone in the editions of West and Fraenkel is the movement in which Iphigenia is transformed into an image as part of the narrative sequence. In Page's text the placement of a single *and* in 242 includes Iphigenia's transformation into an image with the rest of the elements in the narrative: "... *and* standing out as though in a painting." But while all the manuscripts contain this *and,* West and Fraenkel print 242 πρέπουσα τὼς ἐν γραφαῖς—which may be translated in the same way, but without the *and* that connects this simile with the previous words in a continuous narrative stream: "standing out as in a picture." Fraenkel comments, "θ" [and] will not do, for πρέπουσα [standing out], which is purely descriptive, cannot be put on the same level as χέουσα [pouring (her robes down)] (239), which carries on the narrative."[33] Whatever value there may be in a reading of Page's text like the one I offered above, it has less when the edition is that of Fraenkel or West.

There are differences within the critical dossier of the *Oresteia,* some

31. Aeschylus 1950 (ed. Fraenkel); Aeschylus 1990 (ed. West).

32. The use of the accusative singular form αἰῶ is correct and present elsewhere in Aeschylus (*Agamemnon* 715, *Choephori* 350), as is αἰῶνα; see Aeschylus 1990 (ed. West), xxxviii. Behind this passage lurks confusion over the spelling of the word for "paean," which was παιᾶν in Attic (see *Agamemnon* 645, *Choephori* 151, *Persai* 393) but, Page thinks, is occasionally spelled with the omega in Aeschylus (ap. crit. *ad.* 246). The manuscripts universally give αἰῶνα (age) in 246–247 where Page and Fraenkel print παιῶνα (paean). West, more honestly, perhaps, prints <π>αιῶνα.

33. Aeschylus 1950 (ed. Fraenkel), 139.

small and some large. Any of these differences could intrigue someone watching out for details, and all of them challenge the naive idea that a classical text is a simple unity. To someone making a claim like "The *Oresteia* is about..."; the reply should be, "Which Oresteia?"

But it would be wrong to say that each text is a totally different poem, and West's edition has nothing to do with Page's or Fraenkel's; they are all versions of the same play. The critical dossier on a classical text could be compared to the multiple drafts of a work-in-progress, or to an archive of recorded oral performances of the same traditional epic. Clearly all the successive texts have something in common with each other: the idea of an origin—of a version once approved by Aeschylus—and the knowledge that there are a plurality of versions of that origin. A shared problem and the consciousness that no two solutions will be the same.

In Page's version of the sacrifice of Iphigenia at Aulis, the atrocity is never fully recalled. Rather it impels a series of (dis)figurations that gesture to but never quite signify the slaughter. Agamemnon's attempt to transform Iphigenia into a mute beast, the old men's refusal to remember the end of the story, and their transformation of Iphigenia into an aesthetic object at the last moment, even the painting at Pompeii, are all deformed refractions of the act no one can name—just as, according to Freud, some patients suffer from a compulsion to repeat in which they always revisit some forgotten traumatic event, but only in covert, masked, symbolic form: an infinity of partial returns, of disguised representations of a trauma that remains concealed.[34] Perhaps Page's text is another one of these partial, symbolic returns; perhaps West's is too, and Fraenkel's as well. The analytic interest, for the Freudian, is in the masks beneath which a patient is compelled to repeat the initial trauma; for this book it is in the texts through which critics never quite return to Iphigenia's founding sacrifice.

Taking stock of the multiplicity of versions in the critical dossier of an ancient text presents us with what Grigely calls "an overwhelming sense of the burden of textual history. This is daunting, and at the same time it is good: as our awareness of the numbers (and kinds) of textual states and modalities increases, so too do our interpretive possibilities."[35] A reorientation to the multiplicity of critical versions of *Iphigenia at Aulis* is what I propose here. This will open a new perspective, one from which a literary philology will again become possible. Such a literary philology—I would like to call it a *radical philology*—will be reconfigured so

34. See Freud 1958.
35. Grigely 1991, 192.

that, while close textual reading will remain basic and necessary, the meaning of this textual reading will not be contingent on any single critical text. Rather, it will be inscribed within, and in dialogue with, a plurality of texts; this radical philology will ultimately be concerned not with "the" *Iphigenia at Aulis*, located in a specific time and place (late-fifth-century Athens, for example), but with *Iphigenias at Aulis*, essentially plural in form and spatio-temporal position.

But such a radical philology requires that we first strip the critical edition of a number of "metaphysical subtleties and theological niceties"[36] imbued in it by the current division of scholarly labor.

36. Marx 1976, 1:163.

2

The Fetishism of the Critical Text

According to Karl Marx, the physical value of commodities, together with the social basis of the labor that produces them, are eclipsed and replaced by "value relations" based only on exchange. When this happens, commodities seem to take on relationships with each other.[1] What is then seen in the world of commodities is a system of values that operates autonomously and independently of the social relations of production and is measured in terms of exchange-value (money) rather than labor or material value. To illustrate this, Marx has recourse to an analogy:

> It is nothing but the definite social relation between men themselves which assumes here...the fantastic form of a relation between things. In order, therefore, to find an analogy we must take flight into the misty realm of religion. There the products of the human brain appear as autonomous figures endowed with a life of their own, which enter into relations with each other and with the human race.[2]

Marx calls this vivid independent life of the commodity its "fetish character"; as a fetish the commodity "abounds in metaphysical subtleties and theological niceties."[3]

1. Marx 1976, 1:164–165.
2. Ibid., 1:165.
3. Ibid., 1:163.

I invoke the theory of commodity fetishism because it seems to describe the result of the division of labor between textual critics and literary scholars I described above. The critical text comes imbued with a few subtleties and niceties of its own that could well be described as metaphysical; and the manner in which a large proportion of scholars uses them frequently approaches what Marx described, by reference to the "misty regions of the religious world," as fetishism. Many literary scholars concern themselves with establishing relations between critical texts: "meaning," in this kind of scholarship, often arises out of the interrelations between such texts in a manner precisely analogous to the way, for Marx, exchange-value arises out of the relations between commodities.

Critical texts—nearly all classical texts, for that matter, with the possible exception of some inscribed on stone—are produced in a long process of copying, correcting, and publication that affects their form (through corruption, interpolation, conjecture, and emendation, for example). The production of classical texts, in other words, is always located historically, in times and places usually far from their "original" situations. However, the literary scholar nearly always studies texts in the context of their "original" sites of production and reception, with relative disregard for the long tradition that ends in the critical edition he or she cites. Denys Page's edition of the *Oresteia*[4] is treated as a work dated 458 BCE, not 1972 CE, and it may be cited at the exclusion of all other editions. It may also be compared with Euripides' *Iphigenia at Aulis*—in Gilbert Murray's text of 1913,[5] but treated as though dated 405 BCE—or read beside the fragments of the *Proteus*, the satyr play produced at the end of the *Oresteia* in 452 but cited from the *Tragicorum Graecorum Fragmenta* of 1985.[6] Of course each of these texts has a different production history, both in terms of the methods by which it was produced and in terms of the long history of transmission that ends in a printed book; but literary scholars filter all of this out, or they trust the critic to filter all of this out in producing a text "ready for use." Only the specific past of an artificially hypothesized moment of origin interests the literary scholar. The other origins of the text he or she reads are, of disciplinary necessity, ignored.

Literary philologists do this so often that it hardly seems worthy of note or of defense (what else are they going to do?). But while such blindness to the production circumstances of a specific critical edition

4. Aeschylus 1972 (ed. Page).
5. Euripides 1913 (ed. Murray).
6. Aeschylus 1985 (ed. Radt), ffr. 210–215.

may seem self-evident or necessary, it points to a significant fact: the past is the principle of exchange and the condition of comprehensibility for a critical edition. And the past serves this function independently of the properly text-critical concern whether the printed words of an edition are those an author "actually" wrote, a concern that, while vital for textual criticism, has a very limited range and scope. To the finished modern critical edition, the literary scholar often adds the extra property of "pastness"; we treat the printed edition as though it offered us the tangible past. In the finely printed lines of the Oxford or Teubner text (for example), it seems to us that we can read the very words of Euripides or Aeschylus or Sophocles: only energize the imagination and the stones of the theatre of Dionysus arise before us, the masks and costumes, the *mēchanē* and the ten judges in the front row; only coordinate this book with others and with the physical remains of that time and place, and the entire social and political network of ancient democratic Athens, its ideologies and social codes and languages, even its dreams, spread themselves around us in a magnificent phantasmagoria.

It might be simpler to say, The past is the currency in which the critical edition acquires its exchange-value, and through which its specific and historical mode of production is elided; the past provides the system of exchange within which the critical edition becomes a commodity, in a social relation with other commodified critical editions.

Simon Goldhill, for example, predicates his particularly powerful and highly influential approach to the reading of Greek tragedy on the pastness of the past as the currency in which texts acquire their value. Distinguishing himself from an earlier generation of critics who were troubled by the modern philologist's cultural distance from ancient Greece, a distance that seemed to render questionable the possibility of accurately comprehending Greek culture, Goldhill insists (following Jean-Pierre Vernant) that the modern philologist's distance from antiquity is in fact a source of interpretive strength:

> Being alien to a culture meant for Kitto a dangerous increase in the possibility of a reader's misinterpretation or misrepresentation of what the culture itself believed. Vernant, however, rather than repressing his necessarily alien status, insists on the possible advantages of such a position. Like many anthropologists, rather than taking a culture's explicit agreement or recognition as the criterion of judgment for his analyses, Vernant stresses that the outsider's view can investigate the tacit knowledge of a society; it can illuminate the blind-spots of a culture's ideas by investigating what is taken for granted or assumed.[7]

7. Goldhill 1986a, 111.

Goldhill's method is to seek out the things Athenian culture took for granted, identifying its "structure of thought" or, more generally, its "ideology,"[8] which is only visible to the distant philologist, the alien eye.

Goldhill's comparison of the modern philologist with the outsider is particularly telling because it marks Goldhill as belonging to a nostalgic tradition of classicists stretching at least to Johann Winckelmann, for whom (as for Friedrich Schiller, Friedrich Schelling, and many others of their generations) Greece represented a lost region of ideal unity.[9] In the eighteenth and nineteenth centuries, this lost unity was one of content and form, or of idea and expression, but for more recent historians (and for Goldhill) the lost unity has been political. As Alasdair MacIntyre wrote: "The Athenians had not insulated, as we have by a set of institutional devices, the pursuit of political ends from dramatic representations or the asking of philosophical questions from either. Hence we lack, as they did not, *any* public, generally shared communal mode either for representing political conflict or for putting our politics to the philosophical question."[10]

MacIntyre is cited with approval by Moses Finley,[11] who is himself cited as an authority by Goldhill.[12] In this model the philologist's relationship with Greece is similar to that identified by Augustine as the relationship between humans and the city of God; while the city of God exists among us, it does so only as an exile and a sojourn: the Christian dedicated to that other city nonetheless lives in exile in this city. In Goldhill's analysis, the "anthropological critic" becomes the faithful exile, Athens the philological city of God: this sets the stage for a literary philology as nostalgic as German Romanticism. In this scholarship fragments drawn from many disparate texts are reorganized and reiterated to produce an image of that lost unity; that unity in turn becomes the measure of value and the medium of exchange for critical texts.

For Goldhill the name of this unity is *ideology*. Its value to the modern philologist lies in its ability to order fragments of different critical texts according to a system of exchange external to the specific histories of their productions: the result is a vision of lost unity in the mental or discursive field, a philological city of God. For Finley, ideology designates those beliefs and attitudes that ancient political theorists rejected;[13] close readings of works like Aristotle's *Politics* (which Finley is careful to

8. Ibid., 74.
9. See Taminiaux 1993, 89, Ferris 2000, Schmidt 2001.
10. MacIntyre 1981, 129–30.
11. Finley 1983, 125.
12. Goldhill 1986a, 61.
13. Finley 1983, 130.

seclude as a rare exception in ancient political thought) are replaced by a political iconology in which the enthymeme, the image, and the recurrent phrase are the terms of analysis.

> A small number of words and phrases were rhetorically deployed with different nuances and sometimes with divergent and even contradictory meanings. For instance, *eunomia*, a favorite word in Greek ideological debates, had the root sense of "good order," "concord," then became a standard aristocratic slogan which democratic spokesmen in turn refused to surrender to their opponents. Sometimes the sense in any given passage is obvious, but often it can be discovered only by a close consideration of the speaker's outlook and orientation, and of the specific context.[14]

Despite the fact that ideologemes are used differently by different speakers, Finley still manages to arrive at a vision of unity.

> Not all Athenians held the same views, but the evidence is decisive that nearly all of them would have accepted as premises, one might say as axioms, that the good life was possible only in a *polis*, that the good man was more or less synonymous with the good citizen, that slaves, women and barbarians were inferior by nature and so excluded from all discussion....[15]

Although a certain amount of difference in the use of ideologemes is expected by ideologists, the goal and the purpose of their analysis is to uncover a major locus of unity, a catalogue of beliefs ("axioms") held by a majority of Athenians so sizeable that the eccentrics and the dissenters can be left out of the historical reckoning: a lost unity, in other words, a region *below* the "representation of political conflict," in MacIntyre's words, in which there is no conflict but consensus.

Goldhill's readings of tragedy rely on such a consensus. For him, tragedy engages "the strong sense of being an Athenian with its obligations and duties, privileges and honors"—a "complex system of ideological strategies"[16]—in a questioning, challenging mode. While tragedy cannot simply be fit into this sense of identity as into a grid, it does require that this matrix—"the way one's place in the order of things is thought about and organized conceptually"[17]—exist as the background against which the subversions of tragedy are seen. Thus the *Hippolytus* "does not simply reflect a discourse of sexuality but challenges, ironizes,

14. Ibid., 131.
15. Ibid., 125.
16. Goldhill 1986a, 69.
17. Ibid., 74.

undermines the safe use of the language of that discourse."[18] Though this discourse, or "unrecognized system of ideas"[19] about sexuality in Athens is contested, it *must* be there for tragedy's peculiar mode of Dionysian testing to have any sense. In a particularly vivid metaphor, Goldhill describes civic ideology as the echo-chamber or sounding board against which tragedy casts its dissonant voices: Sophocles' plays "echo against the developing civic ideology;" the *Ajax* "resounds" against the "contemporary world and values."[20] Thus, while tragedy is not strictly speaking "ideological," ideology nevertheless furnishes it with meaning by providing it with its negative ground. There is, then, not that much difference between Goldhill and those "conservative and conventional critics"[21] for whom tragedy has lost its power to question and challenge. Both must affirm the existence of an ideological core—only the details of the relation between tragedy and these unstated axioms differ.

If it is clear, however, that for Goldhill Athenian civic ideology functions as the totality against or within which tragedy acquires its meaning, it is also clear that this theory requires him to ignore or elide the specifically modern production of the texts in question and the variation between different editions. Goldhill invokes Foucault: his focus on ideology is said to study "what Foucault would call 'discursive practice'—the way one's place in the order of things is organized and thought about conceptually."[22] It would be a mistake to see Goldhill's work as a mere transference of concepts from the thought of Foucault to the study of antiquity; but Goldhill's work on tragedy does seem to occupy the same general discursive field opened by Foucault. To use a metaphor deployed by Foucault himself: in that "tree of derivation" over which Foucault's works stand as "governing utterances—those that concern the definition of observable structures and the field of possible objects... that reveal the most general possibilities of characterization, and thus open up a whole domain of concepts to be constructed",[23] Goldhill's work on tragedy is located at the tip of one branch, working on a specific locale and transforming the guiding concepts in a specific manner. Despite vast differences in historical object, style of exposition, details of conceptualization, and thematic strategies,[24] it seems to me that, again

18. Ibid., 113.
19. Ibid., 112.
20. Goldhill 1987, 70.
21. Goldhill 1986a, 78.
22. Ibid., 106.
23. Foucault 1972, 147.
24. Ibid., 21–74; Foucault 1988.

in Foucault's terms, the archaeology of knowledge and the ideological study of tragedy take place within the same discursive formation, or (it is the same thing) they obey the same general enunciative laws.

But for all its extraordinary explanatory power and its theoretical sophistication, it is a curious characteristic of the discursive formation in which both Foucault and Goldhill are located that it requires its evidence to behave more like currency than like contested and alterable documents. In the end this poses a problem for any approach to tragedy, since it prevents the development of an adequate interpretation of textual criticism or the editions it produces. To see this we must follow Foucault, for his argumentation in the *Archaeology of Knowledge* decisively conditions Goldhill's approach.

Foucault defines a discursive practice (more frequently he refers to it as a "discursive formation") as a system of dispersion between utterances (*énoncés*)[25] related to each other according to a unitary set of "rules of formation." Essential to his discussion of this order of analysis is the existence of utterances conceived as singular events taking their place within a differential field of other such utterances, and a system of relations between utterances that circumscribes them within a unitary discursive space.[26] Since these relations, Foucault insists, are purely external, that is, since they are relations strictly between (and never within) utterances,[27] the focus of theoretical analysis and historical research must be the utterance itself. This utterance is characterized first and foremost by its self-identity, what could be called its atomic specificity. The utterance "appears with a status, enters various networks and various fields of use, is subjected to transferences or modifications, is integrated into operations and strategies in which its identity is maintained or effaced."[28] How unsusceptible the utterance is to alteration becomes clear when Foucault considers its materiality. "Materiality" for Foucault means neither the materiality of paper, stone, or sound (on or within which the utterance is inscribed), nor of some temporal point

25. The English version translates *énoncé*, "statement," which crucially misses the importance of discourse analysis to Foucault's discussion. I have accordingly retranslated *énoncé* as "utterance" throughout.

26. Foucault 1972, 99 and 125. Cf. Goldhill 2000, 45.

27. "In order to analyze them in an exteriority that may be paradoxical since it refers to no adverse form of interiority. In order to consider them in their discontinuity, without having to relate them, by one of those shifts that disconnect them and render them inessential, to a more fundamental opening or difference" (Foucault 1972, 121).

28. Foucault 1972, 105. "Modifications" here designates modifications in significance and substrate, but not in form: in form, the utterance cannot be modified. It is the selfsame upon which the appearance of discursive dispersion or difference is founded.

(the "now" of the utterance), nor even of a specific language. Rather it consists in a certain range of possible material supports, determined as a set of "possibilities of reinscription or transcription"[29] between contexts, times, and uses. Thus the time, place, language, and institutional context of an utterance may change, but the *utterance itself remains identical* through these modifications: it is only reinscribed or transcribed into different materializations. Foucault gives the case of a literary work as an example and explicitly rules out the possibility of an utterance showing any variation:

> A text reproduced several times, the successive editions of a book, or, *better still*, the different copies of the same printing, do not give rise to the same number of distinct utterances: in all the editions of *Les Fleurs du mal* (*variations and rejected versions apart*), we find the same set of utterances: yet neither the characters, nor the ink, nor the paper, nor even the placing of the text and the positions of the signs, are the same: the whole texture of the materiality has changed.[30]

"Variants and rejected versions" must constitute different utterances or be discarded altogether. The difficulty of using Foucault's approach in the study of classical literature is immediately apparent here: Is not the history of critical editions of a classical text a history of "variants and rejected versions?" Indeed Foucault emphasizes the sovereign importance of "the edition of a book printed with the agreement of the author,"[31] which defines the utterance with respect to its subsequent publications as "that by relation to which there is and must be repetition."[32] The utterance is defined, essentially and even after the admission that its materiality may vary, as that which repeats perfectly and stably through each successive reinscription.

Foucault names this perfect repeatability the utterance's residuality or remanence (*rémanence*), and he is careful to insist that this residuality has nothing to do with the notion of the trace (which would refer back to an origin, an original moment of formulation or inscription) or of memory (in which the utterance would be preserved as the carrier of an "original" meaning, whether this is psychological or contextual).[33]

29. Foucault 1972, 103.
30. Ibid., 102. My emphasis.
31. Ibid., 102.
32. Ibid., 102–103.
33. "This analysis presupposes that utterances are considered in the remanence (*rémanence*) that is proper to them, and which is not that of an ever-realizable reference back to the past event of the formulation. To say that utterances are residual (*rémanent*) is not

Both the notion of the trace and the function of memory would introduce a division internal to the utterance, between what is apparent on its surface and what is unsaid or lost, a primordial silence to which voice would have to be given in a hermeneutic mode.[34] In other words Foucault opposes his conception of the utterance's *rémanence* to the Derridean remainder (*restance*),[35] which treats repetition and alteration as intimately connected to each other and thus introduces a difference *internal* to the written sign or trace. If for Foucault the utterance remains self-identical even when it changes its material, institutional, and technical supports, for Derrida the remainder ("which has nothing in common with *scripta manent*"[36]) is a "differential structure"[37] present both without (here he agrees with Foucault) and within the written trace (here he differs from Foucault), and as a result "renders all absolute permanence impossible."[38]

The difference between *rémanence* and *restance* is a difference between an analytic of identity (Foucault) and one of irreducible and infinite difference (Derrida). The sign's status as a remainder entails not only its relation with a differential other (the signifying relation) but also its own necessary tendency to change through a series of iterations—to differ, in other words, from itself. The remainder thus essentially differs from/to what it signifies, and from/to itself in its next restatement. But if the remainder is fundamentally differential, Foucault's utterance is essentially identical. The utterance is precisely what it is and it is what it is in every iteration (whence Foucault's casting aside of "variants and rejected versions").

Foucault rules out the possibility of fluctuation in a crucial definition. For Foucault the object of analysis (the utterance) is no longer considered a *document*: it is rather conceived as a *monument*:

to say that they remain in the field of memory, or that it is possible to rediscover what they meant; but it means that they are preserved by virtue of a number of supports and material techniques (of which the book is, of course, only an example), in accordance with certain types of institutions (of which the library is one), and with certain statutory modalities (which are not the same in the case of a religious text, a law, or a scientific truth)...This survival in time is far from being the accidental or fortunate prolongation of an existence originally intended only for the moment; on the contrary, this remanence is of the nature of the utterance; oblivion and destruction are in a sense only the zero degree of this remanence" (Foucault 1972, 123).

34. Ibid., 76.
35. See Derrida 1977.
36. Derrida 1977, 189.
37. Ibid., 190.
38. Ibid., 191.

> Scholars have asked not only what these documents meant, but also whether they were telling the truth, and by what right they could claim to be doing so, whether they were sincere or deliberately misleading, well-informed or ignorant, authentic or tampered with. But each of these questions, and all this critical concern, pointed to one and the same end: the reconstitution, on the basis of what the documents say, and sometimes merely hint at, of the past from which they emanate and which now has disappeared far behind them; the document was always treated as the language of a voice since reduced to silence, its fragile, but possibly decipherable trace. Now,... history... has taken as its primary task, not the interpretation of the document, nor the attempt to decide whether it is telling the truth or what is its expressive value, but to work on it from within and to develop it: history now organizes the document, divides it up, distributes it, orders it, arranges it in levels, establishes series, distinguishes between what is relevant and what is not, discovers elements, defines unities, describes relations.... In our time, history is that which transforms *documents* into *monuments*.[39]

The difference between a document and a monument is exactly the difference between difference and identity; between the Derridean problematic of the trace or remainder and the Foucauldian project of archaeology. A document must be mistrusted: it is subject to material and historical forces that make its status as a witness questionable; it may be the last in a chain of other documents in which there have been innumerable alterations, errors, interpolations, and falsifications. The monument, by contrast, simply stands there; it may be weathered, the paint may have come off, or the extremities chipped, but its concrete presence is the same now as it was when the artist first brought it out of its stone encasing. The document, a written trace of what is lost, always differs (both from itself and its transmission and from what it records), while the monument, weathered and transported, defaced or ignored, remains inalienably itself.

A focus on the monument is no serious blindness when one is working with the literary remains of modernity, where first editions and authors' manuscripts exist to be consulted; they can be treated as monuments because they simply are what they are. But in the study of antiquity the objects of analysis are infinitely more complicated; beside the material remains preserved in the earth, we have only documents whose moments of production are radically disjoined from the original moment of inscription, and the problem of the relation between the copy or trace and the original (however that may be imagined) is always front and

39. Foucault 1972, 6–7. See also Foucault 1988.

center. Even critical texts must be read with the same suspicion and care as a thirteenth-century codex or a second-century papyrus, and since each critical edition differs from every other, the self-sameness of some atomic enunciation becomes a highly questionable proposition.

Textual criticism creates objects that must be treated according to the Derridean logic of the remainder rather than the Foucauldian notion of residuality. If, by contrast, the study of ancient discourse is to be undertaken in a Foucauldian mode, some single critical text must be chosen at the expense of all the others and read not as a document produced by modern processes but rather as a monument located within an ancient discursive practice. In other words textual criticism, as a modern art with a history intimately connected with the problems associated with documents, must be elided or set aside.

Thus it seems to me that avoiding the variation between critical editions of ancient texts as a subject in its own right comes not from a desire to maintain the institutional power of editors (see chapter 1), but rather from the logic of the discursive formation that includes methods like Goldhill's ideological analysis. This discursive practice neglects the problematic of the document and the trace in the name of an archaeology of the monument. But in the study of ancient literature, our "monuments" are simulacra, phantasms.

Fetishes. The critical text, taken as a monument, functions as a commodity with a value determined according to its circulation in an abstract economy whose currency is "Athenian civic ideology" or the "discursive practice" of ancient Athens. For Foucault, the utterance qua monument "circulates, is used, disappears, allows or prevents the realization of a desire, serves or assists various interests, participates in challenges and struggle, and becomes a theme of appropriation and rivalry."[40] All of this is measured against the abstract value system of the discursive formation, which Foucault characterizes as an "economy of poverty"; the finite number of utterances within a discursive formation means that the historian is dealing not with a plethora of meanings but rather with a rarity, paucity, or poverty, of monuments:

> To analyze a discursive formation is to seek the law of that poverty, it is to weigh it up, and to determine its specific form. In one sense, therefore, *it is to weigh the "value" of utterances.* A value that is not defined by their truth, that is not gauged by the presence of a secret content; but which characterizes their place, *their capacity for circulation and exchange,* their possibility of

40. Foucault 1972, 105.

> transformation, *not only in the economy of discourse, but more generally, in the administration of scarce resources.*[41]

To transform the document into a monument is thus to treat the utterance not according to the specifics of its production (ancient or modern), but rather according to an abstract economy of exchange: to transform it, in other words, into a commodity.

Under the sign of this transformation of the document into a monument or commodity, Athenian democratic ideology facilitates a literary philology in which due care and careful reading of texts are transformed into a form of consumption. For Goldhill, the realities of textual production—ancient or modern—are completely effaced beneath the exchange system of ideology:

> The spoken word plays an extended and important role that would be hard to underestimate in fifth-century Athens (which is not to ignore the ideological importance of the construction of the many public monuments in the fifth-century *polis*). As much as the civic ideology we have been considering is formed in and through what can be called (in the widest sense) the language of the city, so the exchange of language plays a vital and extended role in the workings of the city. The sense of the city, its order and organization, its boundaries and structure, is formed in language, a language which dominates the various arenas and practices of city life. The city as such is constituted in the medium of language. Fifth-century Athens is truly the city of words.[42]

"The city of words": Can this suggest anything other than that Athens is the Hellenist's city of God, from which one is exiled but to whom one always pays first allegiance in a scholarly nostalgia and a committed philological practice? Ideological analysis is nothing more than a technique of bringing texts into quasi-economic contact with each other (the "exchange of language") according to the law of the past (the city "as such"). Ideology is the value according to which the totality of critical editions is brought into circulation. The real historical circumstances of their varying production is elided in precisely the same way that, according to Derrida's analyses of the late 1960s, written language, the logic of the trace, is elided and effaced by the history of metaphysics.

I imagine a study in which the archive of critical editions is read as a discursive formation in its own right, in which each critical edition is

41. Ibid., 120. My emphasis. See my comments above (n. 28) on the meaning of "modification."

42. Goldhill 1986a, 75.

taken as a discrete monument and the total differential system of texts is treated as what Foucault calls a discursive positivity or practice. It would be the presumption of such a study that the specificity of ancient literature is not based on any geographical, chronological, or linguistic delimitation, but rather on a particular relationship with the modernity that possesses, produces, and invokes antiquity endlessly in its own processes of self-definition. Ancient literature, or any genre within it such as Greek tragedy, would not be treated as a discursive practice as Goldhill and Foucault understand it (that which would present "*one* referential [or system of dispersion of objects], *one* type of enunciative utterance, *one* theoretical framework, *one* field of strategic possibilities"[43]). On the contrary the discursive formation such a study would bring to light would be the discursive formation of *modern classicism*, which is concerned with the self-definition of modernity through its encounter with a complex other named "antiquity" coeval with it.[44] Ancient literature, in this analysis, would be what Foucault calls a *referential*: the "law of dispersion of different objects or referents put into play by an ensemble of utterances."[45] That is, ancient literature would be the law of dispersion that governs different theoretical and text-critical utterances made in modernity for modernity's sake. It would therefore be true, as Goldhill has argued,[46] that the category of ancient literature has no real use when applied to the writings of classical antiquity, not because "literature" is a modern category used anachronistically of the writings of the past, but because there is nothing *specifically ancient* about the texts produced under the names of Sophocles, Plutarch, or Cicero; their production continues, and their antiquity is nothing more than the law according to which each critical edition varies from all others.

But before any such analysis could proceed, there is need for a radical philology capable of assessing the objects in this archive—that is, first and foremost, critical editions—for what they are. And this radical philology must be distinguished in significant ways from Foucault's archaeological method. For every critical edition speaks a language of difference and origin: no critical edition presents itself as *the text* of an ancient author, but rather as a trace, one half of a symbolic relation with an origin. And so, for the reading of critical editions, what is required is not an archaeology of ancient literature or of modern critical practice,

43. Foucault 1988, 321.
44. Such a direction has been embarked upon recently by Goldhill himself: see Goldhill 2002.
45. Foucault 1988, 314.
46. Goldhill 1999.

but rather an analysis of what might accurately be called the deconstructive core of textual criticism. To differentiate it from the fetishism of the critical text I have tried to diagnose in this chapter, such an analysis must oppose variability to stability, plurality to unity, and a concrete to a nostalgic idealism.

Chapter 3 contains the first attempts at a methodology for this radical philology.

3

For a Radical Philology

In the last sentence of chapter 2, I promised a methodology for the study of critical variation. But "method," in the sense of a rationalized, instrumentalizable set of intellectual operations that can be repeatedly performed on the products of textual criticism, is precisely what I cannot offer. Method presumes that the object to be studied is itself rationalized and rule-obeying; a rational method would then uncover the reason beneath the data. But one of the data in this case is the fact that the texts in a critical dossier are *not* the result of some rational, rule-governed logic.[1] The variation between versions of a classical text is instead the product of a force well known to those who have written about textual criticism: the force of freedom, of an irreducible and noninstrumentalizable judgment. This transforms textual criticism into what I term a "cyborg discipline," or into a space characterized by what Paul De Man called the "resistance to theory." Because critical judgment cannot be codified, because it does not obey any axiomatic

1. Here I differ from the diagnosis of Jean Bollack, for whom the productions of textual criticism are the result of an implacable and autonomous system of prejudices: "Les propositions ne sont recevables que si elles restent dans les règles qui fondent le consensus savant. Les conventions tacites qui régissent le débat exercent une autorité anonyme. Ainsi la justification d'une leçon peut ne pas être accuillie, pour convaincante qu'elle soit par elle-même. Elle sera combattue, ou passée sous silence. Les références restrictives se transmettent, en dépit des mouvements de l'idée; du coup, lorsque la fausse continuité enferme, l'invention, qui rompt, n'a pas de fonction" (Bollack 1990, I:xix).

rule of operation, it can produce a plurality of different versions. But, for the same reason, a philology of the critical text cannot itself obey a codified method. What is required instead, after a brief characterization of the domain, is a practice of careful inspection and attentiveness to the specificity of each version.

In this chapter I begin by explicating the cause of critical variation—critical freedom, or, as Housman once called it, "thought." I then turn from this assessment of the internal causes of critical variation and develop a theoretical construction that characterizes the critical dossier as a domain of study and provides an imperative for its philological investigation. In this second part, entitled "Theses for a Radical Philology," I contend that textual criticism is a practice essentially characterized by iteration and dissemination, two pillars of high deconstructive thought, and that its products are essentially implicated in a radical and irreducible textual plurality. Discovering this singular plurality in a critical version I give as the imperative of radical philology.

Freedom: the Cyborg Discipline

"Textual criticism," wrote A. E. Housman, "is an aristocratic affair," and also: "*criticus nascitur, non fit.*"[2] Elsewhere he fulminates against those who believe some method beyond competence in an ancient language and an innate talent for judgment might be a desideratum in textual criticism:

> As the wise man dieth, so dieth the fool: why then should we allow them to edit the classics differently? If nature, with flagitious partiality, has given judgment and industry to some men and left other men without them, it is our evident duty to emend her blind caprice; and those who are able and willing to think must be deprived of their unfair advantage by stringent prohibitions. In Association football you must not use your hands, and similarly in textual criticism you must not use your brains. Since we cannot make fools behave like wise men, we will insist that wise men behave like fools: by these means only can we redress the injustice of nature and anticipate the equality of the grave.[3]

Method, here described as "stringent prohibitions," robs the talented textual critic of his natural advantage, suppresses "thought," and makes

2. Housman 1972, 1069 and 1059.
3. Manilius 1937 (ed. Housman), 1:xxxiii.

for mediocre if not downright bad work. "Thought" is used here to conceal a mysterious power no theorist has ever been able to grasp. In fact, despite Housman's frequent exploitation of the divisions between "wisdom" and "folly," "judgment" and its lack,[4] one searches high and low for a satisfying answer to the question just what "thought" is supposed to be; Housman refuses to define it.[5] But clearly it is not method, not anything that can be codifiable, teachable, rationalized, or worked out in a systematic manner.

Housman is not eccentric in his emphasis on criticism's unmethodical core. In Paul Maas's influential division, the analytic discovery of the archetype or genealogical original from which all manuscripts of an ancient text are supposed to derive (*recensio*) is succeeded by *examinatio*, during which a critic "examines" the archetype and attempts to evaluate whether it is "true" to the original words of the author. This procedure depends largely on conjecture, taste, and judgment, qualities that Maas doubts can be taught or systematized.[6] According to Reneham, "the textual critic is the product of experience, of trial-and-error practice; a man can no more, simply by reading a tidy manual on textual criticism, acquire this craft than he can become a poet by coning an *ars poetica*."[7]

What Housman calls "stringent prohibitions" Kant would call *discipline*, canons of (largely negative) imperatives that prevent a study from overreaching its natural capacities.[8] "Thought" defies such discipline: it overreaches *by nature*, it speculates and extends beyond the limits of human capacity. Perhaps it is for this reason that textual critics so frequently define themselves as prophets.[9] Reneham, whose "reader" in textual criticism is a paratactic series of examples totally devoid of theoretical discussion, celebrates the inspiration of great critics by com-

4. Housman's constant divisions between the idiots and the critics should be a prime candidate for the kind of analyses undertaken by Ronell 2002.

5. Housman 1972, 1058.

6. Maas 1958, 16–17.

7. Reneham 1969, 1.

8. Kant 1998, 2.1 (628–671).

9. The classical statement is that of Richard Bentley: "One must have a very accurate and piercing judgment, a sagacity and acuteness, and, as was said of *Aristarchus* of old, a certain μαντικῆ, and skill in divining; which can never be acquir'd by the utmost industry, or length of time, but are owing to the bounty of nature, and the felicity of birth. And this is the reason, that in other studies the fruits are answerable to the hopes and pains bestowed upon them; whereas, in the school of criticism there have been so very few among the many who have spent their whole life, and grown grey in reading and meditation, that have been able to acquire fame, by engaging in this difficult task" (Horace 1725, 11 [translation of Horace 1711 (ed. Bentley)]).

menting that "the skill of a Porson or Housman at remedying with an easy dispatch *crux* after *crux* ought indeed to be numbered among the *θεῶν ἐρικυδέα δῶρα*; not without reason has this faculty been called in the Latin tongue *divinatio*."[10]

It is telling that while the emendations proposed by textual critics are often celebrated as "right," there is equally often a dearth of reasons why they should be so. Characteristic is James Zetzel's assessment of Housman: "His textual judgments are marked by extraordinary acumen and philological skill, and they are often right: but the reasons for them which he adduces are just as frequently specious."[11] Augustus Boeckh condones Schelling's claim that the philologist "stands with the artist and the philosopher at the topmost stage; or rather, these two pervade the philologist";[12] for Boeckh, the critic's sense for historical truth "is developed into an artistic driving force which *intuitively* hits its target."[13]

It is this drive that makes textual criticism an "aristocratic" affair, as Housman puts it. In a passage from the *Gay Science*, Nietzsche attributes rational calculation to the "common type," and instinct to the "noble":

> The higher type is more *unreasonable*, for those who are noble, magnanimous, and self-sacrificial do succumb to their instincts, and when they are at their best, their reason *pauses*.... They have some feelings of pleasure and displeasure that are so strong that they reduce the intellect to silence or to servitude: at that point their heart displaces their head, and one speaks of "passion."... The unreason or counterreason of passion is what the common type despises in the noble, especially when this passion is directed towards objects whose value seems quite fantastic and arbitrary.[14]

But as Nietzsche makes clear in the following sentences, the instinctual magnanimity of the noble cannot establish a new law. Rather its object is the singular exception. Mistaking this singular and subjective drive for a law or a method would make textual criticism unjust:

> The taste of the higher type is for exceptions, for things that leave most people cold and seem to lack sweetness; the higher type has a singular value standard. Moreover, it usually believes that the idiosyncrasy of its taste is *not* a singular value standard; rather, it posits its values and disvalues as generally valid and thus becomes incomprehensible and impractical.[15]

10. Reneham 1969, 2.
11. Zetzel 1993, 113.
12. Boeckh 1968, 22.
13. Ibid., 126. My emphasis.
14. Nietzsche 1974, #3 (77–78).
15. Ibid.

To the degree that the textual critic reinterprets "drive" as "thought" and establishes its results as "correct," his insight reaches an internal contradiction, since he both advocates the impossibility of "method" and elevates this absence of method to the very level of method itself. Housman's angry invective against those who do not "think," his dismissal of every perspective and practice that varies from his, and above all of those who dare to speak of "method," is, as Nietzsche says, "the eternal injustice of those who are noble."[16] "Injustice" here means the presence, within the same formulation, of two apparently incompatible propositions: first, that as dependent on "thought," textual criticism cannot be based on method; and second, that this nonmethodizable core can itself be elevated to method.

The injustice of textual criticism could be characterized in terms of what Paul De Man called the "resistance to theory."[17] For De Man, resistance to theory is a built-in component of any strongly theoretical approach; "nothing can overcome the resistance to theory since theory *is* itself this resistance."[18] De Man claims that theory remains innocuous and unthreatening so long as it stays within a space characterized by the dominance of logic, grammar, or semiotics, but it increases in complexity the moment it must take into account the necessity of reading. For De Man reading is not "reception," as this might be studied in reception-oriented theories like those of Wolfgang Iser or Hans Robert Jauss.[19] Rather, it designates the response to a residual kernel that remains even after the text has been systematically decoded by grammatical, logical, or other similarly rigorous procedures and does not submit to such forms of analysis; remaining for this reason indeterminate, it demands that a subject actively *generate* sense. In the literary analysis of texts, De Man locates this remainder in a figural dimension, a matrix of meaning based on a rhetoric of tropes that escapes systematic logical or grammatical penetration and demands a subjective act rather than the application of an impersonal system.

A problem arises, however, when strongly theoretical approaches try to take into account not only the logical progression of method *more geometrico* but also the fact of this indeterminable remainder. Taking into account both systematic methods that avoid or are incapable of reading *and* the singular act of reading, such approaches contain the promise of universality, since they address directly what a purely logical approach would denounce as merely subjective. But to the degree that

16. Ibid.
17. For a related perspective, see Gumbrecht 1998, 239, and Gumbrecht 2003.
18. De Man 1986, 19.
19. Iser 1978; Jauss 1982.

such approaches are generalizable and teachable—that is, to the extent that they are theory—they resist and put off the very reading whose necessity they acknowledge in the interest of being theoretical. Strong theory thus resists itself; it is "theory and not theory at the same time, the universal theory of the impossibility of theory."[20]

Similarly, the theory of the editing of classical texts must take into account both its systematic aspects and its unsystematizable core. In doing so it is forced to theorize the necessity of its absence, to conceive of itself as a "theory-free space." When Martin West dismisses the large bibliography of works on textual criticism with the words "Textual criticism is not something to be learned by reading as much as possible about it. Once the basic principles have been apprehended, what is needed is observation and practice, not research into the further ramifications of theory";[21] or when Kenney concludes his history of the theory of textual criticism by asking "whether the world of classical scholarship is now at last on the way to the possession of a general theory of textual criticism, which can be usefully embodied in writing and taught to students," and answers that "the theorists . . . have generally speaking not edited texts or have not done so with much distinction; the best practitioners have fought shy of methodizing and mechanization,"[22] the nobility of textual criticism, its resistance to theory in the sense offered by Paul de Man, is articulated. The terms in which the philological resistance to theory have been deployed vary, but in each case they do the necessary work of limiting "method" within a region of indeterminability and personal intuition that foregrounds the critic's function as irreducible to theoretical mechanization.

"Thought" and related concepts are most often associated with *examinatio*, but a remarkable study performed in the 1930s by William P. Shepard demonstrates that the process of establishing stemmata by comparing manuscript readings, though sometimes celebrated as rigorous and scientific, is no such thing.[23] In fact, it too boasts an irreducible and unpredictable kernel of nobility. Shepard produced stemmatic trees for a number of medieval French texts, using the methods of Greg and Quintin,[24] and compared these with stemmata for the same texts produced by critics relying on the methods of Karl Lachmann. Each of these four critics offered methods intended to be instrumental forms of reason. In other words they proposed to replace subjective and

20. De Man 1986, 19.
21. West 1973, 5.
22. Kenney 1974, 142–143.
23. Shepard 1930–1931.
24. Greg 1927; Quentin 1922, 1926.

individual insight with careful, rationalized, and systematic procedures of observation and deduction. Greg, for example, offered his "calculus" as substituting "symbols and formal rules for the continuous application of reason, thereby not only economizing mental effort, but avoiding, it is hoped, certain confusions of thought which, as experience shows, are liable to occur."[25] The promise was that after mastering some basic techniques of annotation and deduction, stemmatic relationships could be inferred with a high degree of accuracy and a minimum of thought. Shepard showed, however, that none of these systems produced the same genealogical tree for the same set of variants. His experiments demonstrate the absolute self-interest of such logical procedures: each methodological canon produces its own stemma and obeys its own internal laws with autonomous strictness and rigor.

Shepard's experiment demonstrates that the very concept of method is unconcerned with criteria of historical truth. Should any single method acquire complete ascendancy, it could not be said that the logistics of its operation attain to an actual vision of the original: eventually the necessary conclusion would be drawn that notions of "original" and "historical source" are metaphysical and beyond the reach of such an operating procedure—conclusions already drawn for pure reason by Immanuel Kant and for physics by Charles Frank.[26] Method would at that point achieve its own singular autonomy and start producing its own values as, in Marx's analysis, the use of automatized machinery on the factory floor creates a situation in which "the value objectified in machinery appears as a presupposition against which the value-creating power of the individual labor capacity is an infinitesimal, vanishing magnitude."[27]

It is the value of textual criticism to have thrown a *sabot* into the intellectual machinery of textual production. The day of the complete and reliable instrumentalization of stemmatic reason has not yet arrived. Indeed the devastating critique of traditional stemmatics undertaken by Giorgio Pasquali, and the emphasis of recent theorists such as Martin West and Thomas Tanselle on the importance of practice and subjective insight indicates that the hunt has been given up.[28]

25. Greg 1927, 13.
26. Kant 1998, Frank 1998.
27. Marx 1993, 694.
28. Pasquali 1952; Tanselle 1990, 274–321; West 1973, 312–313. It is indicative and characteristic that Tanselle's discussion of classical, biblical, and medieval textual criticism and modern editing is on the whole far more searching and insightful than the recent contributions of professional classicists, which still keep to the well-trodden triumphalist narratives of Wilamowitz (1982) and Kenney (1974); compare Tarrant 1991 and Zetzel 1993.

But this is not to say that method has been completely exiled, that textual criticism should be understood as entirely a matter of impulse and drive. On the contrary, since textual criticism aims at the editing of ancient texts and not the production of new ones, it always remains within a stream of information that is in some portion cybernetic. At the most basic level, this can be seen in the critic's informatic function as a copier and collator of versions and variants. These practices require extreme precision and a complete dedication to exact reproduction; in them the hand of the textual critic is appropriated by the text, just as the labor of the individual worker is appropriated by one of Marx's machines. But textual critics do not allow themselves to be appropriated by the tradition and leave it at that. At a certain point they ask whether what they have copied once is worthy of being copied again (in the pages of a printed text); an individual judgment is exercised that recognizes the contingency of the text and reserves the right to alter it. If to a certain degree the tradition has colonized the hand of the critic in copying, in critical judgment the critic countercolonizes the text.

We must not characterize the work of textual criticism, therefore, as pure, irreducible subjectivity and drive, or as autonomous and mechanized method. Instead we should characterize it as *cyborg*, as a melding of the cybernetic transmission of information and the organic control of these processes. If human and machine coalesce in the cyborg, making the human more mechanical and the mechanical more human, what the human supplies to the hybrid formation is a radical capacity for choice and thought. The difference between mechanized labor and cyborg labor is this: in the latter the potentiality exists that the coalescence of human and machine can break down or change direction of its own volition. In Marx's analysis of the machine, "labor appears as a conscious organ, scattered among the individual living workers at numerous points of the mechanical system; subsumed under the total process of the machinery itself, as itself only a link of the system, whose unity exists not in the living workers but rather in the living (active) machinery";[29] but in the cyborg operations of textual criticism consciousness reasserts itself, throwing a wrench into the works and instituting in place of the monstrous automaton of tradition a new vision of its origin and destiny. The textual critic is not the agent of tradition but its saboteur.

This must lead to a process of free variation in the production of a critical dossier: because the method of textual criticism predicts, even demands, the exertion of an irreducible freedom of judgment, there can

29. Marx 1993, 693.

be no regular progression of textual development, nor any teleologically oriented process of gradual approximation to some ancient "original." Instead, textual criticism produces a field of radical textual plurality, a field exploding with different texts and critical visions.

This field, and its individual members, is the object of the philology I propose under the name of *radical philology*. It has a number of crucial characteristics, which I adumbrate in the rest of this chapter. First, this plural field of textual difference is essentially and characteristically *literary*: that is, it is exactly what one would expect of an art associated with the survival of literary texts. For literary texts do not survive by simply remaining the same; rather they survive by being reiterated, over and over again, on different substances (papyrus, vellum, paper, .pdf) and in different forms. *Iteration* and *Dissemination*, the first two theses that follow, not only characterize any critical dossier, but also confirm the role of textual criticism as an essential part of the natural life of classical literature.

But each critical version is not only a different iteration in the life of a classical text; it is also a model of the essential plurality that characterizes the critical dossier itself. Just as individual freedom contains within itself the potentiality for a countless number of choices and actions, and just as a mind in the process of making a choice could be described as a virtual plurality of outcomes, so too does the critical essay or edition contain within itself a mirror of a plurality of *other* possible forms of the text. The plurality of versions of the *Iphigenia at Aulis* is thus a plurality of pluralities: each version is both a singular member of a plurality and a model and container of that plurality itself. The critical text is thus *singular plural*—a claim I explain and defend in the third thesis of this chapter.

Theses for a Radical Philology

Iteration

The difference, writes Nelson Goodman, between a painting and a work of literature lies in the fact that the painting cannot be copied. Any reproduction of a painting not explicitly named as such would constitute a forgery. By contrast the literary work exists by virtue of its capacity to be copied: indeed, it might be said to exist only through successive iterations. Goodman calls this the *allographic* character of the literary artifact.[30] It is characteristic of literature to exist in successive reproductions or copies, either in scriptural reproductions or in the successive reinscriptions of a text made in the process of reading. The iterability of the literary text reveals that textual flux, in all its forms—scribal, histrionic, text-critical, even translation and imitation—is not the negation or the progressive dissolution of an original work but rather its mode of existence.

But internal to iteration is alteration. Without some alteration we would not be able to identify iteration at all—we would perceive only permanence, *scripta manent*.[31] As Derrida puts it, "The structure of iteration...implies *both* identity *and* difference."[32] Not only does the literary work of art exist through a series of copies, but it exists in a perpetual state of flux, since its iterability necessarily implies that each copy differs from all others. Variation between critical editions is an organic component of the way of being of the literary work.

Thus the succession of critical editions of an ancient work, each of which is different from all others and none of which can claim to be "the" work, is nothing more than the modern form under which ancient literature continues to exist. The set of different versions in a critical dossier are not to be treated as "failures," partial or inaccurate images of an ancient original, more or less "wrong," separated by errors from the one true text. Rather each is to be included *within* the differential set that constitutes the authentic existence of the literary work. Textual criticism is the substance of ancient literature, not a tool used to recover it.

Dissemination

The combination of alteration and iteration instantiated in the proliferation of different critical editions should not be interpreted in terms of multiple meanings or polysemy. Polysemy belongs to interpretation and hermeneutics, to operations that aim to coordinate critical texts within a specific historical context and according to specific methodological axioms and criteria of interpretive "value" (such as ideology). This integrative procedure does not need to account for the alterations produced by the critical tradition. For Derrida, "polysemy always puts out its multiplicities and variations within the *horizon*, at least, of some

30. Goodman 1976, 113.
31. This is the founding thesis of Deleuze 1994.
32. Derrida 1977a, 190.

integral reading which contains no absolute rift, no senseless deviation—the horizon of the final parousia of a meaning at last deciphered, revealed, made present in the rich collation of its determinations."[33] Derrida's use of the term *integral* here is deliberate and illuminating: the metaphor is drawn from calculus, a theme frequent in French thought of the late 1960s and early 1970s. If polysemy is related to the interpretive project of integration, dissemination tracks the opposite movement, that is, toward the differential. It is a matter of the brute production of difference, not of differences in meaning (either as a limited or unlimited field of meanings) but material differences, the multiplication and proliferation through nonhermeneutic, purely textual practices, of alterations and variations.

If deconstruction aims to uncover the pervasiveness of difference, *prior* to meaning as an interpretive category, its first and most literal object is textual proliferation, that is, what is performed in the modern epoch through textual criticism. Textual criticism should therefore join mathematical notation and cybernetics as the forces of which deconstruction is the natural result.[34] From another perspective, I could be taken as proposing that the history of textual criticism in fact constitutes an important major prelude to the deconstructive tradition in philosophy.

To summarize: dissemination lies within the realm of textuality, which is here understood as the proliferation of variants, while polysemy belongs to the realm of literary philology or hermeneutics. Any edition or text may be "polysemous" when read by interpreters; but it is in the hands of the textual critic that texts disseminate themselves. The study of this critical dissemination of textuality is what I propose to call radical philology.

Singular Plural

The point of the first two theses is to emphasize the primary datum of the philology I am proposing: the difference between critical editions, the fact that classical texts continue to change even in the hands of textual critics. Critical editions are to be located within a differential system of texts. This much is (perhaps) obvious. My third thesis, however, may be less obvious: in addition to being contained by this differential system of texts, each edition also incorporates difference and plurality as part

33. Derrida 1981, 350.
34. Derrida 1976, 6–10.

of its essential mode of being. In the modern critical text, this can be seen most clearly in the critical apparatus, a catalogue of manuscript readings and critical emendations that differ from what is printed in the column of text. Although most critical apparatuses are limited and tendentious,[35] the presence of a limited field of difference at the base of the page or the back of the book nevertheless indicates that a critical edition is not merely contained within a system of differences, but also contains that system. To put it differently: the outside (the system of texts) penetrates the inside (the individual text) as its precondition and its origin.

The inner, constitutive plurality of the critical edition disseminates itself along two distinct planes. Contained within each singular edition are (1) a plurality of extant witnesses to a text (manuscripts, papyri, early editions) and (2) a plurality of possible versions of the original produced by textual critics.

First, the critical edition is in an essential relation with manuscripts and early printed editions. These texts lead the textual critic (in his role as stemmatist) to an archetype that differs *by definition* from the text of the critical edition. The stemmatist constructs genealogical relations between texts and determines the form of an archetype by comparing "errors" or "readings of secondary origin," that is, readings judged not to have been present in whatever text the critic wants to print. In general, manuscripts that share such errors share a source. On the basis of this principle, the source of all manuscripts can be determined. But this source must, according to a necessity imposed by the method itself, contain errors. According to West, "what is significant...is not agreement in true readings inherited from more ancient tradition, but agreement in readings of secondary origin, viz. corruptions and emendations, provided that they are not such as might have been produced by two scribes independently. The argument will run like this: There are some errors common to all six manuscripts, therefore they all descend from a copy in which these readings were present."[36] If the archetype did not contain certain errors, it could not be deduced as a common ancestor. Imagine two manuscripts, A and B, that have been securely identified as the sources of all subsequent extant manuscripts. If A and B hold certain errors in common, then they can be supposed to have a common source, C, which contains these aberrant readings. If, on the other hand, A and B had no common errors, C would remain unknown; the introduction

35. West 1973 advises that a critical apparatus should be constructed as an argument, with no more information than is necessary to defend the critic's reading.

36. Ibid., 32.

of secondary readings in A and B would have occurred independently and after the inscription of C. Without errors, an archetype would be impossible to discover.

The necessary presence of errors in the archetype means that the critical text is established on the basis of a difference *internal* to its production; an essential and irremovable difference between it and what stemmatic analysis reveals as the archetype. It is fair, accordingly, to say that the foundation of modern textual criticism is the aberrant nature of the witness or the archetype: whatever is extant, the critic wants *something different.* A critical edition, then, contains an internal and founding rift; like the remainder, the critical edition is split by an inner difference. In it we should see not the tangible past but "a differential structure escaping the logic of presence or the (simple or dialectical) opposition of presence and absence."[37]

However, since the archetype is by definition the last text that can be determined on comparative or diplomatic grounds, that is, according to a more or less determinable method (less: see above), the leap from archetype to whatever is presented as "original" (author's autograph, authorized edition, or performance text, for example) must take place in a theoretical vacuum and according to a measure of probability: this is the phase of criticism identified by Paul Maas[38] as *examinatio.* Though some constraints apply, these are not strong or prescriptive enough to guarantee a "correct" conjecture:[39] in fact, in the space between the archetype or oldest MS and the text "discovered" by the critic, there is room for a multiplicity of possible solutions to the same textual problem. According to Martin West, "the fulfillment of [constraints on emendation] does not logically guarantee that the true solution has been found, and there may sometimes be more than one solution that fulfills them."[40] The multiplicity of solutions to a textual problem, from which or in addition to which a critic may choose a reading to print, is the second plane of plurality constitutive of the critical edition. Though a critic's judgment may select a single reading, the nature of this judgment precludes absolute certainty and requires an awareness that other readings are possible. This is the basis for the presentation in

37. Derrida 1977a, 190.

38. Maas 1958.

39. They are very weak constraints, amounting to the stricture that an emendation should be in the same language as the original. See West 1973, 48.

40. Ibid. For what follows, "but often a reading seems so exactly right that those most familiar with the author can feel absolute certainty about it," and its attempt to elevate membership in a certain group (those most familiar with an author) to an epistemic principle, see above on the "eternal injustice of those who are noble."

the apparatus of the emendations of other critics: it marks the plurality that is a necessary corollary of the indeterminate epistemological status of conjecture.

Thus stemma and apparatus mark the inner plurality of the critical text, the place where the differential system of texts outside an edition takes up residence inside it. According to Derrida, "numerical multiplicity does not sneak up like a death threat upon a germ cell previously one with itself. On the contrary, it serves as a path breaker for 'the' seed, which therefore produces (itself) and advances only in the plural. It is a singular plural, which no single origin will ever have preceded. Germination, dissemination. There is no first insemination. The semen is already swarming. The 'primal' insemination is dissemination. A trace, a graft whose traces have been lost."[41] Such is the critical text: neither the presence of the past nor its absence, but an internally divided and externally divisive graft between present and past, a singularity shot through with a plurality of differences.

Here, with plurality bursting within and without the critical edition, we might recover sense for a radical philology. Though an integrative, "hermeneutical" approach to any single edition is closed off by this viewpoint (see above on dissemination), it does become possible to treat the production of plurality, dissemination itself, as a kind of differential meaning. Though we may not be able to fish a contextual or semantic spread of meanings (polysemy) from the depths of a single text or edition, the very plurality of editions might be called a production of sense, the making of another kind of meaning. "Meaning," writes Jean-Luc Nancy, "is the passing back and forth and sharing of the origin at the origin, singular plural. Meaning is the exhibition of the foundation without foundation, which is not an abyss but simply the *with* of things that are, insofar as they are."[42]

In other words the sense of a classical text does not arise hermeneutically from integration within a horizon (such as ideology, for instance). Rather, it emerges as the passage between editions in the critical dissemination of a classical text, at the point where the plurality outside the book penetrates and disperses the false unity of the edition itself: where the edition becomes a knot of many editions, a tangle of possibilities and a bursting variety of readings and textual forms. This singularity, not its integration into a single horizon but its bursting beyond that horizon in every direction, in a thousand shards, is the sense of the classical text.

41. Derrida 1981, 304.
42. Nancy 2000, 86–87.

If this is true, affirming the sense of (a) critical edition(s) means getting its/their idea. In *De mundi sensibilis et intellegibilis* (1770), Kant distinguished between "concepts" and "ideas" such as time. The former subsumed particulars under them in a hierarchical relationship, while the idea of time Kant considered a singularity that contained every individual time within it.[43] Time as an idea is, in the words of Deleuze, "an organization belonging to the many as such, which has no need whatsoever of unity in order to form a system."[44] An idea is an organization or a constellation of its constituent parts, a single thing that contains and constitutes a plurality that cannot be transformed into a "one." The idea, in other words, is singular plural. When Walter Benjamin claims that "ideas are to objects as constellations are to stars,"[45] it is precisely the singular plurality of the idea to which he refers. The constellation is nothing without the individual points; they, in turn, are organized by the singular constellation. In a similar fashion, a critical edition organizes its multiplicities through stemma and apparatus, and these multiplicities constitute the edition as its differentiated core. The idea is the multiplicity itself, as a multiplicity, the density of the multiplicity that gives the critical edition sense. To put it simply, without a multiplicity of manuscripts or conjectural emendations to a classical text, a *critical* edition would be a senseless undertaking.

I must distinguish my understanding of the idea from what might be termed "two-world idealism." Two-world idealism posits a transcendent ideal realm located "elsewhere," immaculately beyond our world. This kind of idealism is abstractive; the idealism I advocate is concrete. If two-world idealism posits a realm of ideas "there," achieved by removing (abstracting) time and space, the idealism of radical philology locates the idea *here*, in time and space. For Kant, time *is* the idea, not its imitation, as it is in Plato's *Timaeus*, where a distinction is made between "eternity" in this world and "timelessness" in that. To get the idea, accordingly, means to come face-to-face with the concrete embodiment of the world, of this world, in all its rich heterogeneity and difference, not to arrive at a blissful contemplation of another world that is unitary and unchanging, the extreme negation of the here and now. It is to be uncompromisingly—radically—concrete.

What is concrete is not (at least not in any sphere beyond the construction site, and probably not even there) simple, impenetrable, unin-

43. Kant 1922, section 14.2 (415). The distinction is repeated, in nearly identical terms, in Kant 1998, 155–171.

44. Deleuze 1994, 182.

45. Benjamin 1998, 34.

teresting, a "mere" object. The concrete is, on the contrary, a complex collocation, an assemblage—I would like to say a constellation—of elements held together in a force field that does not reduce itself to a governing unity. As an illustrative example, we may briefly consider concrete poetry, a variegated movement that could be exemplified by the "Calligrammes" of Guillaume Apollinaire. Concrete poetry utilizes the full range of possibilities embodied in language (the sound of the word, its disposition in space and time, the dimensions of the page, typography, and so on) to "communicate nothing but its own structure."[46] A reader presented with such texts faces not a message ornamented by poetic devices, but rather a set of linguistic and grammatological juxtapositions on a page shot through with tensions and forces. Eugen Gomringer characterizes this poetic as a method of generating constellations: "The constellation is the simplest possible kind of configuration in poetry which has for its basic unit the word, it encloses a group of words as if it were drawing stars together to form a constellation.... In the constellation something is brought into the world. It is a reality in itself and not a poem about something or other."[47] A founding example of this method of constellation is Mallarmé's "Un coup de dés." In this poem, the construction of the page, utilization of space, and typographical devices are integral parts of the text. On the last two pages, for example, a string of uppercase words (RIEN / N'AURA EU LIEU / QUE LE LIEU / EXCEPTÉ/ PEUT-ÊTRE / UNE CONSTELLATION) is constellated with phrases that are part of, but also juxtaposed against, the central capitalized thread.

Paul Valéry, describing his first encounter with the poem, articulated his reaction as a singular shock in which were crystalized experiences of idea, constellation, and world:

> It seemed to me that I was looking at the form and pattern of a thought, placed for the first time in finite space. Here space itself truly spoke, dreamed, and gave birth to temporal forms....There on the very paper some indescribable scintillation of final stars trembled infinitely pure in an inter-conscious void; and there on the same void with them, like some new form of matter arranged in systems or masses or trailing lines, coexisted the world! I was struck dumb by this unprecedented arrangement. It was as if a new asterism had proffered itself in the heavens; as if a constellation had at last assumed a meaning. Was I not witnessing an event of universal importance, and was it not, in some measure, an ideal enactment of the creation of language that was being presented to me?[48]

46. de Campos 1970, 72.
47. Gomringer 1970.
48. Valéry 1972, 9:309–310.

Valéry suggests that this concrete constellation is ideal, a suggestion prompted by Mallarmé himself, who described his composition as comprising "prismatic subdivisions of the idea."[49]

A passage in Gilles Deleuze, otherwise obscure, is suddenly illuminated when we see it as a reading of the "Coup de dés," and further reinforces the association of the concrete constellation with the idea. Commenting on the proposition that "ideas are pure multiplicities: every idea is a multiplicity or a variety"[50] (we have already seen how the meaning of this idea is latent in Kant's connection of the idea with the singularities space and time), Deleuze writes: "It is... a question of a throw of the dice, of the whole sky as open space and of throwing as the only rule.... Ideas are the problematic combinations which result from throws. The throw of the dice is in no way suggested as an abolition of chance."[51] The throw of the dice, the problematic combination (or constellation) that emerges under (or in?) the "open sky," is the idea, in concrete.

Mallarmé, and the mainstream of concrete poetics after him, reacts to a malaise with the unreflected word, the word that merely signifies, placidly pointing to something else (a narrative or a feeling, for example). While the "poetry of expression, subjective and hedonistic"[52] orders itself in delicate columns determined by the abstract matrices of the printing press, concrete poetry disperses the word throughout the space of the page, unsettling the innocent simplicity of the text block with contradictions, second-guesses, and insipient pluralities. But how different is this from what is accomplished by the modern critical edition of a classical text? Perched over the shifting magma of multiple possibilities in the critical apparatus, no column of text is more fraught with contradiction and tension than the neat column of a classical text. As a constellation of possibilities, manuscript readings, and critical conjectures, it is a concrete idea in its own right.

The concrete idealism of radical philology is also, I hasten to add, a rigorous materialist historicism. "Traditional" historicism aims at a complete reconstruction of a past era—such, I suggested, is at stake in "ideological" analyses of Greek tragedy. This historicism would be the equivalent of two-world idealism: beyond this world, and the texts and fragments to be found here, there is another world: the past, which

49. Mallarmé 1998, 391.

50. Deleuze 1994, 182.

51. Ibid., 198. (The leading thread at the beginning of Mallarmé's poem is "Un coup de dés jamais n'abolira le hasard.")

52. de Campos 1970, 72.

can be reconstructed and contemplated as a neoplatonist might contemplate an ideal unity.[53] A materialist historiography, on the other hand, treats the detritus and the traces present in this world and directs its attention to concrete embodiments. In reading critical editions for their idea, for their singular plurality, I will in effect do nothing more than what Benjamin referred to as materialist historiography: "Thinking involves not only the flow of thoughts, but their arrest as well: where thinking suddenly stops in a configuration [*Konstellation*] pregnant with tensions, it gives that configuration a shock, by which it crystallizes into a monad. A historical materialist approaches a historical subject only where he encounters it as a monad."[54] The critical text is just such a monad, constellating the history of critical variance. On the structure of a monad, Benjamin writes, "This structure first comes to light...in the form of the historical confrontation that makes up the interior (and, as it were, the bowels) of the historical object, and into which all the forces and interests of history enter on a reduced scale."[55] The historical confrontation that takes place in the critical text takes place as a condensed or "reduced" confrontation in the critical apparatus, the "bowels" of the edition. It is the critical edition as constellation—as singular plural, or as concrete idea—that radical philology aims to grasp.

The pervasion of difference within the field of textual criticism, the singular plurality of the critical edition, explains the experience, perhaps more common than reported, of the critical edition as an abyss and of classical scholarship as an attack of vertigo. Martin West quotes some lines that Eduard Fraenkel wrote in 1960:

> I had read the greater part of Aristophanes, and I began to rave about it to [Friedrich] Leo, and to wax eloquent on the magic of this poetry, the beauty of the choral odes, and so on and so forth....When I was finished, [Leo] asked, "In which edition do you read Aristophanes?" I thought: has he not been listening? What has this question got to do with what I have been telling him? After a moment's ruffled hesitation I answered: "The Teubner." Leo: "Oh, you read Aristophanes without a critical apparatus." He said it quite calmly, without any sharpness, without a whiff of sarcasm, just sincerely taken aback that it was possible for a tolerably intelligent young man to do such a thing. I looked at the lawn nearby and had a single, overwhelming sensation: *νῦν μοι χάνοι εὐρεῖα χθών* [now may the broad earth gape open for me].[56]

53. See Porter 2003.
54. Benjamin 1968, 262–263.
55. Benjamin 1999, N10, 3 (475).
56. West 1973, 7.

This particular wish is accomplished the moment it is formulated. When Fraenkel realizes that there is more to a classical text than its neatly printed elegance implies, the ground gives way beneath him. It is in a chasm in which no feet are sure, not even the poetic feet of Aristophanes' poetry, that Fraenkel locates what he calls "the meaning of real scholarship." True scholarship, we can see from this story, is fundamental—not in the sense that textual criticism furnishes the "ground," "bedrock," or "solid foundation" for literary criticism, but in the sense that the critic and the reader of a critical edition experience antiquity *de profundis*, from the interminable depths of a chasm or an abyss: a hell, perhaps, if indeed "hell is others,"[57] the space in which the presence and never-ending demand of other texts articulate themselves inside and outside the "discrete" remainder. And here, perhaps, we arrive again at McGann's distinction between the "angels of hermeneutics" and the "devils" of textual criticism (see chapter 1), though now our understanding could be infinitely deeper than before.

In this thesis I argued that (1) a critical edition is split by an inner rift between itself and the stemmatically determined archetype: as a result, it cannot be described simply as the presence of the past but as an uneasy graft between present and past, a returning ghost with a foot in two worlds. The ontology of the critical text is what Derrida once called a hauntology.[58] (2) Between the archetype and the edition is a gap filled with a plurality of possible readings: those that end up in the text and those that end up in the apparatus. This second plane of difference is produced by the absence of any method for crossing from archetype to edition: criticism is shot through with a human subjectivity that cannot be eliminated. (3) The conjunction of these pluralities within the critical edition allows us to imagine the critical edition as an idea; to conceive this idea is to get its sense.

The third observation of this thesis—that seeing the edition as singular plural constitutes acquiring its sense, having its idea—constitutes a directive for the practice of radical philology: "Get the idea of the critical edition; unpack its sense by perceiving the conjunction of pluralities within it!" I speak of a directive rather than a method because no single line of analysis or method of research will reveal the sense of every critical edition. Rather, each edition demands it own approach: we must be sensitive to the specificity of the edition, listening carefully to its clues and murmured confessions. Only in this way—through a loving and

57. "L'enfer, c'est les Autres" (Sartre 1947, 182).
58. Derrida 1994, 161.

careful attentiveness to each text (i.e., only by being *philologists*)—will its meaning occur for us. Therefore an ethics, not an instrumentalizable method, is required. I try to practice this ethics in my reading of critical approaches to the *Iphigenia at Aulis* undertaken in part 2.

Afterword to Part 1

> οὐ Μενέλεώς με καταδεδούλωται, τέκνον,
> οὐδ' ἐπὶ τὸ κείνου βουλόμενον ἐλήλυθα,
> ἀλλ' Ἑλλάς, ᾗ δεῖ, κἂν θέλω κἂν μὴ θέλω,
> θῦσαί σε· τούτου δ' ἥσσονες καθέσταμεν.
> ἐλευθέραν γὰρ δεῖ νιν ὅσον ἐν σοί, τέκνον,
> κἀμοὶ γενέσθαι, μηδὲ βαρβάρων ὕπο
> Ἕλληνας ὄντας λέκτρα συλᾶσθαι βίᾳ.

> Menelaus has not enslaved me, child, nor have I gone over to his design. But *Greece* has enslaved me, for whom I must sacrifice you, whether I wish to or not. We are less than her. As far as it lies in your power, and in mine, she must be free, nor must Greeks have their wives stolen by barbarians.[1]

That is Agamemnon in Euripides' *Iphigenia at Aulis,* trying to justify to Iphigenia his intent to sacrifice her to Artemis. He holds Greece up here as a massive national collective, assembled for war against the "barbarians" who have allowed Paris to abduct Helen from Menelaus. Agamemnon would have Iphigenia believe that Greece is a supraindividual machine in whose name the lives and deaths of single men and women must be given.

When Agamemnon speaks these lines, Iphigenia does not want this

1. *Iphigenia at Aulis* 1269–1275 Diggle.

death; "He is mad who wants to die," she says; "it is better to live badly than to die well" (1251–1252 Diggle). But in less than one hundred lines, she will change her mind. "I want to die," she will say at 1375. "All of mighty Greece now looks to me" (1378). For the machine, for Greece, Iphigenia's decision to die is salvation, a self-sacrifice that solidifies and assents to the war-machine, a countersignature to the text of the Trojan War and the narrative of identity it engenders. In a way it is the same kind of willing submission to the demands of a foreign system that is performed by the textual critic, who lends his voice to an idea of the past and a dream of literature that would without him only survive in tatters and fragments, who consents to speak in an alien tongue and through an alien voice, and who in doing so dies partly to his own era and languages.

But this self-sacrifice does not quite enable Greece as a fully autonomous system. It is willing and surprising, and not a little disturbing, and that makes all the difference. Iphigenia's willing choice to die is, as Yeats once said, an image that "can bring wildness, bring a rage";[2] the machine trembles with this singular choice, a choice that sets the cost of its construction too high. The force of its shock is felt in the manner in which it is introduced: Iphigenia announces her intent to die midline (1368 Diggle), interrupting a conversation between Achilles and Clytemnestra and surprising them with her new resolution. Surprises are signs of the freedom that resists and opposes the autonomous operation of nationalist or textual machines;[3] the signs that what is produced in the narrative of the *Iphigenia at Aulis* is not an unquestionable national "Greece," but rather a cyborg, one in which the freedom that submits throws a wrench in the machinery and signals the provisionality of what it submits to, the possibility that it may at any point be ruined and reconfigured. Iphigenia sabotages the machine by submitting to it. "The Greeks had a phrase that is still with us today," writes David Rorvik:

> *Theos ek mēchanēs*, better known in the Latin as *Deus ex machina*. It means, literally, *a god from a machine*, and today denotes an entity, be it god, man, or simply thing, that emerges suddenly and unexpectedly to provide a seemingly miraculous solution to a seemingly insoluble conundrum or difficulty.
>
> *Deus ex machina* promises to remain part of the language, since seemingly insoluble problems are more than ever with us. But it will almost certainly assume new significance as the god, or, as some would have it,

2. "Nineteen Hundred and Nineteen," in Yeats 1989 (ed. Jeffares), 314–318, 316.
3. See Nancy 1993.

> the "ghost," in the machine turns out to be man himself, albeit man of an entirely new order.[4]

For Rorvik, the god is humanity in the new cyborg order, an order in which freedom, integrating with and thereby taking greater control of the machinic automation of natural laws, assumes responsibility for its own future in what he calls "participant evolution."[5] The cyborg melding of the human and the machine allows humanity to exert its freedom over the processes that had previously dominated it—both the natural and the machinic. Humanity must continue to change and to evolve, but this evolution becomes the product and the expression of human will. This is not meant to be a utopian vision; it is a terrible vision, a vision of terrible responsibility, and a vision that reveals the shakiness of our foundations—they are only as strong as the next choice. For participant evolution the god in the machine is a terrible, dangerous force at the same time as it is a sublime container of the greatest freedom. For Agamemnon's Greece that god was Iphigenia; for our Greece, it is, perhaps, the textual critic.

4. Rorvik 1971, xxviii.
5. Ibid., 105–138.

PART 2

Introduction to Part 2

The presence of Euripides' *Iphigenia at Aulis* in the modern epoch is like that of an accidental guest at a party, someone who has arrived at a black-tie affair in a sweatshirt and jeans. It looks suspicious: frayed at the edges, unpolished, and dressed in clothes that both the servants guarding the doors and the masters of ceremonies find distasteful and distressing. To make matters worse there are rumors, from trustworthy sources, that this guest is not who she claims to be.

The Alexandrian edition of Euripides' works was completed by Aristophanes of Byzantium in the late third century BCE.[1] What happened to the text of the *Iphigenia at Aulis* between then and the fourteenth century is a matter of conjecture, but it has been described by Zuntz as marked by the activity of "actors 'improving' the wording of their rolls—perhaps on the model of some pre-Alexandrian copy, or also from their own guess; schoolmasters glossing difficult passages, students entering variants from other exemplars, devoted readers jotting down parallels from other plays; and all this copied and recopied." This process of variation was tempered by a "respect for the authentic wording of their literary heritage. Responsible βιβλιοπῶλαι would check the work of their employees, and careful readers their own copies, against a text considered authoritative."[2] The tradition was further affected by

1. See Pfeiffer 1968, 171–209.
2. Zuntz 1969, 253.

historical forces that caused a "selection" of plays to be disseminated through late antiquity and the Byzantine period.[3] The collected works, including the *Iphigenia at Aulis*, survived in forgotten corners of libraries, noticed only by rare and unusual readers. Far out of the mainstream, they would have been lost completely if in the fourteenth century Demetrius Triclinius had not found some portion of them[4] and commissioned the manuscript copy now known as "L." Some time after the creation of L, a copy was made (it is now known as "P"), which went to Italy before 1420.[5] This manuscript became the basis of Musurus's Aldine edition of Euripides in 1503/04, "and thereby, of the text generally used for centuries to come."[6]

Thus did *Iphigenia at Aulis* emerge in modern European awareness. Its arrival might be described as simultaneously successful and scandalous. In 1506 Erasmus published a translation of the *Iphigenia at Aulis* and the *Hecuba* in Paris; Aldus released a second edition in 1507.[7] The choice of the two plays was probably influenced by the subject matter—the pathetic story of a virgin being led to a sacrificial death, shared by both plays, has martyrological overtones that appealed to early modern tastes.[8] Erasmus's translations sparked energetic interest in the plays: Robert Bolgar reports that of the nineteen translations of Euripides before 1600, six were of the *Hecuba* while four were of *Iphigenia at Aulis*.[9] To this accounting we should add the translation of *Iphigenia at Aulis* made by Lady Joanna (Jane) Lumley, probably after 1553.[10]

But with the success of the *Iphigenia at Aulis* came a small kernel of doubt. Erasmus commented: "It has somewhat more naturalness and its style is more flowing [than the *Hecuba*]. For which reason it might seem to be by Sophocles: but again it rather suggests Euripidean paternity by its close-packed themes and a sort of rhetorical ability in marshalling arguments on one side or the other of a question. However it is not my

3. I follow the account of Zuntz, which differs in detail from that of Tuilier 1968, 69–113. Tuilier attributed the selection to the formation of a performance repertoire in antiquity. On the question of the "choice," see also Wilamowitz-Moellendorff 1907, 185 and 196; Turyn 1957.

4. For this stage in the history, see the brief summary of West 1981.

5. Zuntz 1969, 283.

6. Ibid. The Aldine edition is Euripides 1503.

7. See the introduction of Waszink in Erasmus 1969, 195–212. I cite from this edition.

8. On the appeal of *Iphigenia at Aulis* and *Hecuba* in the early modern period, see Purkiss 1999, Erasmus 1969, 207.

9. Bolgar 1954, 512–515.

10. Euripides 1909. First printed in 1909, but missed by Bolgar and Waszink. See Hodgson-Wright 1998.

province to determine to which of the two it should be ascribed, nor do I think it matters much."[11] We can only guess whether this contains a gesture to debates over the authenticity of the *Iphigenia at Aulis* Erasmus had with friends in Venice or England, or even with Musurus himself.[12] But it does introduce the question of authenticity at the beginning of the play's modern career. In Erasmus the doubt feels like a bomb waiting to go off, though the absence of anything concrete to detonate it left its effects latent—and its significance questionable ("nor do I think it matters much")—for nearly 250 years.[13]

Erasmus did correct the text in preparing his translation,[14] but his emendations, like those of the critics who followed, were verbal and sought to bring the text into line with accepted cannons of Greek grammar and usage. Barnes's 1694 edition shows no doubt about authorship, and a note to verse 1550 (part of the messenger's speech describing the sacrifice of Iphigenia) suggests he was certain that the lines were Euripides': "Andreas Schottus (*Obs. Hum.* 1.5 c.17) correctly noted that this passage of *Euripides* inspired that very famous painter Timanthes."[15] By 1934, however, this line of influence was reversed. In *Actors' Interpolations in Greek Tragedy*, Denys Page hypothesized that of three different versions of the play's conclusion circulating in antiquity, the one represented in L was actually *inspired* by Timanthes, and not the other way round.[16]

Intervening between Barnes and Page are two events, separated by a space of forty years, which had a devastating effect on estimations of the authenticity of *Iphigenia at Aulis*, and on the texts as they were imagined and printed thereafter. The first was Samuel Musgrave's discovery (reported in 1762) of two and one-half lines not present in the received text.[17] These were quoted in the third century CE. by Aelian in the *de Natura Animalium* and attributed to Euripides' *Iphigenia at Aulis*:

11. "Et plusculum habet candoris et fusior est dictio. Quo quidem nomine Sophoclea videri queat; at rursus argumentorum densitate quasique declamatoria quadam suadendi ac dissuadendi facultate parentem Euripidem magis refert. Quamquam utri sit inscribenda neque meum est pronuntiare neque magni referre puto." Erasmus 1969, 271–272. The translation is taken from Erasmus 1975, 133.

12. Waszink (Erasmus 1969, 197n.9) conjectures with some probability that Erasmus had consulted Musurus on the text of the tragedies.

13. For editions between Aldus and Barnes, see my bibliography and that of Euripides 1988 (ed. Günther), xiv.

14. See Erasmus 1906–1958 ep. 209 and Waszink ad loc.

15. "Rectissime observat *Andreas Schottus* Observ. Human. I.5. c. 17. hunc *Euripidis* locum *Timanthi* illi celeberrimo Pictori ansam dedisse" (Euripides 1694 [ed. Barnes] ad *Iphigenia at Aulis*, 1550). See Schottus 1615.

16. Page 1934, 203.

17. Musgrave 1762.

ἔλαφον δ' Ἀχαιῶν χερσὶν ἐνθήσω φίλαις
κεροῦσσαν, ἣν σφάζοντες αὐχήσουσι σὴν
σφάζειν θυγατέρα.

And I shall put into the dear hands of the Achaeans a horned deer; slaughtering it they will think they are slaughtering your daughter.[18]

These lines suggested that somewhere in some version of the play a goddess—always assumed to be Artemis—spoke of Iphigenia's transmogrification at the altar, which in the extant play is narrated by a messenger.

The second event to have devastated the received text of *Iphigenia at Aulis* was the publication, in 1802, of Richard Porson's introduction to Euripides' *Hecuba*,[19] where a set of criteria for metrical correctness was established, according to which it became impossible to believe that the iambic conclusion to the *Iphigenia at Aulis* could have been a genuine specimen of Attic tragedy.[20]

These two events had a lasting effect on the text of the *Iphigenia at Aulis*. Before Musgrave and Porson, the text had been sustained in a tradition that varied only slightly. Whatever doubts about its authorship might have circulated between the times of Erasmus and Musgrave were kept at a discrete distance from the business of producing and reproducing the text itself. But after Musgrave's discovery of the lines in Aelian and Porson's suspicion of the end of the play due to metrical irregularities, the tragedy became highly unstable; its form fluctuated wildly in the hands of critics. It is the purpose of part 2 to read some of the more spectacular versions of the *Iphigenia at Aulis* that proliferated in their wake.

In addition to provoking the text's modern critical history, the fragment discovered in Aelian and the metrical irregularities of the final scene encapsulate the terms under which its history unfolds, determine its form, and set out the parameters of sense for each critical version. Together they constitute a binary system whose dynamics energize the dissemination of *Iphigenia at Aulis* at every level of analysis: the *scholarly methodology* that produces its critical texts, the *form of the history* of its criticism, and the *sense* of the play itself.

18. Aelian 1971 (ed. Scholfield) VII.39. "σφάξαντες pars cod." Diggle (422). There is one critical variant of this text, which I discuss below. The translation is mine.

19. Euripides 1802 (ed. Porson).

20. West 1981 contains an excellent and concise recent summary of the difficulties perceived at the end of the play.

Scholarly Methodology

Between them, Musgrave and Porson supply the two forms of evidence essential in every text-critical undertaking: external and internal forms of evidence. The *Port-Royal Logic*, for example, uses textual criticism as a primary example in its analysis of historical knowledge,[21] an explication that continues to characterize the epistemological structures of textual criticism. It can be rephrased as follows. When we are assessing the probability of some event actually having taken place, we must take account of two sets of circumstances: "internal" circumstances and "external" circumstances. The former are circumstances associated with the event itself, while external circumstances are associated with the witnesses to an event.[22] For example, if a known liar tells us that last Wednesday his pet dog recited the first four lines of Homer's *Iliad* in Greek, we must take account of two different sets of circumstances in assessing the probability of this report. On internal grounds, we may reason that it is very unlikely that this dog recited the first four lines of Homer's *Iliad* in Greek, because ancient Greek is a difficult language, and this dog has had no formal education. On external grounds, we take into account the fact that the witness to this event has been known to make up false stories in the past and is therefore not to be trusted. Accordingly, we conjecture that this event never took place.

A similar process of thought must be followed in assessing the genuineness of a work or a passage. Here the event may be specified as a particular author inscribing a particular set of words; the witnesses are the extant manuscripts that contain those words and ascribe them to that author. We must consider both internal and external circumstances to assess the probability that this event of inscription took place. *Internally* we must ask whether this author could have used these words; if he could have known about or referred to such and such an event; if he was in the habit of writing in this particular style. These are questions about the *event of inscription*, not about the product of this event, that is, the words as they appear in the manuscripts. *Externally* we must ask whether the manuscript witnesses to this event of inscription are trustworthy: Do they contain errors that suggest a level of unreliability? Are they contradicted by other manuscript witnesses to the same inscriptional event? Can the evidence of all the witnesses be harmonized? We

21. Arnauld and Nicole 1996, 4:15 (270–273).

22. "I call those circumstances internal that belong to the fact itself; and those external that concern the persons whose testimony leads us to believe in it" (Arnauld and Nicole 1996, 4:13 [264]).

may conclude that, given what we know about witnesses and about acts of inscription in general, the hypothesized event, that is, such and such an author inscribing such and such a set of words, is unlikely to have taken place or, in other words, that it is improbable that this author wrote those words.

These two kinds of circumstance correspond to the two primary operations of textual criticism: *recensio*, an investigation of the manuscript witnesses, considers external circumstances, while *examinatio*, assessing the probability that an author could have written what is in the archetype, considers internal circumstances.

Porson's Law pertains to internal forms of evidence (it pertains to the likelihood that Euripides wrote iambic trimeters with certain prosodic characteristics), while the discovery of a divergent witness in Aelian supplies external evidence on the question of the authorship of the *Iphigenia at Aulis.* Other considerations in the criticism of *Iphigenia at Aulis* can be subsumed under these two headings, as well: seeking external evidence, critics looked beyond the passage in Aelian for any other ancient source that could cast light on the play's form, such as citations by other authors, pictorial representations, and papyrus finds.[23] Internal circumstances, that is, the likelihood that an inscriptional event associated with Euripides and features of the text as we have it should go together, have also played a major role. Evidence of this kind, for example, is supplied by the facts that the *Iphigenia at Aulis* begins with an anapestic dialogue, something usually taken as unparalled in Euripides (The *Rhesus* is usually set aside, and the *Andromeda* debated); that verse 414 contains a messenger speech that begins midline (also unparalleled); that there are numerous linguistic features taken to be suspicious or impossible; and that the play seems to violate general aesthetic criteria of logical regularity and a particular dramatic style.[24]

There is an important second difference between the discovery of Musgrave and the law of Porson: external evidence destabilizes the text, while internal evidence exerts a stabilizing force. A divergent witness to the ancient text (for example, a citation of the play containing lines not found in the manuscripts L or P) causes critics to doubt the traditional forms and initiates a series of conjectural attempts to incorporate

23. A summary of this evidence can be found in Page 1934, 128; Euripides 1994 (ed. Diggle) 3:358, 452; and Euripides 1988 (ed. Günther), passim. On two occasions this evidence led to the hypothesis that the play we have received came not from the hand of Euripides but from Chaeremon (Gruppe 1834; Bang 1867).

24. Page 1934 contains the most influential treatment of the evidence for and against interpolation in the play.

the new evidence; the paradosis breaks apart and mutates quickly in critics' hands. But criteria such as metrical or stylistic regularity serve as a constraint on fluctuation: proposed forms of the text that violate these criteria are excluded. Regularity holds out the offer of a solid criterion thanks to which textual fluctuation might one day come to an end. There is accordingly a tension between the two characteristic functions of textual criticism, in which the one serves as an agent of instability in the modern text while the other serves as an advocate for stability.

Form of the History of Criticism on *Iphigenia at Aulis*

The discovery of the lines in Aelian had a strong effect on critics' thought in the years immediately after Musgrave's discovery. But this effect waned through the nineteenth century, as metrical and stylistic considerations took the fore and the authenticity of the Aelianic fragment came to be doubted. The history of criticism on this text, in other words, displays a gradual favoring of internal over external forms of evidence. But if, as I suggested above, external evidence serves as an agent of textual instability while internal evidence functions as a constraint encouraging reduced textual fluctuation, this suggests that the texts of *Iphigenia at Aulis* between 1762 and the present belong to an *unstable system* tending toward stability and regularity. Favoring the Aelian fragment as an important piece of evidence, which begins early and fades through the nineteenth century, destabilizes the old textual system, while the criterion of systematic regularity points toward an entropic final state of the text in a new textual systematicity.

I believe the fully entropic state is achieved in the Oxford text of James Diggle.[25] Diggle invented a new set of sigla that evaluate each line of text in the *Iphigenia at Aulis* according to the probability of its having been written by Euripides; the edition is modalized throughout by the critic's awareness that his judgments have value only as measurements of probability. But at the same time, the use of a graded canon of probability provides Diggle's text with a matrix that is systematic and stable according to its own logic. But the "stable state" textual system that emerges in Diggle's edition does not mark a return to any pre-Musgravite textual stability. This new stability is based on a systematization of the subjectivity and incompleteness of text-critical insight, replacing the notion of an

25. Euripides 1994 (ed. Diggle).

original, law-abiding, and law-setting cause (Euripides the author) with a systematic calculus of probabilities.

Part 2 traces this historical trajectory. In chapter 4 I track the effects of the initial destabilizing event, the discovery of the fragment in Aelian, which inaugurates a period during which the personal insight and subjective power of each critic produces a new version. In chapter 5 I trace the history that leads to Diggle's systematization of this subjectivity and openness. Neither chapter aims to present a complete survey of all the text-critical investigations into the *Iphigenia at Aulis.* Rather, I aim to give a good account of the two significant moments in this unstable system's history: that of the initial destabilization, and that of its "cold" entropic state.[26]

Sense of the Critical Version

The fragment found in Aelian clearly speaks to the plot—it is universally held that these lines must be spoken by Artemis, either at the beginning of the play (in a prologue announcing her intention to rescue Iphigenia from the sacrificial altar at the last moment), or *ex machina* at its end. The position of these lines bears directly on whether or not Clytemnestra will believe the report that her daughter has been rescued. If she receives this news from a messenger, as she does in the extant ending, there may be room for her to doubt this news, and to suspect that it is a further contrivance of Agamemnon. If, on the other hand, the news is delivered by Artemis herself, such an authoritative witness can leave little room for hesitation: Iphigenia would have been rescued.

Thus major thematic issues are affected by how the critic treats the evidence. But this is not the only place where the nature and value of information is at stake. From beginning to end the play revolves around the timing and nature of messages. In fact, the plot revolves around two modes of informational release that are precisely isologous to the two types of evidence available to text-criticism: on the one hand, the reliability of witnesses (external evidence), and on the other hand the incongruity of Agamemnon's behavior (internal evidence).

Consider, for example, the elaborate precautions taken by Agamemnon and his slave to make sure his second message gets to Clytemnestra (117–

26. I discuss in detail Musgrave 1762; Euripides 1802 (ed. Porson); Boeckh 1808; Porson 1812; Euripides 1813–1837 (ed. Matthiae); Hermann 1816; Euripides 1831 (ed. Hermann); Euripides 1837 (ed. Hartung); Hermann 1877; Euripides 1891 (ed. England); Page 1934; Euripides 1994 (ed. Diggle); and Euripides 2003 (ed. Kovacs).

123 Diggle).[27] Having struggled all night to compose it, Agamemnon hands a letter to the old man and then dictates its contents to him—Clytemnestra should not send Iphigenia to Aulis as previously instructed. Effectively, Agamemnon creates a back-up system: if the written message is intercepted or lost, the other one, recorded in the mind of the old slave, may still get through.

This is in fact precisely what happens: the written message is intercepted by Menelaus (303–315 Diggle). But despite this the old man will, in due course, deliver the message entrusted to him. Thus, while the written tradition is intercepted, the oral one, with which Agamemnon had taken care to supply his messenger, is delivered. That will result in the appearance of an untimely second tradition before Clytemnestra (855 Diggle and following); the story told her by Agamemnon (that Iphigenia will be married to Achilles) is contradicted by the new story told by the old man—that Iphigenia is to be sacrificed.

As a complement to the thematic preoccupation with the transmission of information (external evidence), *Iphigenia at Aulis* contains a number of scenes in which characters show a longing for unambiguous and consistent behavior. Once he has decided to sacrifice his daughter, Agamemnon's behavior becomes complicated and self-contradictory, and the play tracks a series of attempts (by Iphigenia, Clytemnestra, and then Achilles) to decipher his inconsistent and self-confuting presentations. In the first meeting of Agamemnon and Iphigenia, for example, the daughter is troubled by a strange disharmony between Agamemnon's joyful words at seeing her and his mournful behavior; and she struggles to perceive the root of this incongruity. Agamemnon's incongruous behavior in the scene could be interpreted as resulting from a disjunction in what the Port-Royal Logic calls internal circumstances. Reunions of father and daughter are usually attended by unmitigated joy on the part of the father, but in this case Agamemnon shows an unexpected display of grief.

Iphigenia seeks to discern the deeper cause of this, to interpret the event of her encounter with Agamemnon more accurately. The language runs along the surface of Agamemnon's presentation, testing for cracks in his resolve. The imagery is overwhelmingly concerned with vision and sight: there is constant recurrence of verbs of looking (640, 644, 649 Diggle) and references to eyes (637, 650, 658, 684 Diggle).[28]

27. For other comments on this scene, see Lushnig 1988, 19n.6, 38; Gibert 1995, 211–212; Walsh 1974, 301; Chant 1986; Knox 1966; Laurence 1988; Vretska 1961; Siegel 1981.

28. See Fletcher 1999.

She beholds him with joy (640 Diggle), and he her (641 Diggle): but his inner contradictions start to seep out almost immediately. *I don't know how I can say that I have done well in bringing you here and not say it,* he says to Iphigenia (643 Diggle). Iphigenia notices in Agamemnon's face what he is trying to conceal—that he is miserable (644 Diggle). Faced with her critical insight, he wishes she were not so astute. Iphigenia offers to speak ἀσύνετα, if that will make him happy. But even while she seems to see too much, he envies her her inability to understand (677 Diggle). A lack of steadfastness, a willingness to disband the army, is what he wants; but he is now resolved, his mind is made up, and he will not be disuaded, though it destroys him. Agamemnon's inconsistency is expressed at verse 657 (Diggle)—*θέλω γε, τὸ θέλειν δ' οὐκ ἔχων ἀλγύνομαι* ("I want [to stay at home with my family], and not being able to want this I suffer"). The line troubles editors (Diggle obelizes θέλειν). But it is entirely indicative of Agamemnon's situation.

The fact that a concern over internal and external evidence organizes both the forms of the text in modern textual criticism and the major issues of *meaning* in each version points toward an uncanny fact: the literary structure of each version, dependent on an interpretation of these two principles, will echo, often with near-perfect harmony, the manner in which each critical version locates and justifies itself. Thus, for example, the Aelian fragment uncannily means the same thing in any text that includes it *and* in any text-critical use of it: in both cases it represents an authoritative revelation of an actual state of affairs. This uncanny effect can be felt throughout the history of text-critical versions of *Iphigenia at Aulis* and represents a central theme of my discussion. Each version produces a story emblematic of the theory that facilitates it. The conclusion could be drawn that *Iphigenias at Aulis* (singular plural) is/are symbolic of the destiny and condition of textual criticism and its products more generally.

It will become apparent that in addition to producing a harmonious felicity of critical method and literary sense, each version will uncannily reflect its position in the history of criticism on the play. The versions in chapter 4, drawn from the initial period of textual instability, will contain within them reflections on the nature and meaning of textual instability in general, while in the next chapter, where systematicity and stability are the theme, each version will in turn prompt a literary reflection on the nature and cost of such stability. Thus each version can be located according to external relations (by historical position) and according to its internal modeling of these relations (each version tells a story that comments on its context).

That is, just as the two historical moments analyzed in chapters 4 and 5 are a large-scale projection of the binary tensions between internal and external evidence, so also is each version a monadological vision of the whole moment. Leibnizian monads are, in a surprising way, very close in character to Kant's notion of singularity (see chapter 3); every monad, according to Leibniz, contains an infinitely detailed universe within it, even though only certain parts of this universe are fully in focus,[29] just as for Kant a singularity is the container of a manifold. My assumption is that each version is not only a monadological image of the moment to which it belongs, but also that both moments (that of textual destabilization and that of entropic stability) are singular images of plurality. The texts addressed in chapter 4 offer images of textual plurality under the sign of flux: each critical version gives us an image of unstoppable movement and change, a "movement-image," to use the language of Gilles Deleuze.[30] Each text is thus an allegory of textual instability. In chapter 5, the entropic, stable, systematic text will appear to be less a single, "final" text as a method of incorporating textual plurality within a fixed, crystaline configuration.

The Posthumous Text

There is a final factor in the critical history of *Iphigenia at Aulis* that must be considered. A scholion to Aristophanes' *Frogs* (v. 67) reports that this tragedy was produced after Euripides' death by his son (this is "Euripides Minor"; he might also be Euripides' nephew).[31] On its own this need not mean anything—the play could have been finalized before Euripides' passing. But the vast majority of critics since 1813, when Matthiae refined a connection initially made by Boeckh,[32] have assented to the propositions (1) that much of the text's distress is due to its having been left in the form of unfinished drafts at Euripides' death, and (2) the attempts of later generations to work it into acceptable form have created a tissue

29. See Leibniz 1951 and Deleuze 1993.
30. Deleuze 1992.
31. *οὕτω γὰρ διδασκαλίαι φέρουσι, τελευτήσαντος* Εὐριπίδου *τὸν υἱὸν αὐτοῦ δεδιδαξέναι ὁμωνύμως ἐν ἄστει Ἰφιγένειαν τὴν ἐν* Αὐλίδι, Ἀλκμαίωνα, Βάκχας. The text of this passage is not altogether settled; a manuscript variant has *ὁμώνυμον* for *ὁμωνύμως*. The variance influences the critical assessment of its significance. For the identity of Euripides Minor, see also Suidas 1928 (ed. Adler) *s.v.* "Euripides." Willink 1971, 361n.4 suggests that the posthumous "reviser" was Cephisophon, Euripides' actor (See Kovacs 1990 on the identity of Cephisophon).
32. Euripides 1813–1837 (ed. Matthiae) 7:326–327. On Boeckh, see below.

of interpolations.[33] In the 1990s the posthumous condition of *Iphigenia at Aulis* became the starting point for significant technical innovations in the criticism of the play. James Diggle abandoned the imperative of sorting out Euripides' words from later interpolations, opting instead for the fourfold system of probability already mentioned. For his part David Kovacs replaced the question "What did Euripides write?" with the question "What did the audience see at the first performance?" That text was also the product of a posthumous collaboration. Posthumousness, in other words, has become the occasion for text-critical innovations in which the object represented by the critical text has changed from "the authorial original" to something else altogether.

In a sense, then, *Iphigenia at Aulis* presents a singular case in the annals of textual criticism: it is one of a very small class of texts known or suspected to have been left unfinished by their authors. *Iphigenia at Aulis*, even as it appears in one manuscript, contains an incipient plurality of hands *because* it is posthumous. But this is a most illuminating singularity. It means, in effect, that *Iphigenia at Aulis* has always been in need of an editor, that its formation has always been coeval with some text-critical performance. This tragedy, then, presents a special case not merely because it seems to be heavily interpolated, but because the history of interpolation, *from the very beginning*, is a history of textual criticism. Faced with this play, textual criticism looks into a mirror: its work here is always a kind of *immanent critique*, a process of self-knowledge and self-criticism. A singular case, indeed: but a singularity which implicates the entire heterogeneous field of textual criticism. The criticism of the *Iphigenia at Aulis* will always be an act of confession, a working out of the limits—and the powers—of textual speculation.

33. It is easier to count the exceptions: Euripides 1857 (ed. Monk) and Euripides 1897 (ed. Weil) are prevalent in this regard. The importance of the posthumousness theory for twentieth-century criticism is solidified by Euripides 1891 (ed. England).

4

Allegories of Instability

In this chapter I discuss several editions and critical essays by authors who support the authenticity of the Aelianic fragment. In each of these examples, the textual critic produces or hypothesizes a text that could accurately be described as singular plural because it locates itself within a field of plural versions *and* presents itself as an image and allegory of textual instability: each of these *Iphigenias at Aulis* is *an Iphigenias at Aulis.*

Samuel Musgrave's discussion of *Iphigenia at Aulis* is accompanied by a theory of textual criticism that relies on the metaphor of the republic of letters; but the metaphor of the republic of letters unavoidably implies that no single position or critical judgment can be correct or final: another divergent position is always anticipated. Musgrave's critical project is therefore conceived as provisional and subject to imminent correction. It imagines its solutions as part of a plurality of other solutions. And as my reading of the play produced by Musgrave's hypotheses will show, Musgrave's version of the tragedy itself allegorizes this plurality of versions.

August Boeckh's analysis of *Iphigenia at Aulis* depends on the hypothesis of posthumous revision. According to Boeckh, many Greek tragedies, and especially the works of Aeschylus, Sophocles, and Euripides, were significantly revised by family members after their authors' deaths. Boeckh believes that *Iphigenia at Aulis* was first produced during

Euripides' lifetime and then revised by his nephew (or son). He tries to sort out the form of the first version and track how the revised version, represented by the received text, grew out of this. Thus Boeckh's critical vision involves a text that is perpetually in flux.

But Boeckh goes farther: he sees significant similarities between himself and Euripides' posthumous reviser, and he implies that he is himself another reviser of the tragedy. Taking this vision of ongoing posthumous textual difference to a radical extreme, Boeckh even emphasizes the likelihood that he may change his own mind about *Iphigenia at Aulis*: not only does the text mutate from critic to critic, but this mutability may even occur within the mind of a single critic.

I then turn to two critics who enact this mutability: Richard Porson, who changed his mind about the play's form, and Gottfried Hermann, who produced an edition of the play in 1831 but then recanted the position taken there in a long essay published in the 1840s. I dwell on Hermann's case in particular, because he changed his mind on one particular passage not once but twice: this passage, as it developed in Hermann's critical imagination, became an allegory for criticism's capacity to alter ancient texts, its ability to function as an engine of textual flux.

Hermann also engages in the strange technique of printing fragments: at certain points in his analysis, he does not show us an "original" text, but a portion of it, rent by lacunae, tears, and gaps. In an excursus, I set Hermann's rhetoric of critical fragmentation within the intellectual and scholarly context of Romanticism and the increasing importance of paleography, arguing that the critical fragment is not intended to reconstruct some past version of the *Iphigenia at Aulis* but rather to create an image of textual flux. This image of textual fluctuation is no more than an allegory of textual instability.

Finally I turn to the edition of J. A. Hartung, who, like Hermann, printed a text remarkable for its lacunae. What Hartung prints is not a representation of some hypothetical original but a fragment that cannot be associated with any moment in the transmission history of *Iphigenia at Aulis*: in fact Hartung's text does not even harmonize with his own theory of how the play was interpolated. I close this chapter by arguing that Hartung's impossible critical fragment is not an image of some original "pristine" text at all, but rather of the *historical destiny* of an interpolated play. Hartung's fragmentary text, in other words, is a singular representation of the essential plurality of every text that exists in a long process of transmission. It is an image of time itself, of the plurality of forms a text must take in time: it represents *Iphigenia at Aulis* in exactly the same way *Nude Descending a Staircase* represents the scene named in its title.

Samuel Musgrave

Samuel Musgrave's *Iphigenia at Aulis*[1] is a play of high irony in which the audience, equipped with perfect knowledge that Iphigenia will be rescued by Artemis at the sacrificial altar, watches the characters suffer terribly because of their ignorance of the same fact.

Troubled by the unparalleled anapestic dialogue at the opening of the play, and equipped with the fragment discovered in Aelian, Musgrave proposed that Euripides' original began with a prologue in which Artemis set the scene and announced her intentions to save Iphigenia at the last moment. She speaks to Agamemnon—this is deduced from the σήν, "your," in the second line of the fragment. But the story makes little sense if Agamemnon knows what will happen at the end; accordingly, reasoned Musgrave, Artemis must address Agamemnon while he is either absent or not listening.[2]

A prologue in which Artemis tells Agamemnon that the atrocity he is going to commit is no more than an illusion, *but he does not hear*, makes Agamemnon the protagonist in a cruel theater of the gods. The fact that he acts in ignorance of his own ultimate innocence adds a level of tragic inconsequentiality to his struggle.

It also bestows him with an unjust death; for in Musgrave's version Clytemnestra's vengeance (not represented in the play, but surely still anticipated—see 1183–1184 Diggle) would be exacted from an innocent man for a crime that was never committed. While Agamemnon's suffering comes from not hearing the comforting words of Artemis in the prologue, his death in the sequel will be the result of a corresponding deafness on the part of Clytemnestra. Told by a messenger that Iphigenia has been saved by Artemis, Clytemnestra reacts equivocally: πῶς δ'οὐ φῶ παραμυθεῖσθαι τούσδε μάτην μύθους, ὥς σου πένθος λυγροῦ παυσαίμην; (How shall I not say that I am consoled by these words in vain, so that I might cease from my keen grief for you? 1616–1618).

1. I refer to the series of text-critical annotations, published together in Musgrave 1762.

2. "fieri enim potest, ut, quae citat Aelianus, ad Agamemnonem vel absentem, vel non audientem, dicta sint." If Musgrave's conjecture is possible, it must be dramaturgically reasonable to suppose that a prologue speaker could address another character who is absent or inattentive. Musgrave provided a number of parallels: *Hecuba* 55; *Andromache* 221; *Iphigenia among the Taurians* 379.

Musgrave's version of these lines is the same as the wording in the oldest manuscript. But in the eighteenth century, when Musgrave discussed this play, his reading was conjectural. P, and the printed editions before Musgrave contain πῶς δὲ φῶ; (How shall I call you?) where Musgrave gives πῶς δ'οὐ φῶ (How shall I not say). After Musgrave, as well, the passage gave critics considerable trouble.[3] Interpreters of the line, however, have almost universally agreed about its sense: Clytemnestra does not believe the story she has just been told; she will not cease from grief, and Agamemnon remains at risk of vengeance. The humanist translations reinforce this sense. Reading πῶς δὲ φῶ; at 1615 and a period rather than an interrogation mark at the end of the passage at 1618, the Stephanus translation, following but correcting the translations of Melanchthon[4] and Camillus,[5] read as followed:

> O filia cuius deorum furtum facta es?
> Quomodo te appellem? aut quomodo dicam?
> An ad consolationem fingi hos frustra sermones,
> Ut tui luctum acerbum desinam?

> Oh daughter, what god has stolen you? How shall I call you? What should I say? Or has this story in vain been invented to console me, so that I would cease my bitter grief for you?[6]

The supplement *fingi* (invented) removes the ambiguity in the Greek:[7] Clytemnestra says that the story she has just heard was made up to console her and (we presume) protect Agamemnon. This is a slightly more faithful treatment of the Greek than Melanchthon's translation. Melanchthon thought that the story about Iphigenia's transformation was suspect. He has Clytemnestra say,

> Fingi puto ad consolationem frustra hos sermones,
> Ut desinam te lugere.

> I think this story in vain has been invented for my consolation, so that I will stop grieving for you.[8]

3. See Euripides 1872 (ed. Paley), ad loc; Page 1934, 196–199 (these lines "have no redeeming characteristics" [197]).
4. Euripides 1562.
5. Euripides 1550.
6. Varia 1567.
7. Canter and Barnes retain *fingi* as well. Euripides 1602 (ed. Canter); Euripides 1694 (ed. Barnes).
8. Euripides 1562.

Melanchthon expressed his disbelief in Iphigenia's rescue in a marginal note. To the last three lines of the messenger's speech, "Quae a Diis eveniunt, sunt inexpectata, et servant eos quos amant: dies hic vidit mortuam et vivam tuam filiam" (The things that come from the gods are unexpected, and they protect those whom they love: this day has seen your daughter dead and alive) he printed an adscript: "factum incertum" (an uncertain fact).

Not getting the message is the main theme of this tragedy: just as his moral suffering in the *Iphigenia* is the product of his not having heard Artemis, Agamemnon's physical suffering and death in the sequel are the result of Clytemnestra's not believing the words of the messenger. For Musgrave as for many of his predecessors in reading the play, Agamemnon's doom is unjust, the product of Clytemnestra's deafness to a true message. But in Musgrave's play, in contrast to those that came before, Artemis has been on stage and has told the audience the truth: that Iphigenia *will* be rescued, that all the struggles to come are unnecessary. Had Melanchthon read this version, he would not have written *factum incertum* in the margin of his text. That doubt would have remained with Clytemnestra alone. Agamemnon and Clytemnestra suffer in Musgrave's version because they do not or will not hear the truth when it is spoken to them.

This Agamemnon is the figure of Samuel Musgrave himself, who found himself in a situation where he too could be exposed to Artemis's lines without hearing them, could reconstruct the *Iphigenia at Aulis* on their basis without certainty. In fact Musgrave described the intellectual context of his own work in a way that nearly predicted the subsequent appearance of *Iphigenias at Aulis* different from his and suggested that he imagined himself existing in a condition similar to that of Agamemnon.

When, in his introduction to the *Exercitationes*, he defends classical learning, his terminology depends on the regulative metaphor of the republic of letters, a metaphor that, as we shall see, defends against the possibility of any certainty in critical endeavors. Those who read the ancients in translation, he says, can neither appreciate the artfulness of the writing nor clearly appreciate the stories they tell. Rather "they must depend on what their teachers say, like children or women [*sic*], nor do they ever afterwards gain from this the right to suffrage in letters."[9] Knowledge of the ancient languages was a fundamental condition for

9. "Necessario ex ore magistrorum, velut pueri aut mulierculae, pendent, neque unquam postea in litteris suffragii jus consequuntur" (Musgrave 1762, *5v).

citizenship in the republic of letters.[10] Indeed the ancient languages were its official tongues, and textual criticism was one of its fundamental civic practices. The republic of letters had a long-standing role as the context for the correction of ancient texts; according to François Waquet, the first extant use of the term *respublica litteraria* occurred in 1417 in a letter from Francesco Barbaro to Poggio Bracciolini, in which Francesco praises Poggio's editions of Latin authors as contributions to *huic litterariae Reipublicae.*[11] It was by means of editions of ancient texts that the notion of a global community of the learned developed from the Renaissance through the Enlightenment.[12]

By the eighteenth century this republic had become a zone in which ancient and modern could meet as equals. Adrian Marino describes the republic of letters as "A community of letters and literati of all ages and all countries. Its members are contemporaries, fellow citizens, colleagues of all times and everywhere. Solidarity between epochs, generations, and cultures thus becomes feasible; coexistence of ancients and moderns is a reality."[13] This transtemporal community underlies Musgrave's defense of textual criticism: for him the old quarrel between the partisans of the ancients and the moderns was to be replaced by a comparative approach that took both ancient and modern authors seriously as members in a single literary collective.[14]

But the republic of letters, in which Musgrave situates his own work, is an impossibility, a noplace, a project rather than a reality. For H. Jaumann, the republic of letters must be taken only as a notion of what scholarly and literary communication *should* look like. A metaphor

10. See, for example, Heumann 1718.

11. Bots and Waquet 1997, 11–12.

12. In the seventeenth century the perception was that this was changing, that philology was being eclipsed by reason and wit. According to Pierre Bayle, "The XVIth Century produced a greater Number of Learned Men, than the XVIIth, and yet the former was not so enlightened as the latter. Whilst the reign of *Criticism* and *Philology* continued, every part of *Europe* produced prodigies of Erudition. The Study of the new Philosophy, and of the modern Languages, having introduced another Taste, that Universal and Profound Literature has disappeared; but in recompense, a certain Genius more refined, and accompanied with a more exquisite Discernment, has spread itself over the Commonwealth of Learning: People now-a-days are less learned, and more subtle" (Bayle 1734–1738, 1:92 n.d [s.v. Acontius (Aconce)]).

13. Marino 1990, 214–215.

14. "Itaque parum sapienter consulisse mihi videntur, qui facta comparatione inter veterum et recentiorum scripta, alterutros deprimere et ex manibus hominum excutere studuerunt. Neutris enim contentus esse debet, qui literis se addicit; sed sive in recentium thesauris praeclari aliquid exhibetur, sedulo contemplari; sive in veterum monumentis, tanquam gemma in metallis, reconditum est, ne tum quidem negligere, aut eruendi laborem refugere" (Musgrave 1762, *4v–*5r).

rather than a concrete reality, the republic of letters is a regulative concept with only provisional value: "The concept of *republic of letters* is essentially different from scholarly communications and can never be used as a mere synonym or epithet because, as a concept of self-observation, it is already logically different and by definition selective (because it is never the self-observation of *all* observers and of persons involved in *all* communications), normative, even 'kontrafaktisch,' i.e. deliberately fictitious."[15] This was a counterfactuality occasionally felt by those who contemplated it from within. According to DuClos, "letters do not precisely make a *state*, but they fulfill this function for those who have no other, and they procure distinctions for them that men who are superior to them in rank will never obtain."[16] Not really a republic, it was rather a metaphysical organization and a utopian ideal.

Within this metaphorical context, a tension emerges between reason and truth on the one hand, and the absolute freedom of the republic's citizens on the other. For Pierre Bayle, the republic of letters is

> a State extremely free. The Empire of Truth and Reason is only acknowledged in it; and under their protection an innocent War is waged against any one whatever. Friends ought to be on their Guard, there, against Friends, Fathers against Children, Fathers-in-law against their Sons-in-law, as in the Iron Age.
> ——non hospes ab hospite tutus,
> Non soccer a genero [Ovid. Met. I.144]
> *No Rights of Hospitality remain,*
> *The Guest by him, who harbour'd him, is slain.*
> *The Son-in-law pursues his Father's Life, etc. DRYDEN*
> Every body, [*sic*] there, is both Sovereign and under every-body's [*sic*] Jurisdiction. The Laws of the Society have done no Prejudice to the Independency of the State of Nature, as to Error and Ignorance: in that respect, every particular Man has the Right of the Sword, and may exercise it without asking leave of those who govern.[17]

There is a conflict in this characterization between the "Empire of Truth and Reason" and the "innocent war" waged between all its citizens without recourse to any final authority. While reason and truth render war "innocent," they cannot transform it into peace: the freedom of the republic of letters is a freedom of total and continual warfare, without

15. Jaumann 2001, 19.
16. "Les Lettres ne donent pas précisément un état, mais elles en tiennent lieu à ceux qui n'en ont pas d'autre, et leur procurent des distinctions que des gens qui leur sont supérieurs par le rang, n'obtiendraient pas toujours" (Duclos 1769, 141).
17. Bayle 1734–1738; Bayle 1740, *s.v.* "Catius."

possibility of end. Even when reason and truth are named as the sole authority, their authority is reduced to an ineffectual point, a sun that gives no light. In the republic of letters the "Empire of Reason and Truth" functions only as a regulative concept according to which the freedom of the republic of letters is preserved; but it can never be said to appear as such. In other words reason and truth have the same relation to the republic of letters that, according to Jaumann, the republic of letters itself has to scholarly communication. We know of it, we must keep it in mind, but we cannot enact it in any mode other than the fictional, the hypothetical, the ideal.

Perhaps because of the ideality of the "Empire of Reason and Truth," the anomie of the republic became its dominant characteristic. By Musgrave's time it began to resemble the "war of all against all" of Hobbes's precontractarian epoch rather than the universal government of gentlemen of spirit. For the Abbé Irailh, the history of the *Respublica Litteraria* was the history of strife: "Someone said: in the past, beasts fought in the circus to amuse those men who had the greatest intellects; and now intellectuals fight in order to entertain fools."[18] A *dissertatio politica* delivered at the University of Jena in the early eighteenth century on the subject of the government of letters concluded that, since the dominant characteristic of the literary republic was freedom and the absence of any sovereignty, the collective hardly deserved the name of "republic" at all.[19] In this sense the metaphor of the republic of letters had something indigestible about it: to an age reluctant to conceive of statehood without a central sovereign, the notion of a republic of letters was an impossibility—a nice idea, but only that.

For Musgrave, too, reason and truth are ineffectual regulators of the republic of letters. In fact he denies them any regulatory power at all. What rules there instead is a proliferation of indefinite questions. Demonstrative proof and apodictic certainty are not to be had in many of the affairs of men, he writes. "If we were living in some utopia where reason alone ruled, we could easily go without this faculty of interpretation. Now the Most High and Excellent God has deemed to order human affairs differently, so that the two things which are of the greatest moment among mortals, I mean religion and politics, must be judged not by the norm of reason but by another norm, assigned to letters and history: in which it is necessary to resolve questions that require

18. "Quelqu'un a dit, qu'autrefois les bêtes combattoient dans le cirque, pour amuser les hommes qui avoient le plus d'esprit, et qu'aujourd'hui les gens d'esprit combattent pour divertir les sots" (Irailh 1761, vi).

19. Cited by Bots and Waquet 1997, 20–21.

subtlety and interpretation."[20] Musgrave then observes that theologians and lawyers must argue and rely on interpretation: How can the reading of literature and history, another place where reason does not dominate, not behave in this manner also? If theology belongs to the city of God and politics to the city of humans, then philology belongs to the republic of letters; but in the republic of letters, like those of God and humans, there is room only for interpretation and probability rather than absolute certainty.

What does this mean for establishing the context of Musgrave's introduction of the fragment from Aelian into the textual criticism of the *Iphigenia at Aulis*? It means that even as he introduces in the Aelianic fragment a figure of certainty, he dismisses it by setting his work in a context in which certainty is only fictional or counterfactual, the myth of a utopia that will never arrive on earth. Like "Truth and Reason," Artemis speaks authoritatively and is not heard, either by Agamemnon within the play or by the critic who discovers the fragment retaining her voice. She will not put all doubt to rest; those to whom she speaks are neither capable of hearing her nor interested in doing so. The freedom of the republic of letters means that though its citizens hear the oracular voice of truth they must act as though it had never spoken. When the traditional text of the *Iphigenia at Aulis* is destabilized, this takes place in a realm where the possibility of stability is never more than an asymptotic ideal.

Augustus Boeckh

For Augustus Boeckh, whose book on authorship and interpolation in Greek tragedy appeared in 1808,[21] it was a fact of central importance that the earliest known performance of the *Iphigenia at Aulis* occurred in the year subsequent to Euripides' death. But Boeckh believed this performance was not a premiere. Because he believed that the *Iphigenia at Aulis* must have been conceived and performed for the first time before its "sequel" *Iphigenia among the Taurians*, and because he believed

20. "Quod si in Utopia aliqua viveremus, ubi Ratio sola dominetur, facile hac interpretandi facultate carere possemus. Nunc Deo Optimo Maximo aliter res humanas ordinare visum est, adeo ut quae duo maximi inter mortales momenti sunt, Religionem dico, et Rerumpublicarum regimen, non jam ad Rationis normam, sed aliam, litteris historiisque consignatam, exigenda sint; in quibus necesse est quaestiones incidere, quae interpretandi subtilitatemque desiderant" (Musgrave 1762, unnumbered: **9r).

21. Boeckh 1808.

that there were passages in the *Andromache* that imitated it,[22] Boeckh concluded that the tragedy must have had its first performance during Euripides' lifetime, before the production of the *Andromache*.[23] Subsequent to Euripides' death—and the production of Aristophanes' *Frogs*, which, as we will see, Boeckh considers a decisive moment—a revised version of *Iphigenia at Aulis* was produced, along with revised versions of the *Alcmaeon* and the *Bacchae*, by Euripides Minor.[24]

While Musgrave's notes on Euripides aim to establish the text, Boeckh's monograph aims to reconstruct a picture of textual flux, of change as an essential aspect of ancient literature. Rather than constructing a single version said to be the original, Boeckh studies the relations between two versions—that of Euripides Minor and that of the elder—to explain the historical causes and processes that led from the one to the other. It is not, therefore, the model of a finished text "obscured" or "deformed" by later interpolators that concerns him, but rather that of an open genetic dossier, in which an ongoing process of authorship is at work. The life of ancient drama as it is portrayed in his analyses resembles the process of textual generation studied in modern authors by *critique génétique*.[25] His "version" is a "multiversion," a vision of plurality.

Thus Boeckh interprets as historical fact governing the ancient destiny of the play what Musgrave sees as a metaphor defining the context of modern criticism. If for Musgrave the republic of letters had colored his work with an unavoidable provisionality, for Boeckh susceptibility to change is primarily a characteristic of the text in history. Metaphor has become literal, the counterfactual has become historical.

Boeckh will carry this literalization to a radical extreme: not only will he see the *Iphigenia at Aulis* in terms of a plurality of versions, but he will also envision a plurality of other versions of his own model. His is an allegory of instability that is itself unstable. The ultimate result of this radical vision is that while the republic of letters was characterized by innocent war between its citizens (see above), Boeckh's criticism brings the textual critic into unending strife with himself.

Boeckh's emphasis on posthumous revision transforms another metaphorical aspect of the republic of letters into literal history. The republic of letters, "a community of letters and literati of all ages and all

22. Ibid., 223–224.

23. Ibid., 223.

24. On Euripides Minor, son or nephew of the tragedian and possibly an early editor of Homer, see Suidas 1928 (ed. Adler) 3694; Pfeiffer 1968, 72n.4.

25. On the study of the genetic processes of authors, see Lebrave 1986; Hay 1988; Grésillon 1994.

countries,"[26] always had an aura of metaphorical posthumousness. The dialogue between ancients and moderns that had been one of the ideals of the humanist self-conception had always been a kind of "dialogue of the dead" like those of Lucian or Fontenelle.[27] For example, it was surely with the dialogues of Lucian in mind that Lipsius chose the "Menippean Satire" as his literary form when he staged a confrontation between ancient authors and modern "correctors" in the "Senate of the Republic of Letters,"[28] and a similar context of posthumousness was used to great effect by Swift in *Gulliver's Travels*.[29] The transtemporal community of the learned is also a community of the living and the dead.

Behind the Lucianic overtones, perhaps, lies a strong philosophical ambition: the critic who participates in the posthumous dialogues of the republic of letters has found a way to achieve in life what Socrates had looked forward to after death: "What would one not give, gentlemen, to be able to question the leader of that great host against Troy, or Odysseus, or Sisyphus, or the thousands of other men and women whom one could mention, to talk and mix and argue with whom would be unimaginable happiness?"[30] Of course the critic only does this in a *fictional* mode: the community of the living and the dead is never more than imaginary. Its rhetorical basis is the figure of metonymy: the critic has before him not the author but his *text*; the illusion of a community of living and dead depends upon the figural replacement of an effect (the text) by its cause (the author). But Boeckh makes this metonymy real and transforms it into a subject for historical analysis by emphasizing the historical operations of revisers and critics on a posthumous text. In the process of this literalization, posthumousness ceases to be a figure for scholarly community and becomes instead the name for textuality's historical destiny.

This can be seen in the three chapters that begin Boeckh's book and which make a theoretical case for the presence of extensive revisions and interpolations in the texts of Greek tragedy. It begins with a discussion of actors' interpolations: arguing from the law attributed to Lycurgus that a text of the three great tragedians be kept in the city archives at Athens and deviations from it be prohibited, Boeckh makes the case that the plays were subject to some amount of revision by actors after the deaths of their authors, just as Wolf had argued that the epics were changed

26. Marino 1990, 214.
27. Fontenelle 1990, vol. 1.
28. Lipsius 1675.
29. Swift 2002 (ed. Rivero).
30. Plato, *Apology* 41b.

in the recitations of rhapsodes.[31] For Boeckh, this is the product of a culture in which poets are highly valued, the kind of culture in which, as Plutarch reported in the life of Nicias, Athenian soldiers could recite lines of Euripides to their captors during the Athenian expedition against Syracuse and obtain their freedom in exchange.[32] Boeckh takes this anecdote as evidence that there was a paucity of written versions of the plays in antiquity and that as a result of their largely oral transmission the texts were likely to be highly interpolated.[33] The rhetorical language Boeckh uses to describe this destiny for ancient tragic texts invokes the figure of posthumousness:

> For all noble nations, great lovers of song and speech from their beginnings right up to the highest apex of learning, are accustomed to have works given to writing or memory, and they do not lie buried in cabinets [*in thecis*] but walk about, as it were, in the mouths of all. This is the blessed stock of bards and poets, who do not live in their own books, as other learned men live, as is said: these latter have a life in every respect not unlike death, or rather the sad habitation of those madmen who live on in tombs: [the poets, on the contrary,] though dead, are placed in the happy air of day itself, and in the generous light of the sun. But if in these lands, where many public things have been made private, poets still remain public, how much more so must they have been among the Greeks, for whom very few things were private, and many things were public? They paid the greatest attention to performance and recitation, with the result that much must gradually have been improved, corrupted, taken away, and added.[34]

The poems of the ancients resemble those corpses whose bodies are placed in the open air and continue, even after their demise, to take part in the community of the living.[35] In this image Boeckh changes what

31. See Wolf 1795.
32. Plutarch, *Life of Nicias* 542c.
33. Boeckh 1808, 12.
34. "Nam omnes ingenuae nationes, ab incunabulis usque summum eruditionis fastigium carminis sermonisque amantissimae, habere solent opera, memoria sive scriptis consignata, quae non sepulta in thecis iacent, sed in omnium ore quasi obambulant. Haec est beata vatum poetarumque stirps, qui non in libris suis, ut alii docti, quod dicitur, vivunt: sane vitam passim non dissimilem morti aut certe tristi habitationi furiosorum illorum, qui in sepulchris degebant: sed qui defuncti in ipsa diei laetissima aura et in alma solis luce positi sunt. Sin autem in iis terris, in quibus iam publicae res privatae factae sunt, adhuc poetae publici manserunt: quanto magis apud Graecos fuisse debent, apud quos fere pauca privata, communia plurima essent? In quorum actione et recitatione summum apud eos studium positum est, paullatim ut multa necesse sit emendata, corrupta, dempta, adiecta esse" (Boeckh 1808, 9–10).
35. For an excellent recent analysis and performance of this idea, see Šukys 2004.

in the republic of letters had been an imagined community of all times and places into the real historical condition of ancient texts.

But Boeckh is only tangentially interested in the alterations a text might undergo in an oral tradition. His interest lies, rather, in seeing the mutations which a text undergoes as part of its *genetic* process. Boeckh's next two chapters turn their attention from oral dissemination and textual flux to the kinds of alterations that could occur in the process of writing; and here, he notes, there are significant differences between oral traditions and written genetic processes: "In those [epics] the emendor is always someone different from the original poet; in these [tragedies], most rarely. In those chance and opinion reign, in these reason, above all: certainly there is greater liberty in collecting and polishing poems that are rather rustic, than in correcting writings that are more perfected."[36] Even the tragedians themselves can be responsible for variation, and Boeckh argues for the probability that authors might have produced variants in their own texts.[37] For the most part, thinks Boeckh, these variants emerged when a tragedian prepared a second production of a play. This occurred, for example, with Sophocles' *Thyestes, Phineus, Tyro,* and *Lemnian Women,* and Aristophanes points to it in the *Clouds* 542 (Οὐδ' ὑμᾶς ζητῶ 'ξαπατᾶν, δὶς καὶ τρὶς ταὐτ' εἰσάγων (Nor do I seek to deceive you, bringing on the same play two or three times), though here Aristophanes is not altogether sincere, since the *Clouds* is itself a partially revised text.[38] Thus in the remains of ancient tragedy Boeckh claims to be able to deduce and reconstruct not just the original forms of tragedies, but also some glimpses of their gradual growth under the pens of their authors as they wrote and rewrote their works. This is not a theory of interpolations at all, but rather an attempt to formulate a method for the genetic criticism of ancient plays.

The example of authors who rewrote plays for second productions serves Boeckh as an intermediate step between the metaphorical posthumousness of an oral tradition and the constrained variation of a real posthumous textual tradition, which is the subject of his final theoretical chapter and the central theme of much of the book. Aeschylus's vita contains a notice that the Athenians subsidized reproductions of his

36. "In illis [epicis] emendator semper fere differt a primitivo poëta; in his [tragoediis] rarissime: in illis casus regnat et arbitrium, in his ratio potissimum: certe maior libertas est in colligendis et expoliendis rudioribus carminibus, quam in corrigendis perfectioribus scriptis" (Boeckh 1808, 19).

37. "Plurimi igitur auctorum Graecorum scripta sua, etsi edita, posthac accuratius eliminaverunt" (Boeckh 1808, 19).

38. Boeckh 1808, 20–21.

work after his death,[39] and Quintilian records information that, because Aeschylus's tragedies, though popular, were considered unpolished, the Athenians allowed "corrected" versions to be produced posthumously.[40] Boeckh follows these testimonia and develops the thesis that the posthumous performance of revised versions of the three great tragedians was a commonplace practice, and that those most often responsible for the revisions and reperformances were family members of the masters. The program of Boeckh's study is, ultimately, this: to identify where family members interpolated the texts of their famous relatives, perfecting and improving their patrimony as one would polish a family heirloom.[41]

In this context Boeckh introduces his analysis of the *Iphigenia at Aulis*. Euripides Minor's revisions are posthumous in a double sense: they occur after the death of Euripides, certainly, but the major revisions respond to the criticisms of Aeschylus' shade in Aristophanes' *Frogs*. There Aeschylus made fun of Euripides' monotonous habit of beginning his tragedies with iambic prologues.[42] In response, Euripides Minor moved part of the anapestic dialogue, originally placed after Artemis's prologue, to the beginning of the play and gave an altered version of the prologue to Agamemnon, creating the text we now have. Similarly the original opening lines of the parodos, which had been mocked by Aristophanes at *Frogs* 1309 (a scholion to this line claims that it is drawn from the *Iphigenia at Aulis*), were replaced.[43] What Boeckh imagines in Euripides Minor's intervention, in other words, is the writing of a second draft in response to a literary criticism that the public felt to be stringent and damaging.

Here, where the posthumous life of the text becomes the central issue, Boeckh begins to establish a community of textual practices that encompasses both ancient and modern literary culture. Again this community is literal rather than metaphorical: the critic comes to resemble the ancient reviser not in a figural sense but in terms of real prosopologi-

39. See Snell 1971, 3: T1.

40. Quintilian, *Institutionis Orctoriae* 10.1.66.

41. "Nunc quoniam *multi*, Quintiliano teste, interpolatores Aeschyleorum dramatum coronati sunt, quinam ii fuerint, indagare propositum est: in quibus fortasse unus et alter fuit tragico huic genere non coniunctus; sed ii potissimum videntur in censum venire, ad quos ea poemata quodam veluti haereditario iure pertinebant, eius filii et nepotes aliique propinqui, quos affectasse patriarum correctionem fabularum, quibusque mandasse prae aliis magistratus verisimile est" (Boeckh 1808, 31).

42. "Cuius enim sententiae citius recordari theatra poterant, quam toties recurrentis illius Ληκύθιον ἀπώλεσεν?" (Boeckh 1808, 233).

43. Boeckh 1808, 218–221.

cal similarities. In Boeckh's discussion of Euripides Minor, the portrait emerges of a reviser who bears some striking resemblances to Boeckh himself. To the younger Euripides he attributes the *Rhesus*, noting that it and the extant *Iphigenia at Aulis* have a Sophoclean flavor, particularly in their use of anapestic dialogues to begin.[44] Boeckh concludes that Euripides Minor was a lover and imitator of Sophocles. But the major work of Euripides Minor, in Boeckh's opinion, is the production of an edition (ἔκδοσις) of Homer.[45] He thinks that those lines in the parodos of the *Iphigenia at Aulis* which describe the fleet gathered at Aulis but diverge in detail from the catalogue of ships in our text of Homer are to be attributed to Euripides Minor, whose edition of the *Iliad* differed from the received text.[46] Thus Euripides Minor was a textual critic, though his critical judgment might have been clouded by what Wolf calls the "aesthetic" tendencies of antiquity: Boeckh describes him as a *poeta imprimis criticus*.[47] He thus has a profession in common with Boeckh.

The similarities go farther even than this. In a moment of surprising candor, Boeckh admits that he is *himself* a poetical critic. He knows that not all similar passages in literature are due to imitation, since at times two poets arrive at the same idea or form of expression: "I would myself perhaps not be aware of this, unless I experienced it firsthand when I once played at writing verse."[48] Boeckh's own prosopography, in other words, mirrors that of his reviser.

This is particularly interesting because it establishes a line of similarity between ancient and modern keepers of Euripides' text that Wolf explicitly denied in the *Prolegomena ad Homerum*, a work otherwise influential on Boeckh's project. Wolf claimed that the spirit of emendation in antiquity was not critical but aesthetic; the ancients never hesitated to change elements in the Homeric poems if they could make the poet's real excellence live up to his reputation.[49] Wolf uses the Latin neologism *aestheticus* (coined by Baumgarten[50]) to describe the ancient form of emendation. By contrast the modern judgment is *criticus*—rigorous and

44. Erasmus is not mentioned by Boeckh, but he expresed the first doubt over the authorship of the *Iphigenia at Aulis* in the introduction to his translation, where he observed that it seemed Sophoclean; see above.

45. See Suidas 1928 (ed. Adler), 3694. Wolf 1795 was less certain that the edition was to be attributed to this Euripides.

46. Boeckh 1808, 236–240.

47. On the "aesthetic" criticism of antiquity, see Wolf 1795, 173–174.

48. "ipse fortasse ignorarem, nisi quum olim versibus luderem, in me essem ipso expertus" (Boeckh 1808, 243).

49. Wolf 1795, 172–174.

50. Baumgarten 1983 (ed. Schweizer).

careful not to allow anything but the very words of the author into his text (*ne quid aliud quam ab ipso auctore operis scriptum inducetur*).[51]

But Boeckh disagrees with Wolf about the critical character of the modern editor. The chapter on posthumous familial interpolation begins not with an example drawn from Aeschylus or another ancient poet, but rather with the example of modern German literature, particularly Schiller, whose dramatic corpus, Boeckh notes, is filled with the plays of others, attributed to them to be sure, but quietly, as though to downplay the role of translation and imitation. As a result, "now many do not speak of Shakespeare's *Macbeth* or of Racine's *Phèdre*, but of Schiller's, especially because the corrected dramas are more famous in these lands."[52] While Wolf had been unequivocal about the difference between ancient and modern emendation, Boeckh seems equally unequivocal about their similarities. There is an important aspect of the aesthetic and the poetic in all critical judgment.

Boeckh's theory of philology is explicit on this point. In the *Encyclopedia and Method of Philology*,[53] Boeckh made a series of propositions that transformed the critic into an inspired artist. "Criticism," he wrote, "is... that philological performance through which an object becomes understood not by itself nor for its own sake, but for the establishment of a relation and a reference to something else, so that the recognition of this relation is itself the end in view. This performance is signified in the name criticism. The basic meaning of *krinein* is analysis and separation; every analysis and separation is, moreover, a determination of a definite relation between two objects. The expression of such a relation is a judgment."[54] Boeckh's project is thus critical to the extent that it discovers and displays a relationship between the parts of the *Iphigenia at Aulis* in a genetic mode. But, as Boeckh remarks in the *Encyclopedia*, historical reconstruction is as much art as it is science. The philological critic strives to gather knowledge of all things known into an inclusive unity, which Boeckh says exists only as an idea.[55] Citing Schelling, Boeckh contends that philology's goal, as the representation of this idea, must be partly critical and partly fictive or poetic: "'The philologist,' Schelling says truthfully, 'stands with the artist and the philosopher on

51. Wolf 1795, 173–174.

52. "Nunc nonnulli non de Shakespearii *Macbetho*, nec de Racinii *Phaedra*, sed de Schillerii loquuntur, propterea quod correcta dramata clariora sunt in his terris" (Boeckh 1808, 25).

53. Boeckh 1886; I cite from the translation in Boeckh 1968.

54. Boeckh 1968, 121.

55. Ibid., 22.

the topmost stage; or rather, these two pervade the philologist.' His business is the historical reconstruction of artistic and scientific work whose history he must comprehend and display in vivid actual presence."[56] The critic who aims to discover a text's history as a process of genesis and change, to capture history as an idea, needs a *poetical* as well as an analytical capacity.

But (this is the thesis of Boeckh's 1808 monograph) aesthetic critics are agents of textual flux. If that was true of Euripides Minor's work on the *Iphigenia at Aulis*, it is also true of Boeckh and his own critical project. As I outline below, the rhetoric of his introduction reveals that this text about plurality is itself implicitly plural. But that means that the *idea* is curiously realized in the practice of Boeckh himself. In fact it might be more accurate to say that in Boeckh's work on the *Iphigenia at Aulis* the idea has taken bodily form as history, just as his historical vision made literal what in Musgrave had been metaphorical.

A curious diffidence pervades the book on tragedy, suggesting that his analysis of the two *Iphigenias* is not fated to be the only one. In his introduction Boeckh deploys a rhetoric that is pronouncedly skeptical. Echoing Cicero, he claims to feel the same about his own work as Ruhnken felt about the *Prolegomena* of Wolf: "While I read it, I agree, but as soon as I put the book down, all that agreement melts away."[57] Such a claim might endanger his whole project, so long as we expect all claims to be in the indicative mode and uttered with veridical certainty. But Boeckh demands a different kind of thought: "Perhaps some, who tolerate nothing uncertain and think that everything has been explored by them, will call this confession rather absurd. Let them say that I do not know what I am about. But only God seems to me to be safe from error: he is wise, we are philosophers."[58] Truth is not accessible in these matters: there are too many possibilities.

This skepticism derives from an awareness of the plurality of versions criticism can occasion. Boeckh remarks that he may be his own worst critic and claims to be less than certain about his results. A parable drawn from Cicero explains why. When Hiero asked Simonides what God was, Simonides asked for a day to think about it. But when he

56. Ibid., 22.

57. "Dum lego assentior, quum posui librum, assensio omnis illa dilabitur" (Boeckh 1808, x). This is a citation from Cicero, *Tusculan Disputations* 1.11.24.

58. "Fortasse hanc confessionem subabsurdam vocabulunt nonnulli, qui nihil tolerant incertum, nihil sibi non exploratum putant: ii me quid velim nescire dicent. Verum mihi unus Deus ab errore videtur tutus esse: ille σοφὸς, nos sumus φιλόσοφοι" (Boeckh 1808, xi).

was asked the same question the next day, he asked for two more days. Hiero, astonished by Simonides' constant doubling of the number of days required to come up with an answer, asked the poet why it was taking him so long, and Simonides replied that the longer he considered the question, the more obscure it seemed to him. Similarly, remarks Boeckh, had chance not taken the book from his hands, he would probably still be putting off its publication.[59] Behind this pretended reluctance to publish lies an awareness that there may be a multiplicity of other possible theories about the texts he deals with. The story of Simonides and Hiero comes from Cicero's *De natura deorum* and is told by Cotta, a proponent of academic skepticism. Cotta's explanation for the ever-growing extension of time required for Simonides looks directly to a proliferation of contrasting possible answers: "But I suppose that Simonides..., since many acute and subtle things came into his mind, hesitating which of them was most true, despaired of all truth."[60] It is in the face of an infinite number of possibilities that Simonides' *epochē* articulates itself. The deferment of a resolution in Simonides' mind might be compared to the deferment of completion in a written work that an author constantly and compulsively revises: each time the text (or the question) is revisited, another possible course presents itself. Epistemologically, Boeckh is *inside* the genetic dossier.

A curious piece of rhetoric in the chapters that lay out Boeckh's theory of revisions supports this view: after comparing actors to rhapsodes in their ability to alter texts, Boeckh is seized with a bout of shamefacedness and comes close to disavowing this aspect of his theory. "In the preceding discussion," he writes, "I compared actors with rhapsodes. If someone were to understand from this that I thought the same processes were at work for the *Iliad* and a play of Sophocles, I couldn't complain, since he would be reproaching me with midsummer madness. For written things differ by a whole season from songs: which, though many do not see this, cannot remain concealed from someone who thinks about it when these winds are blowing, still less from someone writing through the winter."[61]

59. Ibid., ix.

60. "Sed Simonidem arbitror...quia multa venirent in mentem acuta atque subtilia, dubitantem quid eorum esset verissimum desperasse omnem veritatem" (*De natura deorum* 1.22.60).

61. "In praecedente disputatione actores composui rhapsodis. Hoc si quis ita intelligeret, quasi ego eandem *Iliadis* et Sophocleae fabulae putarem rationem esse, non possem conqueri, quum mihi oestrum dierum obiiceret canicularium. Nam toto coelo distant a cantati scripta: quod, ut multi non perspiciant, tamen ipsis flantibus etesiis nequibat latere cogitantem, nedum nunc per brumam scribentem" (Boeckh 1808, 18).

The placement of this flourish is significant: it lies immediately after the discussion of the effects of an oral tradition on literary texts, in which posthumousness had been invoked as a metaphor, and right before the discussion that opens the properly genetic perspective on the form of ancient tragedies by discussing how ancient authors could revise their own work for second productions. As I have already noted, this section serves Boeckh mainly as a transition to his real subject, revisions done to a posthumous text by the author's descendents. Thus Boeckh figures his own inability to settle on an opinion at precisely the point where genetic textual variation—and the subsequent literalizing of posthumousness for textual criticism—becomes the central subject. The mutability of the tradition and the mutability of Boeckh's own mind in the process of writing about it echo each other in an eerie manner here, suggesting the fundamental similarity between Boeckh's project and that of Euripides Minor. In each case the process of writing and rewriting will never end, and every version is bound to be corrected by a new version.

It is hard to read Boeckh in these passages without thinking of the story of *Iphigenia at Aulis* itself. Appropriately for a theory that aims not at the identification of one original form but rather tries to trace the genetic movement between two versions, Boeckh's text reminds us of the agony of an Agamemnon who, like Boeckh himself, cannot seem to make up his mind or settle on a final resolution:

> εἰ δ' ἐγώ, γνοὺς πρόσθεν οὐκ εὖ, μετεθέμην εὐβουλίαν,
> μαίνομαι;

> If I, having thought wrongly before, change my intent for the better, am I mad?[62]

Indeed the first 543 lines of the play—in either Euripides' or Euripides Minor's version[63]—are a portrait of the kind of wavering and instability characteristic of the genetic process of the play itself. It begins with a change of mind, a revision of intention, as Agamemnon prepares to call off the sacrifice, and continues with the simultaneous change of mind of Menelaus and Agamemnon; Menelaus, who had supported the sacrifice, comes to oppose it, and Agamemnon, who had decided to oppose it, alters his position a second time, agreeing to undertake it. It is easy,

62. 388–389 Diggle.

63. I take the opportunity here to mention a rare and beautiful edition of the *Iphigenia at Aulis* that puts Boeckh's opinions regarding the genesis of the play into the form of a text: Euripides 1845 (ed. Vaterus), produced by a student of Boeckh despite war, famine, and the straightened circumstances of a provincial post in Russia, and proporting to present the text *ex recensione Euripidis Minoris*.

perhaps even natural, to read this portion of the play as a study in the inner processes by which resolve is reached by political leaders out of earshot of the general public—the "private deliberations" of those who will eventually need to present a unified, unchanging front; a genetic process, in other words, that looks toward but always seems just short of the final redaction that will create a single course of action. And indeed the final resolution to sacrifice Iphigenia, which will set the course for both Agamemnon and the Argive fleet for the next ten years or more, comes about less through a gradual approach than from a sudden and surprising external stimulus, in the form of the sudden arrival of Iphigenia at Aulis and her unsuspected accompaniment by Clytemnestra, just as Boeckh claims that chance wrenched the book from his hands.[64] Agamemnon arrives at his resolution because his public has suddenly arrived.

Once the "text" of Agamemnon's policy is established, Clytemnestra and Iphigenia spend the rest of the play trying to deduce its genuine meaning and then, once that is ascertained, trying to reverse it, to return him to an earlier stage in his thoughts when he was unwilling to perform the sacrifice. Their action toward Agamemnon's policy is very much like that assigned by Boeckh to criticism itself: "Criticism is opposed to the spirit that dogmatically presents materials and lays hold of ideas, as it is likewise opposed to imagination and even to memory, which loses its powers as the result of criticism. The analytical and contemplative spirits are continually at strife, since whatever the one proposes the other strives to nullify."[65] What *Iphigenia at Aulis* stages, from this perspective, is the same thing performed in Boeckh's book: a struggle between the desire to keep a presentation solid and the critical enterprise, which aims to deconstruct that presentation, to splay it out and make its fluctuations and disjunctions visible. Just as Boeckh has no text, so does Clytemnestra desire that Agamemnon have no resolve. Thus, in the case both of Boeckh's discussion of the *Iphigenia at Aulis* and the force field of *Iphigenias at Aulis* his book creates, the focus of interest is less the recovery of some original text than it is the possibility that a mind or a text might be in perpetual change.

Gottfried Hermann

The continual strife between analytical and contemplative spirits described by Boeckh brings the textual critic into conflict with himself.

64. Boeckh 1808, ix.
65. Boeckh 1968, 23. On Boeckh's conception of philology, see Horstmann 1992.

The product could be called philology's immanent critique, criticism critiquing itself, just as for Kant critical philosophy was the product of reason critiquing itself. Nor would the analogy with Kant be out of place: Boeckh's distinction between criticism and dogmatism comes from the *Critique of Pure Reason*, where criticism (or critical philosophy) is set up to supercede dogmatism.[66] The notion of a continual strife between the contemplative and the analytic spirit recalls Kant's *Conflict of the Faculties*, where he argues that the role of philosophy in the modern university is essentially critical, that is, its role is to submit the representations of other disciplines to the continual oversight of an autonomous judgment, so that these other disciplines can be saved or prevented from overreaching their capacities.[67]

Applied to texts, the continual strife between criticism and dogmatism means that if a text presented itself as a living memory of the past rather than the product of a tradition of mediation and variation, *the original text* rather than a construct that had passed through many hands, the role of the critical faculty would be to point out the falsification, to analyze the text into its strata and display where and how the mediations and variations had occurred. For this it would appear destructive: "When it falls foul of tradition," writes Boeckh, "criticism is a destructively annihilating force, but it negates only error, and since error is the denial of truth, in this negation it works positively."[68] But it is hard to know when criticism *doesn't* fall foul of tradition; its function is to negate tradition, to question it, to criticize it, to stand over and against what tradition presents as unmediated memory. And, to the degree that criticism is a part of tradition, it must, as criticism, work against itself. Criticism fragments not only the "traditional" text, but also the concept of text itself, the belief that we are narrowing in on the one authorial version. This produces a critical philology that supersedes textual criticism as the mere practice of editing texts, and the philologist enters into an ongoing strife with himself. "Philology," writes Edward Said, "problematizes—itself, its practitioner, the present."[69] That is the source of Boeckh's skepticism: it is not, ultimately, an academic suspension of judgment, but rather an awareness of the self-critical moment in philology and an openness to the ongoing critical procedures directed against philological products.

The power of this self-critical impulse can be observed in the changing

66. Boeckh probably gets his understanding of the conflict of criticism and dogmatism from a reading of the young Schelling's writings on this subject. See Schelling 1980.

67. Kant 1979. See Rand 1992.

68. Boeckh 1968, 123.

69. Said 1994, 132.

positions of two important critics in the years between 1792 and 1848. Both Richard Porson and Gottfried Hermann underwent significant changes of mind concerning the form of the *Iphigenia at Aulis* and the procedures of interpolation or deformation that helped to create the received text, and both looked back at their earlier work and said of it, as Ruhnken had said of Wolf's *Prolegomena*, "Assensio omnis illa dilabitur." Their retractions find an eloquent caption in the opening scene of the *Iphigenia at Aulis*, where Agamemnon says of himself:

> ἃ δ' οὐ καλῶς
> ἔγνων τότ', αὖθις μεταγράφω καλῶς πάλιν
> ἐς τήνδε δέλτον.

> And not thinking rightly on these things before, I again write a new message, a better one, on this tablet.[70]

However, as we shall see, not even these words are trustworthy or free of critical variation.

Richard Porson never produced an edition of the *Iphigenia*, and his annotations in a copy of Markland's edition of the play are concerned with alterations at the verbal level and with collating witnesses in Plutarch, Stobaeus, Clement of Alexandria, and humanist critics.[71] But he does make two topical references to the text of the *Iphigenia at Aulis*. The first is in his inaugural lecture at Cambridge in 1792,[72] where he remarks that the *Rhesus* and the *Iphigenia at Aulis*, alone of Euripides' plays, do not begin with iambic prologues. The *Rhesus* he disregards as inauthentic. On the *Iphigenia at Aulis* he follows Musgrave, claiming that the lines in Aelian must have come from an original prologue:

> The other drama that lacks a prologue is the *Iphigenia at Aulis*; its beginning, as it is today edited, seizes the audience in the middle of the action [*in medias res*], in the Sophoclean style. But here also there is something with which we can retort. For since Aelian cites three verses from this play that are not to be found in the drama as we have it, and since these three verses of Diana setting out the whole structure of the tragedy are most congruent [with the narrative in the extant play], who will doubt that this drama once had a prologue, but that it has been lost by the injury of time?[73]

70. 107–109 Diggle.

71. Porson's notes in Euripides 1771 (ed. Markland) are housed in the library of Trinity College, Cambridge, shelf mark Adv.c.3.39.

72. Porson 1812.

73. "Alterum drama quod prologo caret, est *Iphigenia in Aulide*; cujus sane initium, ut hodie editum est, auditorem, more Sophocleo, in medias res abripit. Sed neque hic deest

Although Musgrave's conjecture that the lines from Aelian belonged to an original prologue was approved by Boeckh, Markland,[74] and (less enthusiastically) Heinrich Eischstaedt,[75] the exodus of the play, which is replete with metrical difficulties,[76] has been a more attractive location. It was by a change of mind that Porson inaugurated this new tradition before 1802.[77] His supplement to the preface to the *Hecuba* in that year revealed that he had come to believe the ending of the play spurious, replacing an original ending that contained the lines cited in Aelian.[78]

Once the voice of Diana had been moved from the beginning of the play to its end, it became possible to defend the extant opening by invoking the notion of an aesthetic singularity: perhaps Euripides had reasons, late in his life, for trying out something new. That was Gottfried Hermann's position in his edition of 1831.[79] While he grants that no other play of Euripides begins with anapests, he observes that many works have not survived. Euripides was an innovator, and therefore we should not be surprised at an innovative anapaestic-iambic-anapaestic opening. His explanation for the presence of iambs among anapests is literary and based on a reading of the emotional nuances of the opening scene: while Agamemnon struggles with the command to kill Iphigenia, he speaks in agitated anapests, but when he narrates the background to his old slave, his mind calms down, and he speaks in

quod regeramus. Cum enim Aelianus tres versus ex hac fabula citaverat, qui in dramata nostro, prout nunc habetur, nusquam comparent; cumque hi tres versus Dianae totam tragoediae constitutionem exponentis aptissime congruant; quis dubitat, prologum hujus quoque olim fuisse dramatis, sed injuria temporis jamdudum periisse?" (Porson 1812, 9–10).

74. "Musgravius admodum probabiliter putat hujus Dramatis Prologum deperditum esse" (Euripides 1783 [ed. Markland], 4).

75. "Isto autem prologo non arbitror eam fuisse tragoediam instructam, quae hodie legitur: in qua poeta, illustriore quodam et ad probabilitatem aptiore *propositionis* genere usus, prologum ita coniugavit cum actione, ut eorum, quae fabulae antecessissent, *narrationem* non praefiguret exordio, sed inseret v. 49–114. Quamquam enim Euripides in seperatis illis Prologis, quos fabulis praeposuit, non acquievit sic, ut dramatica plane supersederet actionis inductione: tamen huius ambitum angustioribus fere limitibus sepsit, quae in prologo esset persecutus, in ea copiosas repetiit. Quid? Quod reperiuntur tragoediae, in quibus, dempto prologo, *expositio* argumenti dramatica, ne satis quidem dulcidine et apte ad communem intelligentiam explicata videri possit. Quapropter Aeliani locus magnam mihi suspicionis movit, duplicem olim extitisse *Iphigeniae* Euripideae editionem, cuius e priore, quae interiit, desumpti etiam videntur versus, quos Aristophanes in *Ranis* v. 1345 facete et perfricate notavit" (Eichstaedt 1793, 99n.147).

76. For an overview of the problems with the end of the play, see Page 1934, 192–197; West 1981.

77. He was followed by Bremi 1819.

78. Euripides 1802 (ed. Porson), 23.

79. Euripides 1831 (ed. Hermann).

calmer iambs; this done, he returns to a more agitated state of mind and speech.[80]

But although Hermann is generally conservative with respect to the opening of the play, he needs to avoid an apparent inconsistency. When Agamemnon tells the old man that only he, Odysseus, Menelaus, and Calchas know of the plot to lure Iphigenia to Aulis under the pretense of a marriage to Achilles, it seems illogical for the old slave to ask immediately after this if Achilles will not be angry at the loss of his bride.[81] So Hermann transposes these lines before the iambic prologue. This produces a theory about the transmission of the play: (1) there was originally a prologue with the structure anapests/iambs/anapests; (2) there was a tradition without the iambs, produced by someone who decided that they were unnecessary or inelegant; (3) the iambs were reinserted wrongly, thus producing the apparent illogicality of lines 124–127. A similar model is used to explain the current state of the exodus: "Either the end was missing in a very ancient book in which this play was preserved, or that more recent poet, not approving that Euripides should introduce a *deus ex machina*, threw the scene out, and substituted for it the one we now have."[82]

Hermann follows Porson in having Artemis come on at the end; Euripides wanted the audience to know about the miracle of Iphigenia's transformation *and* about the transfer to Tauris, something no human could have narrated. Very possibly a late scribe tried to supplement missing pages, using the *Hecuba* as a model.[83]

In time, however, Hermann would come to correct his own text. By 1847–1848,[84] he was led to concede that no Euripidean play could begin without an iambic prologue. This in turn required that he abandon the theory of 1831. Instead he argues that a scribe, faced with a mutilated manuscript, attempted to correct it, filling in sections that were lost and adding lines where he felt something was missing. The beginning of the play was mangled in some ancient copy, and in the process of restoration the order of the opening lines was mixed up: "Just as its ending was lost in that ancient codex, so also was the beginning mangled: for the extremities of books are especially liable to damage. Since the first

80. Ibid., ix.

81. vv. 107–127 Diggle.

82. "Aut in antiquissimo libro, in quo servata est haec fabula, defuit finis, aut ille recentior poeta, non probans quod deum ex machine introduxisset Euripides, abiecit illam scenam, pro eaque substituit illis, quae nunc habemus" (Euripides 1831 [ed. Hermann], xxiv).

83. Ibid., xxvii–xxviii.

84. Hermann 1877.

two sheets, on one of which the prologue was written, and on the other the anapests, being torn out, lay or were glued in inverse order, the beginning seemed to be written in anapests."[85] Once the order had been rearranged, the interpolator had to make some corrections, particularly at the end of the iambs, which now came between two sections of dialogue with the old slave. Hermann thinks in particular that the wording of Agamemnon's speech at the end of the iambs, where he tells of his decision to try to prevent Iphigenia from coming to Aulis, was altered. The original words might have been something like the following:

> ἃ δ' οὐ καλῶς
> ἔγνων τότ', αὖθις μεταγράφω κατ' εὐφρόνην
> ἐς τήνδε δέλτον, ἣν Κλυταιμνήστρᾳ λάθρᾳ
> πέμψω πρὸς Ἄργος. ἃ δὲ κέκευθεν ἐν πτυξαῖς,
> φράσω γέροντι, τὸν τάδ' ἐκπονεῖν θέλω.
> πιστὸς γὰρ ἀλόχῳ τοῖς τ' ἐμοῖς ἐστιν δόμοις.

> And not thinking rightly on these things before, I again write a new message on this tablet by night, and I will send it secretly to Clytemnestra in Argos. And what lies within the folded tablet I will tell to the old man whom I want to fulfill this task. For he is faithful to my wife and my house.[86]

This could, of course, be read just as easily as a moment of self-consciousness on Hermann's part, a translation into the language and meter of Greek tragedy of the sentiment that opens the *dissertatio*, "I myself, when seventeen years ago I edited this tragedy, was more tolerant than I should have been of a considerable amount."[87]

As though aware of some sympathy between the modern textual critic and the man responsible for the deformation of our text, the Hermann of 1847–1848 is mildly tolerant on his behalf. Though he is still called an interpolator, this man is not altogether to be despised. Like a sculptor who restores an ancient monument, the interpolator is a restorer:[88] a textual critic, in other words, undertaking the same kind of work as Hermann himself. And the fact that Hermann is able to change his

85. "Eius ut finis in vetusto illo codice interierat, ita etiam initium laceratum fuit: maxime enim extrema librorum atteruntur: ac prima duo folia, quorum in uno prologus, in altero anapaesti scripti fuerant, quum avulsa inverso ordine adiacerent vel adglutinata essent, exordium visum est anapaestis factum esse" (Ibid., 219).
86. Ibid., 220.
87. "Ego ipse, quum ante hos septemdecim annos illam tragoediam ederem, non pauca patientius tuli quam debebam" (Ibid., 218).
88. Ibid., 219.

mind points to a self-critical moment within his own thought processes, a moment when he is able to read *his own* presentations of the text as he could read the presentations of the interpolator.

This can be illustrated with respect to the fate at Hermann's hands of a single passage. I reproduce the text of Matthiae,[89] the text Hermann worked from in the edition of 1831.

ἔμολες, ὦ Πάρις, ᾗ τε σύ γε   epode
βουκόλος ἀργενναῖς ἐτράφης
Ἰδαίαις παρὰ μόσχοις,
βάρβαρα συρίζων, Φρυγίων
αὐλῶν Οὐλύμπου καλάμοις
μιμήματα πνέων.
εὔθηλοι δὲ τρέφοντο βόες,
ὅτε σε κρίσις ἔμενε θεᾶν,
ἅ σ' Ἑλλάδα πέμπει
ἐλεφαντοδέτων πάροιθεν
δόμων, ὃς τᾶς Ἑλένας
ἐν ἀντωποῖς βλεφάροισιν ἔρωτα δέδωκας,
ἔρωτι δ' αὐτὸς ἐπτοάθης.
ὅθεν ἔρις ἔρις
Ἑλλάδα σὺν δορὶ ναυσί τ' ἄγει
ἐς Τροίας πέργαμα.

You came, O Paris, where you were raised a cowherd among the white Idaean calves, piping alien melodies on your syrinx, playing imitations of the Phrygian aulos of Olympus. And cows with full udders were grazing when the judgment of the Goddesses awaited you. That judgment sent you to Hellas; you who, before the houses inlaid with ivory, your gaze entwined with Helen's, gave love and were yourself set aflutter with love. Whence strife, strife led Hellas with spears and ships to the citadel of Troy.[90]

The passage describes the judgment of Paris: in a play about choices and judgments, this is the one that begins them all, since it was Paris's choice of Aphrodite as the fairest of the goddesses that led to his seduction of Helen. It also offers a point where criticism becomes self-reflexive in contemplating an object: the critic must make a choice about the choice of Paris, and in this process the first choice (the judgment that begins the story of the *Iphigenia at Aulis*) and the last choice (the textual judgment that, if only for the moment, ends its composition) come face-to-face and contemplate each other. The key to reading this passage against the reaction of critics like Hermann is in the word *κρίσις* (judgment),

89. Euripides 1813–1837 (ed. Matthiae), 2:143.
90. Ibid., 563–578.

which could designate either the judgment of Paris or the contest of the goddesses. In antiquity this word would not have had the connotation of any kind of textual criticism—the word for that was usually διορθώσις. But by the time of Hermann the name for correcting texts was criticism, *ars critica, Kritik.* The allegorical force of this passage comes from a resonance between the name of the judgment and the scholarly operation Hermann was performing on the passage.[91] The disapproval or regret the chorus feels over the κρίσις θεᾶν (judgment of the goddesses) here serves as the symbol for a deep ambivalence in the critical text itself over the intellectual technology of its production.

What is particularly interesting about this passage from the point of view of both the thematics of the play and the critical tradition concerning it is the fact that here the chorus expresses regret that the judgment ever occurred. In a single strophic pair, they sing of the dangers of erotic passion, praying "may I have measured love, and holy desires." At the end of this pair, they turn to a mythical exemplum: Paris's judgment of the three goddesses and the destructive love affair with Helen to which this gave rise, and this is the passage we are dealing with here. It is more than just a mythical exemplum finishing off an ode on the ethics of love. The story of the judgment of Paris was told in the Cypria, and it is frequently found on Attic black- and red-figure pottery.[92] Euripides returns to it repeatedly, and it always functions as the beginning of the evils that culminate in the destruction of Troy. In the *Iphigenia at Aulis* the story is told twice: once here, and once much later on, when Iphigenia gives it as the ultimate cause of her own sacrifice on the altar of Artemis.[93] But in addition to being an etiology of the Trojan war, the story of the judgment of Paris also offers an oblique commentary on the scene this chorus of young women has just witnessed: in the long episode leading up to their song, Agamemnon and Menelaus have changed their minds repeatedly; they have shown a remarkable inability to reach a decision on whether or not to sacrifice Iphigenia. To this scene of indecision the *krisis* of Paris serves as an eloquent and ominous foil. The chorus has just seen what damage a decision can do: Agamemnon's ultimate resolution to murder his daughter will wreak havoc on the first family of Argos. So, too, was Paris's decision a terrible one, for it led to this military gathering

91. Compare Wolf 1795, chapter 50, which discusses Aristarchus's athetization of the lines in *Iliad* 24 that discuss the judgment of Paris. Wolf approves, commenting, "Quamobrem et veteres, et recentiores aliqui, in quibus instar omnium Hemsterhusius est, plane probaverunt iudicium illud, quo iudicium Paridis tollitur."

92. See Ackermann and Gisler 1981, *s.v.* "*Iudicium Paridis*"; Stinton 1990.

93. 1382 Diggle.

at Aulis and to the destruction it will inevitably entail. If the judgment of Paris is the first cause of the Trojan War, it is also the first in a series of troubling decisions, including Agamemnon's decision to sacrifice his daughter, and, though the chorus cannot know it yet, Iphigenia's own decision to go to her death willingly.

Whatever the precise wording of this passage, it is clear that, from the chorus's perspective, it would have been better had Paris not made the decision he did, and perhaps it would have been best if he had never made any decision at all.[94] That the judgment is spoken of ruefully by the chorus was felt by Musgrave:[95] he, however, thought it was not brought out clearly enough and proposed to emend the first line to ἀμελὲς ὧν, Πάρις, ἦτε σύ γε (uncaring of which things [that is, the need for moderation in love], Paris, indeed you...")—not a change that has been accepted into any text. Hermann too wanted to emphasize the undesirability of Paris's act of criticism, as though by altering the text of the play he could produce a clearer critical commentary on the provisional nature of all of *his* judgments.

An initial glance through the dossier of Hermann's critical interventions in this passage prompts a few observations.[96] The first is that, from a conservative perspective, Hermann is free in his changes—a lot of what he does here looks more like *inventio* than *emendatio.* Hermann elides the difference between the work of textual criticism and the work of interpolation that this criticism supposedly aims to root out; there is a way, in other words, that criticism does a kind of damage to the text similar to that supposedly done by interpolators and scribes. The second thing we should notice is that as time progresses the texts Hermann prints become increasingly fragmentary. Holes grow, until in the final version we have nearly as many lacunary lines as we have lines of Greek. This fragmentary quality encapsulates the unsettling similar-

94. This regret over Paris's judgment is represented frequently in Attic black-figure vases, which sometimes show Paris turning his back from the three goddesses, as though to avoid what is bound to be a heavy burden. See Ackermann and Gisler 1981, *s.v.* "*Iudicium Paridis*".

95. Euripides 1821, 4:480.

96. Before Hermann, the main interest in these lines had been mythological and musicological (What kind of an instrument is Paris supposed to be playing, and what is the story he is telling?), and the only textual issues had been adjudicating between πνέων (in some editions) and πλέκων (which is the reading in the manuscripts), and deciding whether to print ἔρις ἔρις, ἔριν ἔριν or ἔρις ἔριν in the final lines (the manuscripts read ἔρις ἔριν; Diggle and recent editions read ἔριν ἔριν). Linguistically the first two lines of the passage had given some difficulty to more sensitive readers: as we note below, it is not clear *where* Paris is supposed to be going with ἔμολες in the first line; he is already *at* Ida, where he was raised and where the goddesses came to *him.*

ity between critic and corruptor. Friedrich Schlegel wrote, "Many of the works of the ancients have become fragments. Many modern works are fragments as soon as they are written":[97] Hermann both recovers the fragmentariness considered proper to the ancient text by virtue of the accidents of history and writes in the fragmentary manner supposed, at least by Schlegel, to be characteristic of modernity. Here, then, the fragment is a sign of the antique character of the Euripidean text, lost when the fragment was "ruined" by the scribe who corrected it; but it is also the figure that marks Hermann's own work not as a "recovery" of the past but as a modern act of composition. This fragment is a symbol for the loss of antiquity and for the processes that continue to perpetrate that loss.

By the light of this deeply ambivalent manifestation of the critic's work, it becomes possible to read Hermann waging a campaign against the *κρίσις in* the passage: in each successive version, Hermann makes the chorus's wish that it had never taken place increasingly explicit, until in the final version he has them wishing that the critic—Paris—had never been born.

His relationship with this passage began with the *Elementa doctrinae metricae* of 1816.[98]

(For this version of the text, as well as for the two that follow, I append a genetic apparatus intended to allow the reader a brief synoptic view of Hermann's changes to the text over time. Notes in the apparatus are keyed to the text by a superscript letter. In the apparatus I indicate the reading as it appeared in Matthiae, which Hermann used as a copy-text, or in one of Hermann's earlier versions, if it originated there. I adopt the following abbreviations. "Hermann" on its own indicates that the source is the immediate edition (thus "Hermann" alone in the apparatus to the 1816 text indicates that Hermann (1816) is the source; but "Herman" in the apparatus to the 1831 text indicates that the 1831 edition is the source.) Matthiae = Euripides 1813–1837 (ed. Matthiae); A = Hermann 1816; B = Euripides 1831 (ed. Hermann); Blomfield = Blomfield 1814. MSS = L and P.)

ἔμολες, ὦ Πάρις, ᾗ τε σύ γε strophe
βουκόλος ἀργενναῖς ἐτράφης
Ἰδαίαις παρὰ μόσχοις,
βάρβαρα συρίζων, Φρυγίων
5 *αὐλῶν Οὐλύμπου καλάμοις*
μίμηματα . . . πνέων.[a]

97. Schlegel 1991, 21 (Athenaeum Fragment #24).
98. Hermann 1816, 542–543.

εὔθηλοι δὲ τρέφοντο βόες (antistrophe)
ὅτε σε κρίσις ἔμαινε[b] θεᾶν,
ἅ σ' ἐς[c] Ἑλλάδα πέμπει·
10 τῶν[d] ἐλεφαντοδέτων πάροιθεν δόμων ὃς τᾶς Ἑλένας
ἐν ἀντωποῖς βλεφάροις[e]

ἔρωτα δέδωκας, ἔρωτι δ' αὐτὸς ἐπτοάθης· (epode)
ὅθεν ἔρις, ἔρις Ἑλλάδα σὺν δορὶ ναυσί τ' ἄγει
15 ἐς πέργαμα Τροίας.[f]

(a) πνέων] "vel πλέκων. Versus mutilus est"; Hermann. Scripsit μιμήματα. (b) ἔμαινε] ἔμενε Matthiae et MSS. (c) ἐς] interpolavit Hermann. (d) τῶν] interpolavit Hermann. (e) βλεφάροις] correxit Blomfield; βλεφάροισιν Matthiae et MSS. (f) πέργαμα Τροίας] Τροίας πέργαμα Matthiae et MSS.

You came, O Paris, where you were raised a cowherd among the white Idaean calves, piping alien melodies on your syrinx, playing[a]... imitations of the Phrygian aulos of Olympus.

And cows with full udders were grazing when the judgment of the Goddesses was making you mad[b] and sent you to[c] Hellas; you who, before the houses inlaid with ivory[d], your gaze[e] entwined with Helen's,

gave love, and were yourself set aflutter with love. Whence strife, strife led Hellas with spears and ships to the citadel of Troy[f].

(a) playing] "or plucking. The line is damaged." Hermann. μίμημματα in the same line is a typographical error; Hermann wrote μιμήματα. (b) was making you mad] "awaited you" in Matthiae and the MSS. (c) to] the preposition was inserted by Hermann. (d) inlaid with ivory] an article ("the") was inserted by Hermann. (e) gaze] a shorter form of the same Greek word was proposed by Blomfield and adopted by Hermann; Matthiae and the MSS have a form of the word longer by one syllable. (f) the citadel of Troy] in Matthiae and the MSS the words are transposed ("the Trojan citadel").

Hermann noticed that a series of small changes would make the meter almost entirely glyconic and would produce two responding strophes and an epode. There are six alterations from the traditional readings here plus some changes in colometry, most of which do not significantly change the sense. But two are of particular importance. The usual κρίσις ἔμενε (the competition awaited [you]) in the eighth line has been emended to κρίσις ἔμαινε (the judgment was making [you] mad). The surface reason for this change is metrical: by lengthening a syllable he gets an anaclastic glyconic that will respond with line 2. The new verb emphasizes that the *judgment itself* caused Paris's later erotic misdemeanor and its consequences: *krisis* is the first cause of disaster.

This mad act of criticism is already ripping into the fabric of the text in the sixth line, where a lacuna of two syllables has been introduced. Again, the apparent reason for this emendation is metrical, but it has supremely felicitous consequences in terms of the material of the line: just as the fabric of the text is torn here, so too is Paris's melody interrupted, as though his instrument hiccuped ominously, prophesying the terrible outcome of his choice, but also offering a warning about the deleterious effects of criticism on song in general.

The next time Hermann had dealings with the judgment of Paris was in the edition of the *Iphigenia at Aulis* printed in 1831.[99]

ἔμολες, ὦ Πάρι, μήτε[a] σύ γε — strophe
βουκόλος ἀργενναῖς ἐτράφης
Ἰδαίαις παρὰ μόσχοις,
βάρβαρα συρίζων, Φρυγίων
5 αὐλῶν Οὐλύμπου καλάμοις
* * μίμημα πλέκων.[b]
* * * * * *[c]

εὔθηλοι δὲ τρέφοντο βόες — antistrophe
εὖτε[d] σε κρίσις ἔμηνε[e] θεᾶν,
10 ἅ σ' ἐς Ἑλλάδα πέμπει
τῶν ἐλεφαντοδέτων πάροι-
θεν δόμων, ὃς τᾶς Ἑλένας
ἐν ἀντωποῖς βλεφάροις
ἔρωτα δέδωκας,

15 ἔρωτι δ' αὐτὸς ἐπτοάθης· — epode
ὅθεν ἔρις, ἔρις
Ἑλλάδα σὺν δορὶ ναυσί τ' ἄγει
ἐς πέργαμα Τροίας.

(a) μήτε] ἦ τε A; idem Matthiae et MSS. (b) μίμημα πλέκων] μίμηματα [sic]... πνέων A. (c) * * * * * *] lacuna interpolavit Hermann. (d) εὖτε] ὅτε A. (e) ἔμηνε] ἔμαινε A.

I wish you didn't come, O Paris, nor[a] were raised a cowherd among the white Idaean calves, piping alien melodies on your syrinx, [...] plucking[b] an imitation of the Phrygian aulos of Olympus. [...][c]

And cows with full udders were grazing when[d] the judgment of the Goddesses made you mad[e] and sent you to Hellas before the houses inlaid with ivory, you who, your gaze entwined with Helen's,

gave love and were yourself set aflutter with love. Whence strife, strife led Hellas with spears and ships to the citadel of Troy.

99. Euripides 1831 (ed. Hermann), vv. 575–592.

(a) nor] "where" A, Matthiae, MSS. (b) plucking an imitation] "playing... imitations" (with a misprinted plural form of "imitations") A. (c) ...] the lacuna was added by Hermann. (d) when] an alternate word was used in A. (e) made you mad] "was making you mad" A.

Here, while he continues to assert that these lines constitute a strophe/antistrophe/epode set, Hermann feels that he needs to emend differently than before. In particular, the first line bothers him. Why, he asks, should the chorus say, "You came, O Paris, there where you were raised?" How can he *come* to where he already *is*? "Surely," he remarks, "no one, once he has been shown, will doubt that this verse should say, 'Would that you had never gone there, nor pastured cattle, there where you were the judge of the three goddesses.' "[100] After all, Paris's presence at Ida, and his function as judge in the competition of the goddesses, led to the Trojan War. So ἦτε becomes μήτε, and we are instructed to take it twice, once with ἔμολες and once with ἐτράφης. We are now unequivocally focused on the *undesirability* of the scene described. Again, as though in a symptomatic reflection of the terrors of criticism, the surface of the text becomes increasingly fragmentary: to the two-syllable lacuna in line 6 has been added a whole new lacunary line, line 7.

This process of increasing fragmentation comes to fruition—or one might rather say, reaches a maximum state of dissolution—in the 1847–1848 dissertation "De interpolationibus Euripideae *Iphigeniae in Aulide*."[101] Between this text and the 1831 edition, there intervened what can only be described as a firestorm around the criticism of the play. In 1834 Otto Gruppe, in a massively controversial work, argued that the *Iphigenia at Aulis* was not the work of Euripides at all, but was rather written by the fourth-century poet Chaeremon.[102] In 1837 Johann Hartung printed a version of the text that freely rearranged lines throughout, inserted long stretches of asterisks where the original had supposedly been lost, and produced a text that was nearly unrecognizable.[103] The general response was described by Hartung in 1844 as *Quanti undique clamores*![104] Into the midst of a widening cyclone of essays, dissertations, and arguments about the play's form and authenticity, Hermann released his last statement on the matter. And in it the main

100. "Nemo, opinor, semel monitus dubitabit quin hoc dici debuerit, utinam ne venisses illic, neve armenta pavisses, ubi iudex fuisti trium dearum" (Euripides 1831 [ed. Hermann]), 53.

101. Hermann 1877.

102. Gruppe 1834; Bang 1867.

103. Euripides 1837 (ed. Hartung).

104. Hartung 1844, 515.

plotline, the governing metaphor, and the object of philological inquiry is the fragment, fragmentation, and fragmentariness, and the culpable hand of the critic.

The story of the judgment of Paris is one of the passages severely mutilated and then fixed up by an early critic. Hermann prints what the mutilated page might have looked like; he reconstructs not Euripides' text, but a fragment of it. In this version, fully half of the second antistrophe is lost, as well as the first line of the epode.

[μή μοι φῶς πότ᾽ ἐς ἁμέρας][a]
ἔμολες, ὦ Πάρι, μηδὲ[b] σύ γε — strophe
βουκόλος ἀγραύλοις[c] ἐτράφης
Ἰδαίαις παρὰ μόσχοις,
5 βάρβαρα συρίζων, Φρυγίων
αὐλῶν Οὐλύμπου καλάμοις
[πολυπλόκον][d] μίμημα πνέων.
* * * * * * *
εὔθηλοι δὲ [πλανώμεναι — antistrophe
10 κατὰ νάπας][e] τρέφοντο βόες,
εὖτε κρίσις σ᾽ ἔμηνε θεᾶν,
ἅ σ᾽ [εἰς] Ἑλλάδα πέμπει.
* * * * * * * *
* * * * * * * *
15 * * * * * * * *
* * * * * * *
* * * * * *[f] — epode
ἐλεφαντοδέτων[g] πάροιθε θρόνων,[h]
Ἑλένας [ἵν᾽][i] ἐν ἀντωποῖς βλεφάροις
20 ἐρωτά τ᾽ ἔδωκας,[j] ἔρωτι δ᾽ αὐτὸς ἐπτοάθης·
ὅθεν ἔρις, ἔρις
Ἑλλάδα σὺν δορὶ ναυσί τ᾽ ἄγει
πρὸς πέργαμα Τροίας.

(a) μή μοι φῶς πότ᾽ ἐς ἁμέρας] versum interpolavit Hermann; fortasse scripsit μή μοι φώς πότ᾽ ἐς ἁμέραν. (b) μηδὲ] μήτε B; ἦ τε A (c) ἀγραύλοις] ἀργενναῖς A, B, Matthiae et MSS. (d) πολυπλόκον] interpolavit Hermann. (e) πλανώμεναι κατὰ νάπας] interpolavit Hermann; εὔθηλοι δὲ τρέφοντο βόες A, B, Matthiae et MSS. (f) ...] lacuna add. Hermann. (g) ἐλεφαντοδέτων] τῶν ἐλαντοδέτων A et B. (h) θρόνων] δόμων A et B. (i) ἵν᾽] interpolavit Hermann; ὃς τᾶς Ἑλένας ἐν κτλ. A et B. (j) ἐρωτά τ᾽ ἔδωκας] Blomfield; ἔρωτα δέδωκας A, B, Matthiae et MSS.

[I wish you never came to the light of day][a] oh Paris, nor[b] were raised a cowherd among the rural[c] Idaean calves, piping alien melodies on your syrinx, blowing a [complex][d] imitation of the Phrygian aulos of Olympus. [******]

and cows with full udders [were ranging through the dells][e] and grazing, when the judgment of the Goddesses made you mad and sent you to Hellas. [****************]

[********][f] before the thrones[h] inlaid with ivory[g], [where,][i] your gaze entwined with Helen's, you both gave love[j] and were yourself set aflutter with love; Whence strife, strife led Hellas with spears and ships to the citadel of Troy.

(a) I wish you never came to the light of day] Hermann added this line; he may have written "I wish you had never come into the day as a mortal." (b) nor] a different particle, with similar sense but a different shade of syntactical meaning, was used in B; "where" A. (c) rural] "white" A, B, Matthiae, and MSS. (d) complex] Hermann added this word. (e) ranging through the dells] Hermann added this line; A, B, Matthiae and the MSS have "and cows with full udders were grazing." (f) ...] Hermann added this lacuna. (g) inlaid with ivory] Hermann had added an article ("the") in A and retained it in B. (h) thrones] "houses" A and B. (i) where] Hermann added this; A and B had a relative pronoun ("who") and an article before "Helen." (j) you both gave love] Blomfield; "you gave love" A, B, Matthiae and MSS.

A thought experiment can help us to see how in this fragmentary printing of the passage Hermann and his interpolator-critic approach each other. If all versions of the *Iphigenia at Aulis* were lost, all papyri, MSS, and critical editions, with the exception of Hermann's last version of this passage, later generations would have a text that significantly misrepresented the textual tradition as we have it. But that is what Hermann thinks the interpolator-critic himself did; he misrepresented the text as *he* received it. This text is both the representation of a fragment *and* a fragmentary representation, an act of fragmentation perpetrated on the received representations of Euripides' text.

Hermann reproduces the activity of his interpolator-critic in another way as well. If Hermann fragments a text that seems whole in the tradition, the interpolator-critic makes whole what was a fragment—he ruins the fragment by not reproducing it, fragments the fragment by making it seem intact. But so does Hermann, when he supplements the fragment he has "recovered" in verses 1, 7, 9, 10, 12, and 19. As both the recovery of a fragment *and* its critical supplementation, this text does the work of the critic and *works against* criticism, negating and affirming its role at the same time. Not only is the text fragmenting but so, we might say, is the critic, engaged in an argument with himself he doesn't know how to resolve.

This text emphasizes with nearly unbearable clarity the chorus's wish that the primal act of criticism had not taken place: they now wish that Paris had never been born at all. Hermann supplements his fragment with a new first line, one that was in fact lost in the copy the scribe worked with, *μή μοι φῶς πότ' ἐς ἁμέρας / ἔμολες*, which according to Hermann should mean, "I wish you had never come to the light of day."[105] This new line produces a strophe one line longer than in his previous editions, and to create a responding antistrophe he supplements the ninth and tenth line, which turns one line into two. But because he is unable to make *ἐλεφαντοδέτων* and what follows respond with the new structure, he shucks the rest of the extant lines into the epode and prints a lacuna of four lines in the antistrophe.

There is a challenge in all this fragmentation and supplementation—a challenge to think through the implications of the modern practice of textual philology. Particularly the first line [*μή μοι φῶς πότ' ἐς ἁμέρας*], which requires a violent hyperbaton, and it almost seems that we are being dared to try to find a correction that would yield an easier construction. In fact such an emendation might be possible: we could take the circumflex accent in *φῶς* as a printer's error and read it with an acute instead, *φώς*,[106] and then we could emend *ἁμέρας* to *ἁμέραν*, giving, "I wish you had never come into the day as a mortal, oh Paris." That would mean treating Hermann's critical endeavors as the same kind of (somewhat incompetent) corrections he attributes to his medieval scribe: as though, in this late revisitation to the *Iphigenia at Aulis,* Hermann were inviting us to see critic and interpolator, corrector and corruptor, as figures for each other, as members of the same destructive tribe. It would also mean that we had been provoked into a continuation of the processes of *écriture* that criticism studies and performs, been drawn into what had already taken place: an explosion of varying theories about the authorship and form of *Iphigenia at Aulis.* We would have begun to produce a plurality of versions of *Hermann*'s text, just as there was already a plurality of *Iphigenias at Aulis.*

Excursus: The Critical Fragment

When, in his engagement with the *Iphigenia at Aulis,* Hermann showed us texts in fragmentary states, what precisely was he trying to display? What does his fragment mean? Clearly it is not the original form of the *Iphigenia at Aulis,* not the words "as the author wrote them." Some of

105. Hermann 1877, 230.
106. Cf. *μίμηματα* in Hermann 1816, 253.

those words are presumably present in the fragment, but not all of them; the holes Hermann prints represent places where what Euripides wrote has been lost. Nor is what Hermann shows us meant to be ancient. The mutilated copy he reconstructs is supposed to be located somewhere in time between the end of antiquity and now. Perhaps the surviving *words* are ancient: the *fragment itself*, the object of Hermann's conjecture, is not. It is a single medial moment in the textual tradition, of no particular interest beyond the fact that here the *Iphigenia at Aulis* was decisively defaced.

Hermann might have supplemented the holes and tears in his imaginary fragment; he might have printed a text "fully restored." But he does not. Instead, he wants us to contemplate the fragment itself, the tattered, sad, debased object halfway between classical inscription and scholarly edition, as though he wanted us to put our fingers in the tears as Thomas put his on the wounds of Christ, as though this artificial fragment presented something more concrete than any fully restored text could do.

What does the critical fragment aim to present? As I have already suggested, an answer to this question can be found in Romantic discussions of fragments and fragmentariness. When Schlegel wrote: "Many of the works of the ancients have become fragments. Many modern works are fragments as soon as they are written,"[107] he specified two very different kinds of fragment, which Hermann's critical fragment synthesized. The first is a diplomatic fragment, a real, documentable scrap of parchment, papyrus, or stone with a tangible materiality; indeed, its materiality is essential to the fragment, since the decay of the material causes the text to become fragmentary. Clearly this is the kind of thing Hermann wants to imitate: his is a simulated diplomatic fragment. But the fact that it is simulated indicates a second important kind of fragment that Hermann's text also resembles: the melancholic or sentimental fragment, the artificial ruin that never had an intact form. I claim that Hermann's critical fragment uses the form of the diplomatic fragment and the rhetoric of the melancholic fragment to present us with an image not of an original text but rather of time itself, of the certain loss of antiquity.

The Diplomatic Fragment

When Schlegel remarks that "many of the works of the ancients have become fragments," he articulates an awareness that had become

107. Schlegel 1991, 21 (Athenaeum Fragment #24).

increasingly concrete in the eighteenth century. While publishing fragments of ancient poetry had been an integral part of text editing from the beginning, developments in scholarly methodology and the first attempts to publish papyrus fragments meant that in the seventeenth and eighteenth centuries the fragmentariness of ancient literature was increasingly considered in terms of its actual material deterioration.

The rise of paleography, for example,[108] focused scholarly attention on the forms of alphabets and the effects of the material on which they were written. Part of the significance of works like Mabillon's *De re diplomatica* and Montfaucon's *Palaeographia graeca* is in the fact that they present the fruits of a scholarly vision that treated books and documents not only as traces of events and signs of things but also as concrete objects in their own right. In short the *reality* of written traces is affirmed; the manuscript is transformed from a document into a monument.

This has its effect in a number of significant new practices coeval with the emergence of a diplomatic awareness. First the addition of books and libraries to travel itineraries: the *iter litterarium* is interested first and foremost not in the ruins and statues of Italy, a point of interest since at least the Middle Ages (as evidenced by the popularity of the *Mirabilia urbis Romae*),[109] but in the contents of libraries and the condition of old books. Indeed, other antiquities could be treated almost as an afterthought. "Though the principle Motive of our Journey," writes Montfaucon, "was to gather some particulars never published, out of the Manuscripts of the Holy fathers, and by them to amend any Errors, there might be in former editions, it would have been a crime to neglect other curiosities."[110] While other guides of Rome and Italy could read like lists of places and architectural remains, the diaries of Montfaucon and Mabillon[111] are leavened with lists of remarkable old books, themselves transformed into material objects as important as ancient columns or the relics of saints.

Together with a focus on libraries and books as material sites and objects, the rise of awareness in the materiality of the MSS from which ancient works are drawn effects changes in the scholarly use of bookmaking techniques. The presentation of Latin and Greek, previously a

108. In the works of Mabillon 1704; Montfaucon 1970 (a reprint); Maffei 1727. See Knowles 1963; Momigliano 1966; Reynolds and Wilson 1991, 131.

109. Gardiner and Nichols 1986.

110. "Etsi porro nobis princeps isthaec fuerit migrationis causa, ut ope manuscriptorum, SS. Patrum anecdota eruere possemus, et sarcire si quid peccatum in priscis editis est; religio tamen fuisset ab aliis abstinere" (Montfaucon n.d./1702, 1–2; English translation in Montfaucon 1712, 2).

111. Mabillon 1687.

problem for type-designers and type-setters, became an aspect of book illustration as well, and techniques formerly used for the engraving of architectural and technical images had to be deployed in the strange service of representing writing (see fig. 1). In this move the materiality of the written artifact is fully acknowledged: the abstract reproduction of text using movable type is replaced by concrete techniques of pictorial representation.

In addition to pictorial representation of inscriptions (see, for example, the beautiful books of Maffei),[112] more "regular" typesetting processes also needed to address the difficulty of representing fragments of papyrus. Montfaucon's *Diarium Italicum*, for example, utilized rows of periods to mark missing text on a stone inscription (borrowed from the marking of conjectural lacunae)—apparently a technique beyond the ken of his English translator and printer, who left the passage out.[113] Nicola Schow's 1788 edition of a papyrus found in the Museum Borgianum[114] uses similar typographical conventions to represent tears and holes in the papyrus (fig. 2). Other editors, like Hermann, used asterisks instead of ellipsis points.

These practices complicate the meaning of printed lacunae. Whereas a line of dots or asterisks previously marked something the critic conjectured to be missing on metrical, linguistic, or logical grounds,[115] the typographical representation of papyrus in Schow and other early papyrological editions[116] made it possible for a more creative critic such as Hermann to use the same signs to represent not necessary lacunae but rather imagined lacunary documents. Type has begun to serve the function of illustration: we are meant to imagine the physical contours of a torn original, represented in typographical abstraction.

The diplomatic fragment, then, uses the lacuna, the tear, and the elision to give a strong sense of the materiality of an inscription on papyrus or stone. *Fragment*, here, means "real, coarse, immediate"; a direct object of the senses. Above all such a fragment signifies the

112. Maffei 1749, 1977 (reprint).

113. Montfaucon n.d./1702, 99–100. According to the translator (Montfaucon 1712, 103), "The epitaph is imperfect in the house of the renouned Danesius, and shall therefore be omitted."

114. Schow 1788.

115. There are countless examples. One is Callimachus 1761 (ed. Bentley and Ernestus), fr. LXXI (p. 443), v. 3.

116. Publications of papyrus are scarce in this period. Schow 1788 is normally considered the first, but see Maffei 1727, 130–176. After Schow but before Hermann's last version of the *Iphigenia at Aulis* were published Peyron 1827, 1829; Reuvens 1830; Forshall 1839. See Gallo 1986. For a broader history of elipsis points, see Henry 2000.

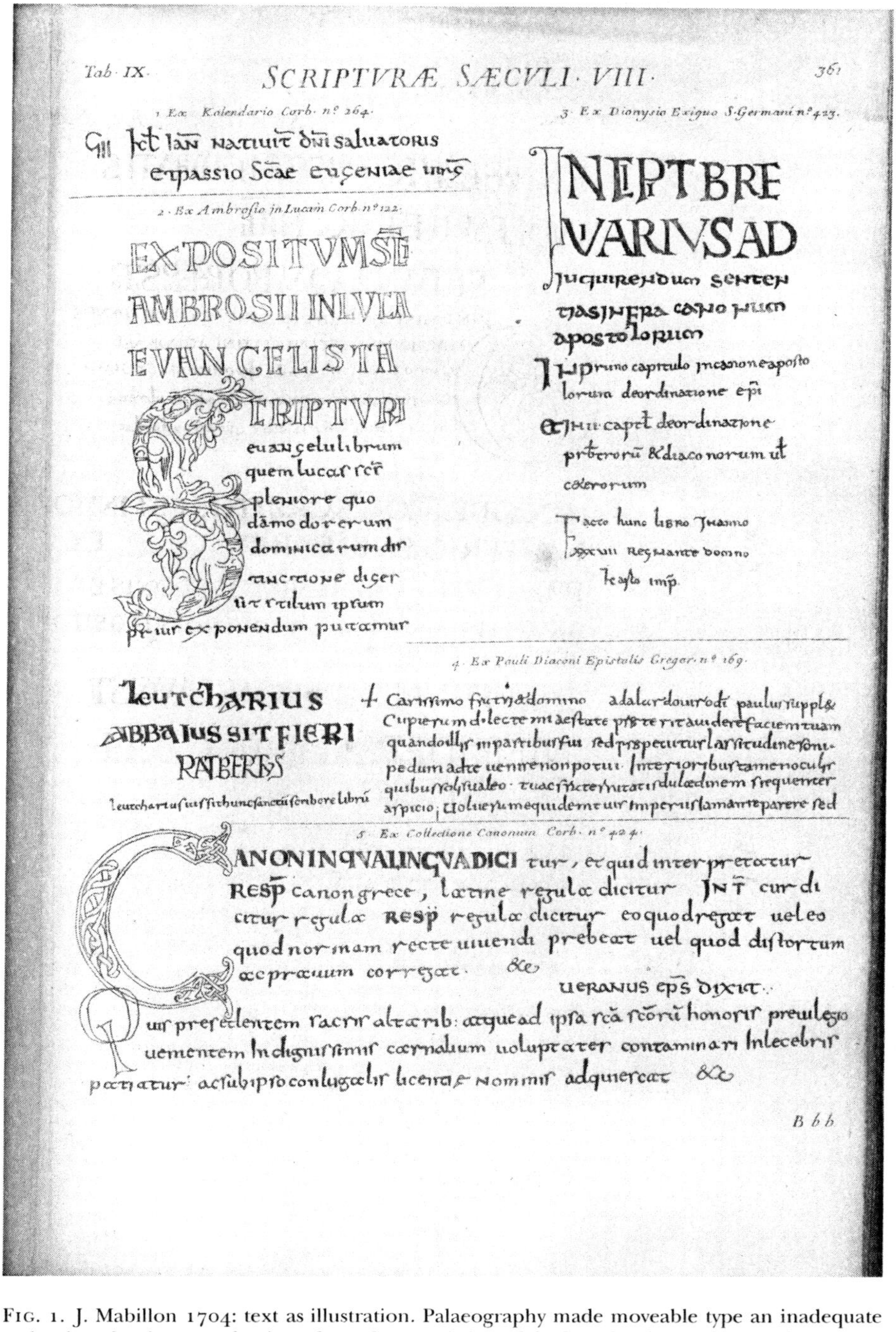

Tab. IX. SCRIPTVRÆ SÆCVLI VIII. 361

1 Ex Kalendario Corb. nº 264.

2 Ex Ambrosio in Lucam Corb. nº 122.

3 Ex Dionysio Exiguo S. Germani nº 423.

4 Ex Pauli Diaconi Epistolis Gregor. nº 169.

5 Ex Collectione Canonum Corb. nº 424.

Bbb

Fig. 1. J. Mabillon 1704: text as illustration. Palaeography made moveable type an inadequate technology for the reproduction of text. By permission of the Rare Books and Special Collections Library, University of Sydney.

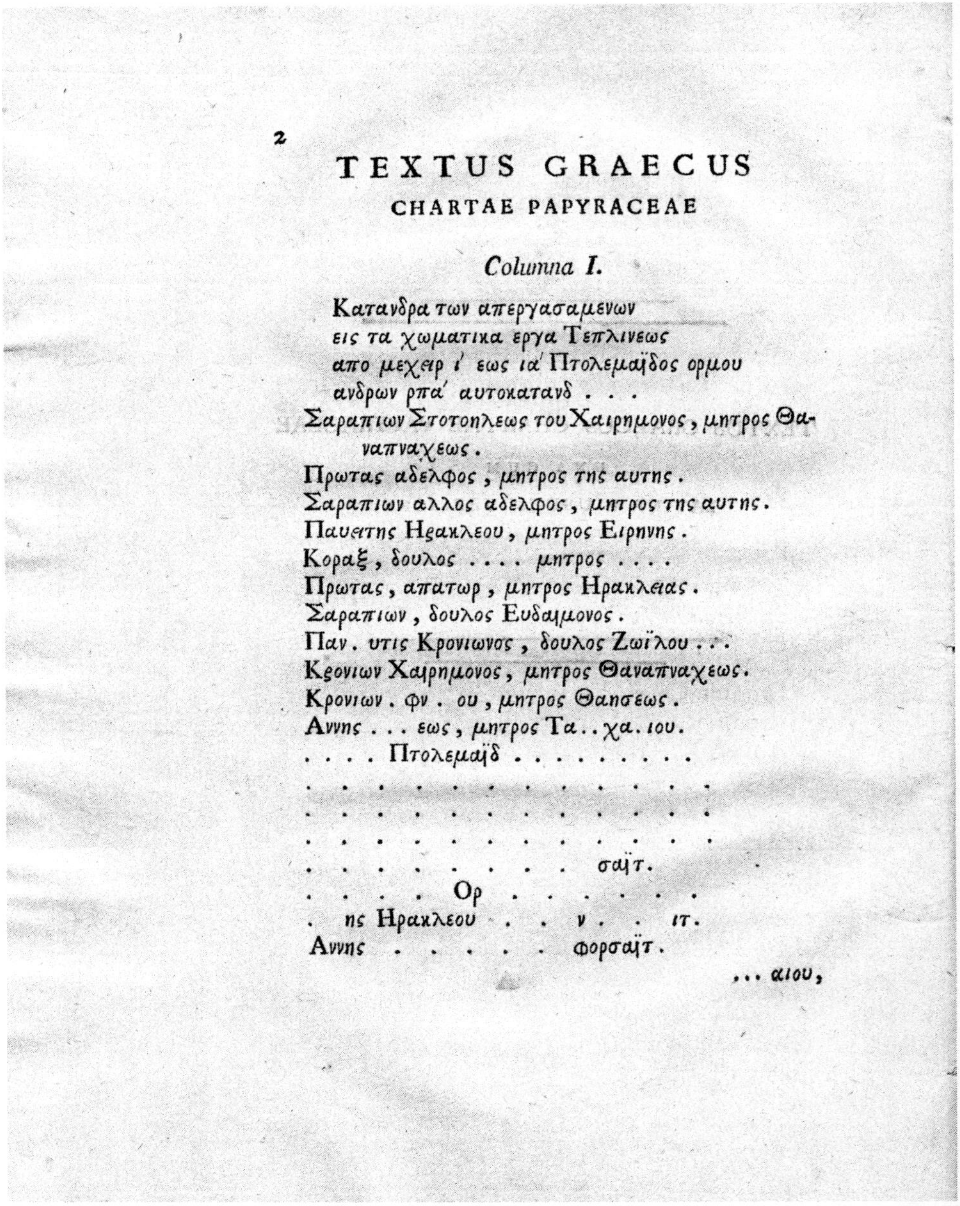

2

TEXTUS GRAECUS

CHARTAE PAPYRACEAE

Columna I.

Κατανδρα των απεργασαμενων
εις τα χωματικα εργα Τεπλινεως
απο μεχειρ ι' εως ια' Πτολεμαΐδος ορμου
ανδρων ρπα' αυτοκατανδ . . .

Σαραπιων Στοτοηλεως του Χαιρημονος, μητρος Θα-
ναπναχεως.
Πρωτας αδελφος, μητρος της αυτης.
Σαραπιων αλλος αδελφος, μητρος της αυτης.
Παυσιτης Ηρακλεου, μητρος Ειρηνης.
Κοραξ, δουλος . . . . μητρος . . . .
Πρωτας, απατωρ, μητρος Ηρακλειας.
Σαραπιων, δουλος Ευδαιμονος.
Παν. υτις Κρονιωνος, δουλος Ζωΐλου . . .
Κρονιων Χαιρημονος, μητρος Θαναπναχεως.
Κρονιων. φν. ου, μητρος Θαησεως.
Αννης . . . εως, μητρος Τα . . χα. ιου.
. . . . Πτολεμαΐδ . . . .
. . . .
. . . .
. . . .
. . . . σαϊτ. .
. . . . Ορ . . . . . .
. πς Ηρακλεου . . . ν . . ιτ.
Αννης . . . . . . φορσαϊτ.
. . . αιου,

FIG. 2. N. Schow 1788: the typographical representation of a fragment. The ellipsis points mark physical gaps in the text. By permission of the McCormick Library of Special Collections, Northwestern University Library.

tangible presence of the past, as a monument does. In his introduction to *Antiquity Explained,* Montfaucon defines antiquity as "only what may be the object of the sight, and may be represented by figures";[117] antiquity is the real, the tangible fragment, the monument. Hermann's critical fragment exploits this increasingly paleographical consciousness to show us a simulacrum of the material past.

The Melancholic Fragment

A growing awareness of the materiality of writing may have provided Hermann with the iconography of the fragment—he reconstructs a paleographical artifact, something all the more "real" for its fragmentariness. But a second stream of thought about fragmentation influences the critical fragment as well, for a critical fragment is also, after all, an *artificial* fragment: it copies no real object, as papyrus publications or corpora of inscriptions do. Rather the critical fragment is a philological fantasy, artfully conjuring the melancholic tatters of a forgotten page, analogous to an artificial ruin in a picturesque garden or a painted ruin by an artist like Hubert Robert:[118] According to Denis Diderot, "the effect of these compositions, whether good or bad, is to leave you in a state of sweet melancholy. We fix our gaze upon the remains of a triumphant arch, a portico, a pyramid, a temple, a palace, and we come back to ourselves. We anticipate the ravages of time and in our imagination we scatter across the earth the very buildings we inhabit. Immediately solitude and silence prevail around us."[119] Though Hermann's critical fragment takes the form of a paleographical representation, its rhetorical effect is much closer to the one recorded here. The critical fragment reminds us of time, of mutability, of textual flux and ruination.

But first it reminds us of copies. A central element of romantic Hellenism was an acute awareness of the role of the copy, the artificial, and the simulacrum. Winckelmann never saw Greece, and he wrote of the Roman copies he studied for traces of their Greek originals: "We too have, as it were, nothing but a shadowy outline left of the object of our wishes, but that very indistinctness awakens a more earnest longing

117. Montfaucon 1721–1722, 1:iii.

118. A very large bibliography now exists on ruins and fragments. See McCaulay 1953; Mortier 1974; Goldstein 1977; McFarland 1981; Levinson 1986; Szondi 1986; Lacoue-Labarthe and Nancy 1988; Janowitz 1990; Gasché 1991; Seyhan 1996; Verstraete 1998; Nochlin 2001, 64–65.

119. Diderot 1994, 274–275.

for what we have lost, and we study the copies of the originals more attentively than we should have done the originals themselves, if we had been in full possession of them."[120] Copies excite the imagination, speaking of realities forever beyond view. It is not actual ruins that cause Diderot exquisite melancholy but Robert's painted ruins. The medium, the refraction, and the copy are the surfaces on which the melancholic imagination sees its distance from antiquity inscribed. Indeed the experience of sentimentality was in many ways a symptom of a culture of the copy. According to Gillen D'Arcy Wood, romantic Hellenism's representations "consisted principally of literary translations, paintings and prints of ruins or mythological scenes, the travel writing of dilettantes, and, after Winckelmann, the new scholarly discipline of Art History. The idealizing refractions of these media inspired the sentimental imagination of the eighteenth-century Hellenist."[121]

Related to an awareness of the copy was an impression of irretrievable loss, of an incommensurability of experience and insurmountable difference between antiquity and modernity. Greece represented a perfect and unique integration of idea and substance, a historical moment in which the ideal illuminated the artistic form, and a region of aesthetic harmony; modernity, irrevocably exiled from this, was a time of shattered fragments and unattainable unities. "Everlastingly chained to a fragment of the whole, man himself develops into nothing but a fragment,"[122] wrote Schiller. "United with themselves and happy in the feeling of their humanity, [the Greeks] had to stop at humanity as their highest value and try to bring everything else nearer to it, while we, in discord with ourselves and unhappy in our experience of humanity, have no more urgent interest than to flee out of it and to remove such an unsuccessful form from our eyes."[123] Fragmentation specifies the inaccessibility of the ancient ideal; all that is left are broken, partial copies that emphasize the distance between their lost wholeness and our present brokenness. From this, perhaps, originates Hermann's interest in a fragment from an indeterminate moment sometime between antiquity and modernity: as a copy it incites a sentimental reflection on what has been lost.

Of course the critical fragment is not actually a copy: it is an imitation copy, a fake remnant, signifying nothing real. Rather, the artificial fragment signifies the destructive force of time itself, the very loss that is the core of romantic melancholy. To the sentimental mind, the ruin serves

120. Winckelmann 1872, 4:292.
121. Wood 2001, 128.
122. Schiller 1967, 35.
123. Schiller 1981, 34.

as the "hypostatization of his own difference from the vanished culture of antiquity."[124] Like the ruin, the fragment, an "aesthetically controlled shape of temporal transience,"[125] signifies the impossibility of Greece's revival just as the literary fragment of Schlegel signifies the inexpressibility of the ideal in temporal language. If we contemplate a lost Greece in the ruins of the Parthenon, we contemplate *history itself* in the paintings of Hubert Robert or the fantasies of the Garden at Stowe.

> Here columns heap'd on prostrate colums, torn
> From their firm base, encrease the mould'ring mass.
> Far as the sight can pierce, appears the spoils
> Of sunk magnificence: a blended scene
> Of moles, fanes, arches, domes, and palaces
> Where, with his brother horror, ruin sits.[126]

In other words, the artificial fragment is meant to seduce by signifying the processes by which the diplomatic fragment is created. "There is a grandeur in the thoughts that ruin awakens in me," writes Diderot. "All things vanish, die, and pass away. Only the world remains. Only time persists."[127] Hermann's critical fragment signifies not an original "whole," but time itself. The subject of this kind of fragment is nothing but fragmentation.

An image of time and a figure for irrevocable loss, such a fragment might be described as a radicalization of what Barthes once called the "reality effect."[128] By an exponential increase in intensity or a further twist of logic, the fragment moves beyond the effect of the real to its inverse, an unreal effect. Barthes traces the manner in which narrative (which he understands to be a systematic textual economy) incorporates the nonsystematic, the superfluous, the singular, or the fragmentary (in Barthes's discussion, "details": a barometer, the dimensions of a door) and reappropriates them as signifiers of the category of reality. This category allows the unincorporable, the fragmentary, to be incorporated and supplemented. The romantic fragment, by contrast, has the fragment signify not "reality" but rather "reality's irremediable loss." "Here is the real," says the fragment in Barthes's analysis; "No real here," says the romantic fragment. Concealment unconcealed is its central signification.

124. Wood 2001, 122.
125. Janowitz 1990, 1.
126. Wharton 1747, 21.
127. Diderot 1994, 277.
128. Barthes 1982.

If this is the case, then we can make one further observation: the fragment reveals the structure of the sign as such and reveals it essentially as difference, as the infinite deferral and essential inaccessibility of the signified (the "original," the "whole," the "real") in the sign. A signifier, by virtue of its need to signify, is by definition removed from the signified: to become conscious of this separation is to introduce into the sign a radical hiatus and division, to transform the signifier into a fragment. For Schiller, this self-conscious fragmentation articulated itself by the introduction of oblique grammatical cases, the transformation of an intransitive verb into a transitive one: "The feeling of which we are speaking [sentimentality] is, therefore, not that which the ancients had; it is rather one with that which we have *for the ancients.* They felt in a natural way, we feel the natural."[129] The ancients *feel*; we feel *for*; Schiller uses the preposition to mark the difference between the natural self-identity of antiquity and the directed intentionality of modern consciousness, which by virtue of its having to signify something different (we have a feeling *for the ancients*) makes it fragmentary, splits it off from its object. According to Jean-Luc Nancy and Phillipe Lacoue-Labarthe, the modern fragment, as a simulacrum of the ancient or diplomatic fragment, is essentially *about* antiquity and the philological work of recovering it.[130] The fragment, we could say, invents the relation "about," using it as a wedge to separate us from the real presence of antiquity. If for Montfaucon, writing in the early eighteenth century, it was possible to define antiquity as "only what may be the object of the sight," and to boast of the ability to compact all of antiquity within the covers of a series of books, by the early nineteenth century the book itself would become the focus of attention, and its difference from the monuments it copied would be taken as a sign of its internal, essential fragmentariness. Henceforth there can only be *signs* of Greece; there can be no Greece itself.

This experience inflected the theory and practice of philology as well. In Boeckh's famous definition, philology "is the knowledge of what is known. Within the phrase 'what is known' are comprehended all conceivable ideas, for frequently it is ideas alone that are recalled to mind, as in poetry, art, or political history. In these areas, as in scientific concepts, ideas are only in part laid down, ideas which the philologist has to reconstruct."[131] Boeckh interprets "knowing things known" in terms of the Greek verb ἀναγιγνώσκειν, which, he reminds us, can mean

129. Schiller 1981, 34.
130. Lacoue-Labarthe and Nancy 1988, 47.
131. Boeckh 1968, 9.

both "to read" and "to recognize." But in reading or recognizing, philology reveals itself to be empty of any knowledge of its own. Rather it is pure signification, a relation to knowledge essentially and unequivocally removed from it. Boeckh continues: "If, however, one does ascribe a knowledge to philology, it is not merely something learned; such information belongs to a branch of learning and as such is alien to philology. Philology thinks *about* this knowledge.... Philology stands over against this reproduced knowledge so as to view it objectively."[132] Philology is essentially characterized by the "*about*," by the separation and difference of the signifying relation. The production of philological work, as a production irrevocably alienated from its objects, is deeply and essentially fragmentary.

To summarize: Hermann's critical fragment, his artificial archetype, by imitating diplomatic fragments produces a document whose significance lies less in the recovery of an original than in its ability to gesture toward the irrevocable loss of the historical real. In Hermann's fragment the concealment of antiquity is revealed.

J. A. Hartung

Hermann was not the only textual critic who deployed the rhetoric of fragmentation in the service of a melancholic textual criticism. Denys Page ended *Actors' Interpolations in Greek Tragedy* (1934) with a tour de force of conjectural criticism, the uncovering of the fragmentary ending that served as the basis for what is in our manuscripts (fig. 3).[133] Page's work is, as I discuss in the next chapter, acutely aware of the fact that textual criticism has a history at times unkind to the ancient remains, and his invocation of a fragmentary archetype may well utilize the same kind of rhetoric deployed by Hermann.

In 1837 Johann Hartung used typographical markers of fragmentation to similar effect. His edition opens in a melancholic mode that transforms the *Iphigenia at Aulis* into an image of the ruinous forces of history.

> Whenever I consider the fate of the plays of Euripides in my mind, I seem to see an example [*exemplar*] of the iniquity of fortune (which detracts from all outstanding things) placed before my eyes, and the perversity of human affairs, in which great things are only rarely born and once born

132. Ibid., 18.
133. Page 1934, 198–199.

* * *

1585 ἄελπτον εἰσιδόντες ἐκ θεῶν τινος

* * *

1587 ἔλαφος γὰρ ἀσπαίρουσ' ἔκειτ' ἐπὶ χθονὶ

* * *

1590 κἂν τῷδε Κάλχας πῶς δοκεῖς χαίρων ἔφη·
1591 Ὦ τοῦδ' Ἀχαιῶν κοίρανοι κοινοῦ στρατοῦ,

* * *

1595 ὡς μὴ μιάνῃ βωμὸν εὐγενεῖ φόνῳ.

* * *

1597 δίδωσιν ἡμῖν 'Ιλίου τ' ἐπιδρομάς.
1598 πρὸς ταῦτα πᾶς τις θάρσος αἶρε ναυβάτης,
1599 χώρει τε πρὸς ναῦν· [
1600 λιπόντας ἡμᾶς Αὐλίδος κοίλους μυχοὺς
1601 Αἰγαῖον οἶδμα διαπερᾶν. ἐπεὶ δ' ἅπαν
1602 κατηνθρακώθη θῦμ' ἐν 'Ηφαίστου φλογί,
1603 τὰ πρόσφορ' ηὔξαθ', ὡς τύχοι νόατου στρατός.

* * *

1605 [1] λέγειν θ' ὁποίας ἐκ θεῶν μοίρας κυρεῖ
1606 καὶ δόξαν ἔσχεν ἄφθιτον καθ' 'Ελλάδα.
1607 ἐγὼ παρὼν δὲ καὶ τὸ πρᾶγμ' ὁρῶν λέγω·
1608 ἡ παῖς σαφῶς σοι πρὸς θεοὺς [ἀπέπτετο]
1609 λύπης δ' ἀφ[
1610 ἀπροσδόκητα [
1611 σώζουσί θ' οὓς φιλοῦσιν. [
1612 θανοῦσαν εἶδε καὶ βλέπουσαν [
1613 Χο. ὡς ἥδομαί τοι [
1614 ζῶν δ' ἐν θεοῖσι [

* * *

1621 Αγ. γύναι, θυγατρὸς [
1622 ἔχει γὰρ ὄντως ἐν θεοῖς ὁμιλίαν. [1]
1623 χρὴ δέ σε λαβοῦσαν [
1624 στείχειν πρὸς οἴκους· ὡς στρατὸς πρὸς πλοῦν ὁρᾷ.
1625 καὶ χαῖρε· χρον[
1626 Τροίηθεν ἔσται· καὶ γένοιτό σοι καλῶς.

* * *

FIG. 3. The fragmentary end of *Iphigenia at Aulis* according to Page 1934. Reprinted by permission of Oxford University Press.

> are even more rarely regarded with esteem, causes me pain. For that poet [Euripides], whom ancient men put behind no tragic poet in order of estimation, and whom they preferred to all others in imitating and in carefully reading, is disparaged and destroyed.... When I consider the reasons for this, I seem to myself to conceive of two especially, of which the one is located in the iniquity and injury of time directed against the poems themselves, and the other is in the mentality of modern men [*in nostrorum hominum ingeniis*].[134]

This passage could be read as a philological translation of Schlegel's comment on fragments cited above: the poor condition of the *Iphigenia at Aulis* is the result (1) of time's ravages and (2) of the essentially degraded and fragmented condition of modernity. Though it appears whole, in other words, the tragedy's paradosis is in fact a fragment. Under the guise of printing the original (which it does not do at all: see below), Hartung's criticism instead reveals the essential fragmentation of *Iphigenia at Aulis*: his text, riddled with hiatuses, asterisks, and transpositions, literally displays the play's fragmentary essence. Its concealment, in other words, is revealed.

[. . .]	ἃ δ' οὐ καλῶς
108	ἔγνων τότ', αὖθις μεταγράφω καλῶς πάλιν
109	ἐς τήνδε δέλτον, ἣν κατ' εὐφρόνην * *
110†	* * * * * *
111‡	* * * * * *
1	ὦ πρέσβυ, δόμων τῶνδε πάροιθεν
2	στεῖχε.
	ΠΡΕΣΒΥΣ
3/4	στείχω. μάλα γὰρ※ γῆρας
5/6	τοὐμὸν ἄϋπνον καὶ ἐπ' ὀφθαλμοῖς
7/3	ὀξὺ πάρεστιν· τί δὲ καινουργεῖς,
4	Ἀγάμεμνον ἄναξ;

† λύοντα και συνδοῦντά μ' εἰσεῖδες, γέρον. Diggle
‡ αλλ' εἶα χώρει τάσδ' ἐπιστολὰς λαβὼν Diggle
※ τοι Barnes

134. "Quotiescunque Euripidis fabularum sortem animo mecum considero, exemplar quasi iniquitatis fortunae, obtrectantis praestantissimis quibusque rebus, ante oculos positum mihi conspicere videor, ac poenitet pravitatis rerum humanarum, in quibus magna quum rarissime nasci tum nata rarius etiam observari soleant. Deprimitur enim atque despicitur poeta is, quem antiquorum temporum homines aestimando quidem tragicorum nemini postponebant, imitando autem atque assiduitate legendi vel omnibus praeferebant.... Cujus rei cum requiro caussas, duas potissimum mihi deprehendere videor, quarum altera in ipsorum carminum depravationibus injuriisque temporum, altera in nostrorum est hominum ingeniis posita" (Euripides 1837 [ed. Hartung], 1–2).

And not thinking rightly on these things before, I again write a new message, a better one, on this tablet. It by night [*********] Oh old man, come from out of the house.

OLD MAN. I come. For my old age is very sleepless and there is still some sharpness in my eyes. What new thing is afoot, lord Agamemnon?[135]

Of the numerous gaps that populate Hartung's text, not one is meant to mark hiatuses in an actual mutilated manuscript. In fact Hartung's theory of the historical deformation of the *Iphigenia at Aulis* has very little room for a damaged archetype.[136] Instead, he proposes that the received form of the play results from the contamination of two texts: "It was not interpolation so much as corruption that was committed, and by a man who was neither a poet nor a scribe, but a stupid versifier [*versificatore stupido*], at the very end of antiquity, certainly after Stobaeus."[137] This *versificator stupidus*, a barbarian with a poor understanding of Greek meter and a Christian, wrote his own verses in the margins and between the lines. A later scribe, who was copying the manuscript, could not tell the genuine from the fake and created a new text that promiscuously kept now the graffiti and now the genuine text. The beginning and end of the play are in particularly bad shape because the open spaces at those locations in the manuscript gave the versifier room to write.[138] A new ending was composed, and the scribe copied most of it (only five and one-half lines of the original made it into the new version); the lines cited by Aelian were among those left out.[139]

This theory suggests that the most appropriate method of textual presentation would be to bracket or remove the words of the versifier, leaving regions where the original is lost. But this is not how Hartung proceeds. In addition to revealing gaps by removing lines deemed inauthentic, Hartung interpolates gaps between authentic lines of verse, freely transposes lines, and inserts new gaps where his transpositions do not immediately generate sense. These critical procedures cannot be justified by his theory. It is easier to imagine that a scribe combining two different texts into one would proceed sequentially than to imagine

135. Euripides 1837 (ed. Hartung) vv. 59–66. The numbers to the left of the text are those given in Diggle.

136. He raises, but does not seriously entertain, the possibility that the end of the play was missing in some manuscript. Euripides 1837 (ed. Hartung), 76.

137. "non interpolationem tantum, verum etiam corruptionem factam esse ab homine neque poeta neque scriptore, sed versificatore stupido, extremis antiquitatis temporibus, certe post Stobaeum, vivente" (Ibid., 71).

138. Ibid., 76–77.

139. Ibid., 85–87.

him freely moving verses around; he would in this case become a second composer, not merely a copyist.

The contradiction between Hartung's historical theory and his critical practice might lead one to accuse him of illogicality or methodological laxity. But I believe his 1837 text can be read differently, as a two-part rhapsody on the theme of textual instability. The first part, a one-hundred-page introductory essay on interpolations, offers an explanation of the historical mechanisms by which ancient texts are obscured and fragmented, and the second part, a text, is intended to stimulate sentimental reflection on the loss of the literature of antiquity. We should read this *Iphigenia at Aulis* not as a failed attempt to recover Euripides' play but rather as an image of absence itself, an artificial simulacrum that stages a drama of loss by cutting off our access to the original. It is a picturesque textual ruin.

This image of loss emphasizes the fragmented—and fragmenting—condition of modernity. The major sources of conscious change to Euripides' texts are threefold: learned men who live in solitude and want to erase Euripides' populism; those who want to teach the origins of religious practice; and, finally, those who want to insert *subtilitates philosophorum* into the text. Thus the major sources of corruption are scholars and schoolmen, intellectuals, and historians.[140] In this way Hartung includes interpolators within the general set of textual critics.

This community of critics and "interpolators" surely includes Hartung himself. His own work on the *Iphigenia at Aulis* is gestured toward in a discussion of the opening scene, where the process he hypothesizes is out of sync with his own theory of contamination. Here the versifier is thought to have disapproved of Euripides' use of prologues, a position he shares with some of Hartung's contemporaries. Accordingly the versifier moved it into the midst of the anapests, making alterations in an attempt to create a smooth transition.[141] Such a critical transposition is hard to reconcile with the image Hartung paints elsewhere of a versifier scribbling doggerel in the empty spaces of a manuscript. Did he cut out the early pages and rearrange them? Did he write out his new order beside the old one? If he did this, would the scribe not have produced here, as elsewhere, a contaminated text? But as discordant with his general theory as it is, Hartung's vision of an interpolator who thinks critically about the text before him and then rearranges lines to suit his own aesthetic sense does describe what Hartung does, making

140. Ibid., 35–43.
141. Ibid., 85.

a new text by transposing lines and interpolating gaps. Thus, in his description of the fate of the opening lines of the tragedy, Hartung reflects the moment of his own intervention in the *Iphigenia at Aulis.* His dissertation on interpolation offers a vision of textual flux that includes Hartung's own time.

A history of textual variability that includes the critic precludes criticism from ending that history and becomes a narrative of catastrophes, the continuing reconfiguration and progressive fragmentation of an original poetic utterance now irretrievably lost. This is the object of Hartung's critical text; through the presentation of an artificially constructed fragment, he shows a simulacrum of the catastrophic forces of history (*exemplar iniquitatis fortunae*) that could inspire not an aesthetic appreciation of Euripides' tragedy, but a melancholy mediation on time itself.

It could be said that Hartung's text misses its target (Euripides' original), only to strike another one, more difficult to hit. Using techniques aimed at reconstructing what Euripides wrote, he achieves instead an image of history as a ruined landscape, a sentimental reflection of the irretrievability of the past and of the ideality of the ideal. In this way Hartung's textual criticism could be described as a wager that pays off in an unexpected manner, or as a hallucinogenic delusion that nevertheless contains more truth than what is seen by the cold, intentional, clinical eye. We could say of his text that it is what Schlegel once called for, a genre of writing "fragmentary both in form and content, simultaneously completely subjective and individual and completely objective and like a necessary part in a system of all the sciences."[142] A "completely subjective," methodologically impossible text, the 1837 edition of *Iphigenia at Aulis* nevertheless attains an objective vision of the mutability of texts in general.

As though obeying an unconscious law, as though confirming Boeckh's belief that criticism can only arise out of a sense of history that *intuitively* hits its target,[143] Hartung's text comments not only on the force of history (through its fragmentariness) but also on the unintentional method by which this commentary is achieved. Hartung's transpositions frequently produce scenes in which dramas of divination, lucky guesses, and fortuitous suppositions unfold. In the opening scene, for example, Hartung believed that the original play began with the iambic speech

142. Schlegel 1991, 27 (Athenaeum Fragment #77).
143. Boeckh 1968, 127.

of Agamemnon, and he accordingly printed the iambs first in the text. One of the effects of this transposition is that the two anapestic passages where Agamemnon converses with the old slave were brought together (I have printed the suture above). Another consequence is that the new order requires of the old man a conjectural prescience usually only expected of textual critics. In this version Agamemnon speaks a traditional prologue to the audience and then summons the old man from his tent; as a result, the old man is never told of the plot to kill Iphigenia. This threatens the fabric of the entire story, for it is the old man who reveals the plot to Clytemnestra (845f; 855–895 Diggle). More locally, this order leaves the old man's lines at 133–135 (133–135 Diggle) unexplained:

δεινά γε τολμᾷς, Ἀγάμεμνον ἄναξ.
οὔτω τῷ θεᾶς σὴν παῖδ' ἄλοχον
φατίσας ἦγες σφάγιον Δαναοῖς;[144]

You dare a terrible thing, Lord Agamemnon. Did you thus bring your daughter as a sacrifice for the Danaans, calling her the bride of Achilles?

Hartung finds no difficulty in this, commenting: "For it was necessary that the old man, sharp of eye, watchful, and suspicious, should either have understood by conjecture or received by speech what the whole host was murmuring. Therefore we should not marvel that now he cannot restrain himself from openly pronouncing what he has discovered, though Agamemnon would rather he didn't, and is showing reluctance, concealing, and staying silent."[145] The old man guesses what is afoot after having put Agamemnon's current behavior together with the rumors he has heard bruited abroad. Stunningly he arrives at his insight with the help of witnesses and a personal incisive vision—by *recensio* and *examinatio*, we could say, or by a combined consideration of external and internal circumstances. It is characteristic of Hartung's play that the conjecture is correct. This *Iphigenia* celebrates more than any other version of the play the triumph of the hopeful conjecture, the fulfillment of faith in the eventual revelation of divine benevolence.

144. These are the lines as Hartung prints them. He retains *οὔτω* against Canter's far more popular emendation *ὃς τῷ*. My translation of this questionable Greek obeys Hartung's instructions: "Verte: *siccine filiam, Achilli uxorem dictitans, victimam adducebas Graecis?*" (112).

145. "Necesse enim fuit, aut conjectura assequutum esse senem acutum oculis, vigilem, suspicacemque, aut fando accepisse quae universus populus susurrabat. Non est igitur mirandum, quod jam retinere se non potest, quin, quae invito rege resciit, tergiversante, dissimulante reticenteque illo, aperte pronuntiet" (Euripides 1837 [ed. Hartung], 112).

Appropriate to this theme is Hartung's ending, which provides unambiguous closure. After Iphigenia's exit Artemis appears on the *mēchanē* and declares to Clytemnestra her intent to save Iphigenia: Clytemnestra receives the news with gratitude, and the play ends. Artemis's words serve a triple function here. To be sure, they provide Clytemnestra with uncontestable proof that her daughter will not die and thus make impossible the suspicion she feels in the extant ending, a suspicion that could lead to the eventual murder of Agamemnon. But they also redeem and justify Agamemnon's decision to sacrifice his daughter in the face of what had appeared to be an impossible situation: his eventual resolution to kill her and thus to lead the armies against Troy becomes the tragic equivalent of Abraham's "God will provide." And as a revelation delivered to the textual critic from the pages of Aelian, they justify the critic's suspicion and facilitate his own sacrifice of the traditional forms of the text in the name of a new reconstruction.

But at the very moment when the role and the value of conjecture is triumphantly confirmed, Hartung's 1837 text seems to falter, even to fail, in its hymn to critical insight. For its conclusion contains as many lines marked lacunary as lines of Greek. There is just enough to inform us as to the nature of the ending: Artemis will rescue Iphigenia and replace her with a deer; she will be spirited away and celebrated henceforth as blessed, and Clytemnestra will put aside her anger against Agamemnon. But no more.

ΑΡΤΕΜΙΣ

* * * * * * *
ἔλαφον δ' Ἀχαιῶν χερσὶν ἐνθήσω φίλαις
κεροῦσσαν, ἣν σφάξαντες αὐχήσουσι σὴν
σφάζειν θυγατέρα * * *
* * * * * * *
(*καὶ δόξαν ἔσχεν ἄφθιτον καθ' Ἑλλάδα*
* * * * * *
λύπας δ' ἀφαιροῦ, καὶ πόσει πάρες χόλον
* * * * * *
ἀπροσδόκητά τοι βροτοῖς τὰ τῶν θεῶν
σώζουσί θ' οὓς φιλοῦσιν * *
* * * * *

ΚΛΥΤΑΙΜΝΗΣΤΡΑ

* * * * *
* * *οὐ μάτην λόγους,*
ἄνασσα, παρεμυθοῦ * *)[146]

146. The lines in parentheses are salvaged from the condemned exodus, in order, vv. 1596, 1599, 1600, 1601 (1606, 1609, 1610, 1611 Diggle [emended differently]). Clytemnestra's lines are freely altered from 1607 (1617 Diggle).

ARTEMIS. [***************] And I shall put into the dear hands of the Achaeans a horned deer; slaughtering it they will think they are sacrificing your daughter. [***********] And she has immortal fame throughout Greece [*********] Set aside your grief, and cease to be angry with your husband. [********] the gifts of the gods are indeed unexpected—and they save those whom they love [******]

CLYTEMNESTRA. [*********] You do not vainly soothe me with words, mistress.

But perhaps this fragmentary text is in fact the true result of a happy conjecture: Hartung has hit upon a representation far more true than any reconstruction of an original would have been. The fragmentary condition of Artemis's speech and Clytemnestra's response reveals the irretrievability of the Greek ideal; though we cannot fully hear what Artemis has to say, we *can* hear its inaudibility. And thus, if we do not know the details of Iphigenia's election to happiness, we do know the historical condition that gives us the loss of antiquity as an essential object for our thought.

Hartung's text reveals the concealed nature of the ancient tragedy and the history of textual flux as a history in which the original is progressively effaced. Concealment unconcealed is the theme of this criticism of the fragment, this criticism through the fragment. Uncannily this aspect of Hartung's enterprise finds unintended confirmation in the 1857 edition prepared by James Monk.[147] In Monk's opinion Hartung's edition displayed an audacity unparalleled in the history of textual criticism. Monk also finds Hermann's text poor: in Hermann's edition, because of his overzealous emendations in some places and his refusal to emend in others, "it has come about that this play seems to me to be less Euripidean after the recension of Hermann than it once was."[148]

Monk himself finds the evidence for early interpolation, especially by Euripides' son or nephew, unconvincing. On the question of the unprecedented anapestic prologue, Monk is of the same opinion as Hermann (in 1831): Euripides might have had his own reasons for an innovative beginning. Nevertheless he finds passages that are so bad that they might have prompted the desire for a theory of a double recension or multiple ancient versions. Monk concludes that there is indeed corruption in the text, but it is a result of lazy scribal work followed by an incompetent attempt at correction. All of this happened long before the

147. Euripides 1857 (ed. Monk).

148. "Evenit, ut haec fabula post Hermanni recensionem mihi quidem esse videatur minus, quam olim, Euripidea" (Ibid., 219).

extant manuscripts were written: they show a remarkable agreement in places where there is interpolation.[149] He agrees with Hartung, Porson, and Hermann that the exodus is spurious but does not believe that the interpolator filled in an unfinished manuscript. Rather the interpolator wanted to show off his own skills and used Euripides' words when they suited him.[150] The opening lines of the messenger speech might easily have been said by Artemis to Clytemnestra *ex machina*; the interpolator kept them for his own ending.

In the end, however, despite his attack on Hartung, Monk arrives at a position vis-à-vis the exodus which is essentially the same. Monk opposes the notion that the printed edition should hypothesize what the original text might have been; instead, the printed edition presents the reader with the text as a problem, one that requires his own active intervention. Careful to avoid the charge of having become an interpolator where a critic was called for, Monk places conjectural emendations in the margins and not in the text since he himself would not dare to change a word.[151] Thus, while Hartung revealed an illegible text, and the substance of the ending remains hidden from view, Monk's refusal to reproduce the original exodus leaves the reader with an illegible end. Here we read a text obscured by interpolation rather than by holes and gaps; it is a fragment in reverse, no more a recovery of the "original" than Hartung's or Hermann's texts.

As though to prompt the reflection that a whole and conservative text conceals as much as a fragmentary and aggressively interventionist text like Hartung's, Monk provides us with a hypothetical ending for the original play in which nothing is clear, not even to the agents in the drama. Monk reads the fragment from Aelian slightly differently from other critics:

> *ἔλαφον δ' Ἀχαιῶν χερσὶν ἐνθήσω λάθρᾳ*[1]
> *κεροῦσσαν, ἣν σφάζοντες αὐχήσουσι σὴν*
> *σφάζειν θυγατέρα.*
>
> 1. *φίλαις* ceteri.

> And I shall secretly put into the hands of the Achaeans a horned deer; slaughtering it they will declare they are sacrificing your daughter.

Monk's emendation of *φίλαις* to *λάθρᾳ* in the first line recommends itself because it appears to improve the sense of the subsequent clause:

149. Ibid., 216–217.
150. Ibid., 321.
151. Ibid., 217.

without it, one is bound to wonder how the Achaeans could slaughter a stag but declare that they have killed Iphigenia. Monk's solution is to have Artemis replace Iphigenia without the Achaean's knowledge: thus they sacrifice what they *think* is Iphigenia when in *fact* it is a stag. As a result, Clytemnestra is pacified by the god from the machine, but Agamemnon continues to believe in his guilt and now pays a subjective price for the choice he has made. Here the concealment of the ending that has been at issue since Musgrave's revelation of the Aelianic lines reaches its most extreme state: just as the ending is veiled by an evidently interpolated simulacrum of the original, so is the true ending of the story hidden from its most central agent: the father's salvation is concealed by the pathetic simulacrum of his executed daughter.[152]

152. In light of the counterfluxions of concealment and unconcealment traced in these pages, it might be important to point towards Heidegger's analysis of truth as ἀ-ληθεία, and note that Hartung, in his 1852 bilingual edition of the works of Euripides, supplemented the metrically deficient line 61 with this same λάθρᾳ, translating it *unheimlich* (Euripides 1852 [ed. Hartung]). See Heidegger 1996 and 2000.

5

The Entropic Text

In the introduction to part 2, I outlined two major factors at play in the *Iphigenias at Aulis* produced by modern critics: the destabilizing role of external evidence (represented by the fragment discovered in Aelian), and the importance of internal evidence (symbolized by the discovery of Porson's law). I noted there that in treating internal evidence, textual criticism showed a strong bias toward regularity of system over singularities or idiosyncrasies; that is, where internal evidence is decisive, systematic predictability or uniformity tends to be a determining value. In this chapter I substantiate this claim by outlining the role of systematicity and internal criteria in the formation of several *Iphigenias at Aulis.* In the texts addressed here, external evidence loses its priority to internal evidence as a factor in the formation of the text.

This is symbolized by a tendency to doubt that the lines quoted in Aelian pertain to the tragedy. A school inclined in this direction is coeval with their discovery: the first critic to take such a position was Heath, whose *Notae sive Lectiones ad Tragicorum Graecorum Veterum*... were published in 1762, the same year as Musgrave's *Exercitationes.*[1] But mainstream scholarship in the nineteenth century took them to be the words of Euripides. Even Gruppe and Bang, who believed that the extant *Iphigenia at Aulis* was written in the fourth century by Chaeremon,

1. Heath 1762.

thought that these lines were from Euripides' *Iphigenia*, which they believed was otherwise lost.[2] It was not until the later decades of the nineteenth century that serious skepticism arose about the provenance of the Aelianic fragment, most notably in the work of Girolamo Vitelli and Edwin England,[3] but also in many critics after them, among whom I will discuss Denys Page, David Kovacs, and James Diggle.[4]

The tendency to disregard Aelian as a reliable witness is related to a more general willingness to devalue external evidence. According to Denys Page, in *Actors' Interpolations in Greek Tragedy*, for example, the fact that a passage is cited by an ancient author, even a comparatively early one, only provides a *terminus ante quem* for interpolations. Internal evidence, in Page as elsewhere in the critics studied here, trumps the evidence of witnesses in determining authenticity.

With the rise of internal evidence comes a corresponding rise in the importance of system and regularity. In contrast to the versions I addressed in chapter 4, where an awareness of the provisionality or temporariness of critical judgment could be detected, each of the versions addressed here depends on the belief that a critic can produce a stable, systematic, and (to the degree that it conforms to certain criteria) final version. This does not mean that critics of the late nineteenth and twentieth centuries became arrogant where previous critics had been modest, or that modern critics frequently claim that *their* text is *the* actual Euripidean text. In fact most recent critics show extreme skepticism about the possibility of reconstructing the original words of Euripides.[5] But when the possibility of recovering an authorial text is abandoned, there arises a search for other criteria on the basis of which a stable, permanent, and positive text can be produced. This causes an alteration in the basis of change between editions: while previously readings and models of the original fluctuated between critical enterprises, now conceptual underpinnings and the criteria for textual systematicity vary from critic to critic. While none of the major versions sketched here represents the original words of Euripides, neither can any be described as representing the same object. Variation between texts in this case is the result of different notions of system rather than different attempts to solve the same problem (that of an authorial original) according to the same criteria.

2. Gruppe 1834; Bang 1867.
3. Vitelli 1877; Euripides 1891 (ed. England).
4. Page 1934; Euripides 1994 (ed. Diggle); Euripides 2003 (ed. Kovacs).
5. See Euripides 1994 (ed. Diggle) I:iv; Kovacs 2003, 77–78; Euripides 1988 (ed. Günther), ii; Hennig 1870, 185.

There are two major streams within this general trend:

(1) England and Kovacs, for example, aim at a text they believe to be *stylistically regular.* That is, they rely on models of what was aesthetically possible and impossible for Euripides or for tragedy. These texts are defined not by having come from Euripides' hand (Euripides, after all, might have written something completely idiosyncratic, avant-garde, or bizarre), but by conforming to abstract stylistic laws.

(2) Diggle's Oxford text, on the other hand, without disregarding linguistic and stylistic criteria, presents a version of the *Iphigenia at Aulis* that is prominently and predominantly inflected by the critic's attempt to systematize and represent the probability of *his own conjectures.* In the final analysis, Diggle's text is not a presentation of Euripides' original text, or even of a stylistically regular drama. Rather it aims for a systematic presentation of the critical dialogue between the received text and Diggle himself. In this, as we shall see, Diggle follows Page.

Far from representing movements aimed at eliminating the principle of plurality in the name of a single overarching methodical law, each of the systems outlined in this chapter serves as a transformer that opens the edition to further and more radical pluralities. Each text discussed here is, if anything, more explicitly singular plural than the experiments discussed in chapter 4. These texts accomplish this by thematizing and basing their procedures on the text's participation in a multiplicity of acts of reception.

The emphasis on stylistic regularity displayed in England and Kovacs (and a few other critics whom I discuss incidentally) does not derive from the assumption that Euripides was absolutely predictable as an author, but rather from the idea that literary style, like language or social norms, is a shared, intersubjective set of expectations: any violation of this set of expectations would produce a text incomprehensible to its audience. The text is formed as much by (what the critic believes to be) the dominant aesthetic and stylistic expectations of fifth-century Athens as by any subjective desire on the part of an author. In other words the leading criteria for Kovacs and England is not that Euripides' texts must all be Euripidean in nature, but rather that any ancient text must be comprehensible to a contemporary audience; that is, it must participate in the shared expectations of a historical culture just as it participates in a shared language. Similarly, Diggle and Page explicitly thematize the reception of the text, but not by its ancient audience (though this is often a factor in the thought-processes that lead to a conjecture); rather, they emphasize modern critical reception. In both approaches the idea of reception serves not as the unitary carrier of a number of possible meanings but as the locale where multiple possibilities of textual form contest and share space. In each of these approaches, the text functions as an event that crystallizes textual plurality within a singular container.

It is remarkable that the emphasis on reception as a basis for new systems in the representation of an ancient text and the denial of the authority of the fragment in Aelian occur at the same time, in the same texts. What is even more striking is that the division between these two approaches (that is, between emphases on ancient and modern acts of reception) coincides with a contrast in the nature of the relation between these two factors. In the approach that strives to represent stylistic or aesthetic regularity (England and Kovacs), the emphasis on reception *precedes* the rejection of the lines in Aelian; by contrast, the approach that aims to codify the critic's judgment (Page and Diggle) *begins* by rejecting the lines in Aelian. In other words in the former case an emphasis on ancient response causes the rejection of the lines in Aelian, while in the latter case the rejection of the lines of Aelian causes an emphasis on criticism as a modern act of reception. Clearly these two trajectories are not mutually exclusive. One might easily progress from a concern over stylistic regularity to a rejection of the Aelianic fragment, and from there to a concern over critical reception. In effect this is the path followed by Diggle and Page.

Exemplary of the complex relationship between the critical emphasis on reception and the rejection of the fragment in Aelian is the edition of Augustus Matthiae.[6] A concern with stylistic regularity leads him to reject the Aelianic fragment, and this in turn leads to a crisis in reception emblematic of the modern critical condition.

Matthiae initially approached the fragment with a question about the dynamics of response. What, he asked, is the right time for the release of certain kinds of information to an audience? His answer was that it was inappropriate for a tragedy to give the ending away at the beginning: "It is also the case that in Euripides the one who delivers the prologue only ever expounds the condition things are in at that very moment. If by chance he indicates the outcome of the action to the audience right at the beginning, he does so in general terms, as Venus does in the prologue of the *Hippolytus,* and he never gives away the actual ending, commonly called the catastrophe, where the *dénouement* of the action

6. Euripides 1813–1837 (ed. Matthiae), 7:320–327.

takes place."[7] A degree of suspense is needed. The prologue's business is to set the scene and bring the audience up to speed, but not to dispel the narrative interest that arises from our ignorance of the ending. This consideration of the dynamics of response leads Matthiae to doubt that the lines from Aelian, in which Artemis announces that Iphigenia will be rescued at the end, belong in a prologue.[8]

But Matthiae is not sure the lines from Aelian can come from a lost ending, either. Euripides only uses the *deus ex machina* to untie a knot in the plot that cannot be resolved any other way, and there seems no reason for such a device at the end of the *Iphigenia at Aulis.* This argument is based on an assessment of Euripides' regular practice of narrative construction; here, Matthiae thinks, a divine intervention would be uncharacteristic of Euripides.

But if the criterion of stylistic regularity (underpinned, as Matthiae's discussion of the prologue shows, by a concern over audience response) compels him to reject the fragment in Aelian, its removal leads in due course to a crisis in reception that, though it is located in antiquity, emblematizes and foreshadows the condition of modern textual critics. Matthiae is troubled by the fact that in the *Iphigenia among the Taurians* Orestes thinks Iphigenia was killed at Aulis. If the mythical content of the *Iphigenia among the Taurians* is supposed to be consistent with that of the *Iphigenia at Aulis,* this must mean that the same disjunction between reality and perception prevailed at the end of the *Iphigenia at Aulis* as prevailed at the beginning of the *Iphigenia among the Taurians.* If, years later,

7. "Accedit, quod apud Euripidem is, qui prologum agit, semper illud tantum exponit, quo statu res sint eo ipso tempore, aut, si forte, eventum rei generatim et infinite tantum significat, ut in *Hippolyti* prologo Venus, nunquam ipsum fabulae exitum, quam καταστροφήν vulgo vocant, et in quo λύσις actionis posita est, statim ab initio spectatoribus enunciat" (Euripides 1813–1837 [ed. Matthiae], 7:321).

8. Matthiae, like Musgrave, is troubled by the opening of the play. He is worried by the unparalleled anapestic dialogue, by the abrupt and uncharacteristic transition to iambics (7:322), and by lines 115–161 (because Agamemnon has no reason to narrate the contents of the letter aloud to the old man when he has already explained their substance [7:322–323]). In addition he observes that 124, where the old man asks Agamemnon how Achilles will not be angered at having his fiancée taken away from him, seems to be out of sync with what came before, since Agamemnon had already explained that only Calchas, Odysseus, Menelaus, and he himself were aware of the situation. It goes without saying, Matthiae implies, that if only these four know what is going on, Achilles, who knows nothing, not even about the use of his name, can hardly become angry about the loss of something he never knew he had (7:323). The lines attributed to the play in the *Frogs* of Aristophanes and in Hesychius worry him as well (7:323). Although he does not believe as Boeckh does that there was ever a production of the *Iphigenia at Aulis* by Euripides during his lifetime, he is nevertheless inclined to think that the play was left incomplete after his death and arranged for the stage by his son, but with gaps and inconsistencies that led to later interpolations and additions.

Orestes believes his sister was killed at Aulis, we can extrapolate that Clytemnestra must have believed this at the time, since in the *Iphigenia among the Taurians* Orestes is on the run because he murdered his mother, who killed Agamemnon in revenge for the killing of Iphigenia.[9] Since Matthiae thinks the transformation should have been narrated by a mortal rather than a god, this must mean that the announcement was doubtful enough for Clytemnestra to disbelieve it (as in the extant ending, which Matthiae believes is probably spurious). If it is reasonable to suppose that it was possible for Clytemnestra to doubt it, it must also have been possible for the audience to doubt it (otherwise how could it seem credible that Clytemnestra could doubt it?). This means that in Matthiae's version of the play, *the audience does not really know how the play ends.* If they knew about Iphigenia's transformation at the altar from other sources, and they knew Euripides was going to use this ending, that would put the lie to the principle Matthiae used to disqualify the lines from Aelian from the prologue—that an audience should not know the end of the play at the beginning. That the ancient audience cannot have known how the play "truly" ended is a crisis in reception that effectively allegorizes the condition of the modern critic. Just as they did not know how the play ended, neither do *we* know, because we have a manuscript ending full of metrical errors, stylistic slips, and unlikely diction.[10]

If in Matthiae we can witness both (1) a movement from a consideration of reception to a denial of the lines in Aelian, and (2) a subsequent movement from its denial to a crisis in reception, other critics have relied on one or the other. But in every case, as I will show, the main and consistent emphasis is on reception and its dynamics; either (1) the

9. Euripides 1813–1837 (ed. Matthiae), 7:321–322.

10. A similar observation may be made with respect to Vitelli's explanation of the state of the text in 1877 (Vitelli 1877). Vitelli adopts Heath's suggestion that the lines in Aelian were those of Euripides Minor, but draws very different conclusions. For Heath, the lines belonged to another play by another Euripides; Vitelli spliced this attribution with the idea that that the younger Euripides had had a hand in the composition of the play. In his account the fragment in Aelian belonged to an ending added by the younger Euripides, lost from what we have by accident, and replaced by the poetasting of some late Byzantine. This damns the reconstructive efforts of the critic to the most tenuous possible: trustworthy comparanda being lost, all reconstructions will be of singular texts which, so long as the criterion for evaluating a reconstruction is that "every emendation be in agreement with the genius of the language and the style of the writer" (omnis emendatio linguae ingenio aut scriptoris stylo consentanea esto" [Le Clerc 1778, 2:270]. I quote Le Clerc, who is neither remarkable nor out of date on this matter), cannot be satisfactorily evaluated. The increase in complexity that the history of interpolations begins to show—Vitelli has two non-Euripidean hands in the exodus of the *Iphigenia*—is coupled with an increase in uncertainty of the critic's conjectures, a crisis in reception.

desire for stylistic regularity causes a methodological reliance on ancient response, or (2) an awareness of the difficulties of critical reception leads to a systematic presentation of the critic's own judgments. In every case the critical edition produced is the reception of a reception.

I begin with a discussion of some critics who present versions of the *Iphigenia at Aulis* conceived as stylistically or aesthetically regular. I then conclude with a discussion of the approach that emphasizes the probability of the modern critic's conjecture and culminates in the edition of James Diggle.

Stylistic Regularity

The proposition that an ancient text should be stylistically regular is not an invention of the late nineteenth and early twentieth centuries: it dates at least to ancient conflicts between analogists and anomalists. Musgrave raised doubts over the opening anapestic dialogue on the grounds that such a beginning would be unparalleled in Euripides;[11] because of similar worries, Hermann recanted on his position that Euripides might have written an innovative beginning.[12] But in the versions I address here, the criterion of stylistic regularity is given particular importance, due in large part to the methodological dominance of reception. I focus particularly on David Kovacs's edition and its rationale,[13] but I begin with a few illustrations from earlier critics.

In 1891 England presumed that Euripides left the *Iphigenia at Aulis* in a more or less unfinished condition, that "the man or men who prepared it for [presentation on stage] not only added passages at the end and in the body of the play, but rearranged the prologue,"[14] and that the play contains many later casual interpolations. England does not think there could have been an irregularity like the anapestic opening even in Euripides' drafts. A scholion at the beginning of the *Hecuba* informs us that Euripides began all his plays with a prologue; such a sweeping statement would make the extant beginning of *Iphigenia at Aulis* impossible.[15] Therefore England moves Agamemnon's iambic speech to the beginning and places the anapests together after it. The possibility of any authorial idiosyncrasy has been removed.

11. Musgrave 1762, ad loc.
12. Hermann 1877, 218.
13. Euripides 2003 (ed. Kovacs).
14. Euripides 1891 (ed. England), i.
15. Ibid., xxiii.

While personal regularity serves as one constraint, a second is provided by the notion of generic regularity. There is a strange and troubling redundancy in the prologue: at verses 106–107 Agamemnon tells his slave that only he, Calchas, Odysseus, and Menelaus know of the plot to sacrifice Iphigenia, but at 123–126 the old man asks how Achilles will not resent being deprived of his promised bride, a question that implies that he has not heard 106–107. Henri Weil remarked, "If the old man lacks a little bit of attention or intelligence, this is because the poet wanted to make sure the audience did not, so that would be no obscurity in the mind of the spectator."[16] Though Weil gives a parallel in the *Orestes* (v. 757), England remarks, "This does not sound like tragic art."[17]

England's notion of generic and authorial regularity depends on a strong concept of audience response. His discussion of the play's ending makes this clear. In addition to having concerns over its metrical and linguistic irregularity, England objects on the basis of "the fitness of the Exodus from the point of view of Euripidean dramatic construction." "Euripidean dramatic construction" here means how and when Euripides likes to release information to his audience, a reprise of Matthiae's response-oriented question of what an audience should know and when. Euripides, more than any other tragedian, was the sort to give the whole picture. But the extant exodus does not definitely state whether Iphigenia was slaughtered or not: this allows for a dramatic irony in which the spectators know something about the true ending but the agents in the play do not. For England such a degree of dramatic irony is unacceptable in a Euripidean play.[18]

To make a claim about the acceptability of dramatic irony in an ancient tragedy is implicitly to make a claim about the state of knowledge of the audience, a claim about reception; to base one's text on such a claim is to change its signification radically.[19] If the text represented is not what was written down but what prompted and received some response by an audience, then that text no longer represents a written document. Instead it represents something that floated between author and audience, something emergent from a collaboration between sender and

16. "Si le vieillard manque un peu d'attention ou d'intelligence, c'est que le poëte craignait que le public n'en manquât, afin qu'il y a aucune obscurité dans l'esprit du spectateur" (Euripides 1868 [ed. Weil]), 329.

17. Euripides 1891 (ed. England), xxiv.

18. Ibid., xxvi–xxvii.

19. It is instructive to compare the texts in this chapter with the work of Musgrave (see chapter 4); Musgrave makes claims about dramatic irony *on the basis of* a textual emendation, while these critics make emendations on the basis of propositions concerning dramatic irony. The process, in other words, has been completely reversed.

receiver. The resulting product is not a material text but *textuality*, the sort of thing produced, according to the reader-response theorists of the later half of the twentieth century, as a cognitive or ideal object in the process of reading.[20] If this were not so, then the argument from what an audience may or may not know would have no cogency: a written document might well be incomprehensible, unconventional, even bizarre, especially if that written document is an unfinished script left behind after an author's death. A shared text, on the other hand, or one produced in the process of reception, will very rarely be so. England's edition, justified in terms of audience-response, presents an *ideal* text, a text interpolated not by a scribe but by an entire culture with its codes and its expectations.

It could be said against this claim that what is represented in such an edition is the only thing *possible* for a tragic writer to write, because a tragic writer was constrained to write with the expectations of his audience in mind. This can be granted without retracting the claim that the edition presents an ideal or intersubjective text. In this case we would have to imagine a process of writing in which an author engaged in an unspoken dialogue with his audience, negotiating between what he wanted to express and what he believed an audience was capable of receiving. What he arrived at should then be described as the material representation of an ideal text; that is, a redaction or actualization of the intersubjective text that itself remains ideal or imagined. Of course, a material document can never be an intersubjective text—it is a thing, shared between people only as an object. Its textuality, to the extent that this is intersubjective, must be ideal, and not in the manuscript. But then even the autograph must be described as a representation of the ideal text. In this case we would have to speak of England's text (or the text of anyone else who used audience response as a criterion) as a representation of a representation of an ideal text that cannot be made extant, because it cannot be made into a material object. Any critical edition of an ancient text that uses an audience's response as a criterion does not represent an objective material text—a sequence of signs on paper or papyrus—but rather an ideal and intersubjective textuality.

In this light the mere text—the tradition of signs on the page, stemming from Euripides' hand—becomes a highly questionable object. *That* we do not have, if it ever existed at all. And so England's belief that the lines quoted in Aelian do not come from Euripides' *Iphigenia at Aulis* acquires a surprising felicity. Though he thinks Euripides might

20. See Iser 1978; Fish 1980, 2: "The reader's response is not *to* the meaning: it *is* the meaning." The critical editions discussed here substitute *text* for *meaning* in this formulation: the reader's response is not *to* the text: it *is* the text.

have intended an ending with a deus ex machina, England is still not inclined to treat the fragment in Aelian as genuine. He thinks it is the product of what happens with "a quotation which, owing to some prominent feature, has acquired an independent existence in the memory, loses its hold on its original context and easily makes new connections—i.e. becomes associated in the mind with some other slightly similar context."[21] Just as ruling this fragment out as evidence for the end of the play leaves no evidence for what the original ending looked like, so too does the emphasis on an ideal text rule out every material text, from any hypothetical authorial inscription onward, as a recoverable object. We can recover only the *spiritual* communication of the ancients, not their *material traces*; textual criticism becomes an archeology of the psyche, a paraphysical pursuit.

This surprising turn has increased in importance.[22] According to David Kovacs, for example, textual criticism must take into account not only the rules of grammar and metrics, but also those aesthetic canons provided by "literary criticism." By literary criticism Kovacs means knowing the laws and conventions that govern ancient literature, that is, axioms of literary style. These include criteria such as "symmetry" and "aesthetic regularity."[23] Where such criteria appear to be violated and a simple emendation can be found, then the critic should emend the text.

Despite surface differences, Simon Goldhill advocates an exactly identical use of "literary criticism" as stylistic axiomatics. His diagnosis of Kovacs's position is elucidating: "I am not sure how 'textual criticism' can proceed without 'literary criticism': certainly when Kovacs basis his argument on what constitutes a 'logical,' 'consistent,' or 'meandering' speech, or on 'good taste,' he is involved in strictly literary questions. In regretting 'how little Euripides' critics and editors are disturbed by violations of the formal regularities of tragedy,' he seems particularly unaware of the extensive and detailed discussions precisely of Euripides' 'violations of the formal regularities of tragedy.' "[24] In question in this debate is whether Kovacs's axioms of style are better or more appropriate than Goldhill's. "I am not suggesting," writes Goldhill, "that there

21. Euripides 1891 (ed. England), xxx.

22. Similar assumptions underlie the contributions of Willink 1971; Knox 1972; Bain 1977. The importance of response-oriented criticism in classical studies in the last thirty years can hardly be overestimated: that individual or societal matrices of comprehension and expectation are significant for the study of ancient culture is an assumption so pervasive as to be difficult to point to adequately. For explicit discussions, see Pedrick and Rabinowitz 1986; Rabinowitz 1986; Gentili 1988; Erp Taalman Kip 1990; Goldhill 2000.

23. Kovacs 1987.

24. Goldhill 1986b, 158n.4. He is referring to Kovacs 1986.

can be no interpolation in Euripides. Nor am I suggesting that Euripides wrote incoherent nonsense that can be defended only by the application of anachronistic literary awareness fostered by Sterne, Joyce, or Artaud. Rather, I am asserting the importance of recognizing the way in which Euripides' literary technique works through the deformation and transgression of his audience's literary, theatrical, and social expectations and norms."[25] Kovacs and Goldhill agree on the rule that a critical emendation must be based on some systematic and elaborated stylistic operating as a constraint on the possibilities of expression for a Euripidean drama. But, as I have argued, any such axiomatics cannot be a *diplomatic*, textual matter. It must instead be a spiritual one, defining the text as something hovering in an intersubjective ether; this ether dominates literary expression as both means and meaning.

Kovacs's *Iphigenia* represents the most extreme elaboration of this antimaterialist notion of the classical text. Here is his position on the major issues:[26] the anapests at the beginning of the play are spurious, while most of the iambic prologue (except 106–114) was part of the first performance. Most of the first episode, including Menelaus's first speech, Agamemnon's reply, the Messenger's speech announcing the arrival of Clytemnestra and Iphigenia, and the speeches in which Agamemnon and Menelaus both change their minds a second time, was not seen at the first performance. The play ended with Iphigenia departing to die and a final choral farewell. Neither the fragment preserved in Aelian, nor the ending preserved in the manuscripts is from the original; the manuscript ending is probably a very late (postclassical) addition.

Kovacs situates the text far from the influence of authorial idiosyncrasies and represents it not as Euripides' personal work but as a social construct. The first step in this process is a decision not to treat the question, "How much of the *Iphigenia at Aulis* was written by Euripides and how much was written by other hands?" Since he believes it would be extremely difficult to separate the words left by Euripides in his posthumous papers from those added by others in the preparation of the piece for performance,[27] Kovacs proposes to answer a different question: "*What did the audience at the first performance of the play hear and see*, whether genuine Euripides or lines written to complete what he left unfinished?"[28] As becomes clear in the development of his argument,

25. Goldhill 1986b, 171.
26. Euripides 2003 (ed. Kovacs); Kovacs 2003. I am grateful to David Kovacs for allowing me to review his text and arguments before their publication.
27. In this he follows Hennig 1870, 185.
28. Kovacs 2003, 77. The emphasis is mine.

this first audience is totally determinant of the form of this text. Indeed, in Kovacs's analysis, what the audience saw and heard is not synecdoche for "what was produced"; it is the object itself, the thing represented by Kovacs's edition. Deviation from traditional patterns and expectations is not possible for such a version: it interfaces perfectly with categories already placed in the audience's minds by previous tragedies and by other forms of storytelling. Even if the production was unconventional, the audience's matrices of comprehension would have filtered out any singularity: because Kovacs depends on understanding these comprehensional grids for his textual criticism, he is also incapable of recovering any unconventional aspect of the first performance.

Kovacs relies in particular on traditional narrative expectations to root out interpolation. In his model the form of the first performance was lost when, sometime in the century after its premiere, a revival was prepared. For the revival, a reviser added numerous passages and substantially changed the play. He used a high degree of repetition in his language, was given to unnecessary but "picturesque" scenes like the entrance of Clytemnestra with Iphigenia and Orestes on a chariot (606–634 Diggle), and favored psychological portraiture that added little to the progress of the plot but served an emotional purpose, such as the changes of mind of Agamemnon and Menelaus in the first episode.[29] Identifying and removing these addition will, Kovacs believes, uncover the "text" of the "first performance."

Crucially Kovacs's reviser is responsible for one particular innovation in the story, which Kovacs calls the "secret prophecy theme." Kovacs finds two contradictory stories concerning the prophecy requiring Iphigenia's sacrifice in the text. In one Calchas made his prophecy to the whole army, and the entire fleet knows about the imperative to sacrifice Iphigenia.[30] In the other Calchas made his prophecy to the Atreidae and their councilors alone: no one else knows of the plan to sacrifice Iphigenia.[31] But the "secret prophecy" motif cannot be genuine, since

29. Ibid., 78.

30. Evidence for this story is gathered from 87–91, 324, 538–540, 814–818, 1259–1275 and 1345–1357.

31. This version is gathered primarily from 518, *Κάλχας ἐρεῖ μαντεύματ' Ἀργείων στρατῷ* (Calchas will tell the prophecy to the army of the Achaeans), which obviously implies that he has not done so yet. It is only inference from 106–107, 590–597 (which Kovacs, following Murray, puts in the mouth of a secondary chorus of Argive soldiers [they greet Clytemnestra warmly: this is cruel irony if they know of the prophecy: therefore they must not]), and 425–434, where the army wonders at the women's arrival and therefore must not know of the prophecy (a comparison with Willink 1971, 362 is instructive: he takes 425–434 as evidence that the army knew of the sacrifice, that is, as part of the "public prophecy" theme).

"neither in Homer nor elsewhere in tragedy are important prophecies affecting an army or a people delivered, as it were, behind closed doors, and one would not expect them to be in our play either."[32]

The "one" in this sentence names no modern reader. Rather it designates any one of those Greeks with normal expectations who went to the theater to see the first performance of Euripides' last tetralogy. When Kovacs elevates the absence of a parallel for the secret prophecy theme to a text-critical principle, he makes it impossible for a text to present any singularity that might break with precedent or tradition: such a singularity would be inassimilable by an audience's matrices of comprehension. And in fact intersubjectivity regulates Kovacs's text, not the "secret prophecy" motif. The critic's ability to identify this motif as spurious depends on his or her having a prior knowledge of a certain axiomatics of style, that is, it depends on his or her knowledge of an ideal set of intersubjective expectations shared by Euripides and his Athenian audience.

We can trace Kovacs's dependence on intersubjectivity in his treatment of the two prophecy motifs. All of those passages that are summoned to identify a "public prophecy" theme depend on probable inference rather than intuitive certainty (see appendix). But though even the strongest evidence for the public prophecy is circumstantial, lines 517–518 are clear, literal evidence that the prophecy was secret:

> MENELAUS. Don't be too afraid of the army.
> AGAMEMNON. Calchas will tell his oracles to the Greek army.

This cannot be interpreted away; rather, it must be excised. Kovacs does so on stylistic grounds, arguing that the entire passage is afflicted by sentiments inappropriate for tragedy. His discussion of this passage differs significantly from his practice in the rest of the 2003 *Journal of Hellenic Studies* article that defends his theory of the text. In striking contrast to the rest of the article, where he cites the Greek exclusively and without translation, here Kovacs cites only a translation. (That translation, it should be noted, does not correspond exactly with the one in his edition.) Further, Kovacs avoids the usual practice of discussing his objections to the text discursively, opting instead for a series of objections interpolated between square brackets. These singularities may suggest the central importance of this passage for the logical structure of his argument. I cite his discussion in full: the comments in parentheses and brackets are both his.

32. Kovacs 2003, 78.

AG. We have reached a point where I must kill my daughter.
ME. How so? Who will force you?
AG. The whole Achaean army.[33]
515 ME. Not if you send her back to Argos.
AG. I could manage *that* without detection but not this other thing. [What is the other thing *to be managed* by Agamemnon? None appears in the sequel.]
ME. What other thing are you talking about? Don't be too afraid of the army.
AG. Calchas will tell his oracles to the Greek army.
ME. Not if he's killed, which can be easily arranged.
520 AG. Seers are a worthless lot.
ME. (emended with Murray) Yes, useless where they are needed, and where they are useful, causing pain. [Both lines irrelevant.]
AG. Aren't you afraid of a consideration that has just struck me?
ME. How can I be unless you tell me what it is?
AG. Crafty Odysseus is in on this plot.
525 ME. We have nothing to fear from Odysseus. [Pointlessly false statement implicitly retracted in what follows.]
AG. He is always of variable nature and on the side of the rabble.
ME. Yes, he's in the grip of ambition, a terrible bane.
AG. Don't you think that he will stand in the midst of the Argives, tell Calchas' prophecies, and say that I promised the sacrifice and then reneged? Won't he gather up the army and order them to kill you and me and then sacrifice the girl? [How is this a different point from 518?][34]

The comments Kovacs inserts in square brackets are meant to indicate that the passage does not conform to the aesthetic laws of proportion, consistency, and decorum he sees as necessary constraints on tragic expression. A passage will be excised because it breaks the aesthetic law that is the common property of author and audience and that constitutes a public horizon of expectation. Thus it is not the necessity of a public prophecy that determines Kovacs's critical decisions, but *the public as necessity*: intersubjectivity has become the determining ground of textuality.

Just as the epistemic construction that facilitates the creation of Kovacs's version of the *Iphigenia at Aulis* makes it a public, common

33. "513–514 could in themselves belong to [the first performance] as they seem to presuppose the public prophecy. Just where they would fit in the original structure of the episode is unclear" (Kovacs 2003, 87n.49).

34. The translation printed here from Kovacs 2003 varies in nuance and detail from Kovacs's translation of the same passage in the Loeb edition (Euripides 2003 [ed. Kovacs]). In Kovacs 2003 the Greek corresponding to these lines does not appear.

text with no room for secret, idiosyncratic, or singular expression, so too, in Kovacs's *Iphigenia at Aulis*, does the plot turn on the bringing to fruition of a common and public intention. The plan to sacrifice Iphigenia is, in this version, known to all. Agamemnon's agony, and the wrangling between himself and his brother, are reduced to an unobtrusive minimum. These aspects of the play are largely confined to the long first episode, where Kovacs finds the hand of the reviser particularly active. He brackets both the speeches of Agamemnon and Menelaus at the opening of the episode and the subsequent change of heart of Menelaus toward its end, as well as the messenger's entrance (335–441, 469–537). Rather than the complex psychological twists and turns presented in the paradosis, Kovacs envisages a scene in which

> we must suppose, first, that Agamemnon comes to see that the sacrifice of his daughter is inevitable: in later scenes he is resigned to it. Second, it seems necessary that both he and the audience should be prepared for the entrance of his daughter and his wife. This is desirable on grounds of dramatic intelligibility, and it surely contributes something to the sense that the sacrifice cannot now be avoided. There need not have been set speeches by the brothers at all, or they might have been much shorter than those we have. In our present text the Old Man stands around saying nothing for nearly a hundred lines before the entrance of the Messenger, and for another hundred lines after his departure. This is poor stagecraft. The crucial thing is that Agamemnon should see that there is no chance now of averting the sacrifice. This could be accomplished by having Menelaus reveal that while he was keeping watch over Agamemnon's affairs (*cf.* 328) he saw the arrival of Clytaemestra and Iphigenia. The discussion of this, particularly if it involved mention of the army's having seen them, would probably have contained material that the Reviser had to delete if he wanted to carry out his design. Agamemnon at this news sees that his brother has won and goes inside (his exit seems to be suggested by his instructions to the Chorus).[35]

That is, Agamemnon is checkmated into accepting the inevitability of a course of action decided upon by the entire army; rather than coming, with difficulty and a great amount of struggle, to an unhappy resolution, he submits quickly to the will of the army, the vengeful command of Artemis, and the persuasion of Menelaus. But Kovacs's use of an intersubjective a priori makes the first performance's circumstances of production tell a similar story of submission to public overdetermination. The focus on the collaborative nature of the genesis of this text removes

35. Ibid.

from consideration any worry over Euripides' nonconventionality. In its stead it asks us to consider a posthumous collaboration between Euripides Minor and his late father (or uncle) which regularized the play into a positive, collectively acceptable aesthetic object.

It might be possible to detect a residual Platonism in the assumptions that underlie this version of the *Iphigenia at Aulis*, a belief in some set of ideal notions concerning what is possible and what is not possible with respect to the composition of a Greek tragedy. The assumption that there are formal regularities of tragedy might require that these formal regularities reside in some immaterial (mental or metaphysical) sphere, common to all Athenians (if not to all of humanity), and serving as the form that all extant Greek tragedies imitate. To put it in different terms that hardly change the general import: some schematism governs the presentation of tragedy within the system of cultural exchange that forms the fabric of Athenian life, through which all presentations must be filtered and without which no sense can be made at all.[36] It might also seem that these forms or schemata *existed* and are merely to be discovered by the literary historian, perhaps through an essay in literary grammar aimed at discovering the "deep structure" of tragic expression, then used as criteria to divide the spurious from the genuine in the textual criticism of a tragedy.

The discovery of such transcendent literary forms (should they have existed) on the basis of the texts that have been left to us involves an irresolvable circularity. Since there is no independent testament to the formal regularities of style in Attic tragedy (as there are, for example, for Greek lexicography and grammar), these must be deduced from the extant texts.[37] But there are—this is the facilitating assumption of all modern textual criticism—irregularities and transgressions of these norms (whatever they are) in the texts themselves. We thus find ourselves in a circle: we can only deduce tragedy's regulative norms from the texts, but we can only do *that* if we know which parts of the texts are genuine, which parts of the texts conform to the regulative norms.[38]

Kovacs proposes an expedient designed to allow us to get around this circle: emendation, provided that is supported by a "different and

36. See Iser 1993.

37. Kovacs 1987, 257. Aristotle's *Poetics* is, of course, nowhere near precise enough for work at the level of detail required for text criticism.

38. It does not matter here whether Euripides is supposed to be "transgressive" of formal norms (Goldhill) or to conform to them (Kovacs); in either case one must *know* the norms before one can determine this, and *knowing* the norms at all involves the circularity.

likelier explanation."[39] If circular reasoning is to be avoided, "likelihood" can have nothing to do with the schemata regulating tragic expression. Rather it will need to depend on auxiliary considerations—the technical armature of textual criticism (stemmatics, paleography, a knowledge of the dynamics of interpolation, and so on), or a preference for simple, elegant explanations over tortured, complex ones (nominalism),[40] or some external standard of style—a modern one, for example. This means that every emendation aimed at removing an irregularity depends on a decision in each case as to whether a norm is obeyed or transgressed that has *nothing to do with the ancient norms themselves.* Enforcing the norms of Greek tragedy by textual emendation, in other words, is a performative act that *produces* them on the basis of *extraneous* considerations. Textual critics produce the norms for tragic expression at the very moment when they appear to be enforcing them.

This is what, in another realm, Iphigenia does: she produces Greece as a historical positivity the moment she submits to its demands and legitimates its authority. Agamemnon argues before Iphigenia that it is not the private interests of Menelaus that have bound him to his terrible resolution but the longing of the army as a whole for war against Troy, and thus "it is not Menelaus that has enslaved me, nor have I gone over to his purpose: it is Hellas. To her I must sacrifice you, whether I will or no: she is my ruler. As far as it depends on you, my daughter, and on me, she must be free, and we Greeks cannot have our wives forcibly abducted" (1269–1275, trans. Kovacs). This does not seem (as it does in other versions) a desperate last-minute argument that carries little persuasion; rather, it names the central theme of the play. Iphigenia's decision to die willingly represents a fundamental poetic act that creates Greece as a national project and identity. According to Kovacs, "Just as the deaths of Menoeceus, Macaria and the daughter of Erechtheus were the necessary price for the success of their cities in war, an effective remedy for a problem that is real, so too are we meant to see Iphigenia's death as a necessary precondition for a necessary war."[41] This is a defining contribution: by her free submission, the war's necessity is confirmed, and the last remnant of an alternative view on historical events converted to the concerns of a now-dominant public community.

But (as I discussed in the afterword to part 1) this sudden suicidal submission is fundamentally disruptive of the system it aims to inaugurate; coming from a radically unpredictable source (Iphigenia's mind)

39. Kovacs 1987, 258.
40. See Kovacs 2003, 82: "*inepti non sunt multiplicandi praeter necessitatem.*"
41. Kovacs 2003, 100–101.

and producing an action of terrible proportions, it forces us to remind ourselves that it might have been otherwise. This is the tragic element in Kovacs's text: that "Greece," though successfully inaugurated as a national identity, is nevertheless based on a terrible act of self-sacrifice. In this version that self-sacrifice is real. There is no transmogrification at the altar, no final happy revelation that she has not been killed. The first audience witnessed Iphigenia's death, and Greece terrorized herself with the possibility that another outcome might have been better—that Greece itself, as the entity that fought and won the Trojan war, *not* have been granted existence.

Kovacs's *Iphigenia at Aulis* allegorizes the circumstances of its own production, first by staging the imposition of a choice that is radically other in provenance, and second, by invoking its own contingency. The criteria might have been different; the text might have been otherwise. To illustrate this we must remember how Kovacs brings the intersubjective a priori to bear as a force in the production of his text. I have already pointed out that he levers the text apart with the hypothesis that the paradosis contains two stories concerning Calchas's prophecy: the "private" and "public" prophecy motives. But the public prophecy motif, which Kovacs favors as belonging to the first performance, in fact does not originate from intuitive certainty but from a set of possible inferences dependent on interpretive choices made by Kovacs himself.[42] In other words, by means of an interpretation that, while possible, is not certain, Kovacs produces a double text and then selects a single alternative as original. Against a *plural* text is brought to bear the intersubjective a priori. The production of plurality thus precedes the critical performance as its precondition and its ground, and the critical performance itself stages for us the same kind of troubling inauguration narrated in the death of Iphigenia. The text, in other words, is tragically plural: it invokes its other possibilities as lost and presents itself as an unstable raft on an ocean of flux.

Toward a Systematics of Critical Reception

The final approach addressed here bases its principle of system not on the play's reception by some ancient audience but rather on the adventure of textual criticism itself. It does this by quantifying and concretizing the epistemological basis of textual criticism, what might be termed its

42. See appendix.

logical organon: probability. So doing, James Diggle presents *Iphigenia at Aulis* as an image of multiple possible texts and in the process generates the most explicitly singular plural edition in the critical dossier.

Throughout its modern history, textual criticism has been intimately and inextricably linked to probability. The particular technique that infuses the critical edition of an ancient author with the tincture of probability is the conjectural emendation, one of the twin pillars of textual criticism throughout the modern period. "Bivium enim ad corrigendum: libri, et conjectura," writes Lipsius (The road to emendation is double: books, and conjecture).[43] The sentiment is frequently repeated, and it is not obsolete.[44] Although post-Lachmannian textual criticism self-consciously privileges the history of traditions and a sophisticated knowledge of circumstances of manuscript production (*libri*), the advent of stemmatics did not make obsolete the discourses and epistemological assumptions associated with *conjectura.* Even the fullest knowledge about a text's tradition eventually leaves the critic with the task of *examinatio,* evaluating the quality of the text the witnesses provide, and then exercising his or her own intelligence to conjecture the status of the original (see chapter 3).

Dependent on the judgment of the critic and the faith of the reader, the conjectural emendation self-consciously reinserts the work of contemporary minds into the transmission and reception of ancient texts. It does this in two ways: by valuing the role of the researcher as a producer of possibilities, and by accomplishing a dispersal of *new variants* that are taken under the sign of doubt. Conjecture, in other words, represents one moment at which the resistance to theory in classical philology is instantiated, because conjecture inserts the free judgment of the subject into the process of textual transmission.

There is no sense in which a conjecture can be described as certain.[45] The theory of conjecture has deep roots in modern epistemology, where it is consistently characterized as a matter of probability.[46] According to these theories conjectural emendation is based on the interpretation of signs,[47] and its results cannot be given the stamp of certain truth. Rather, conjectures introduce into the discourse of and about ancient literature

43. Lipsius 1675, 986.

44. Robortello 1662, 100; See Kenney 1974, 25 for further examples.

45. Le Clerc's final law of emendation stipulated that all emendations must be expressed with modesty and not with the surety of truth (Le Clerc 1778, 2:300).

46. "From 1500 to 1900, no noun is more often found beside the adjective *probable* than *conjecture*" (Patey 1984, 47).

47. See Patey 1984 and Hacking 1975, 32; Franklin 2001.

further possible textual forms. We may accept them with some degree of probability, but we must not understand them to achieve the certainty of mathematical deductions or of sense-evidence.

For Thomas Hobbes, writing in 1650, a sign is something regularly concomitant with the thing it signifies: thus fire may be a sign of ashes, and vice versa, because we know from experience that fire and ashes are usually closely related. We are able to infer the future presence of ashes from the present appearance of fire because we know from experience that ashes follow fire. Similarly, from the present appearance of ashes, we conjecture the past existence of fire. But because these conjectures depend on frequency of experience, conjectural knowledge cannot be said to be certain, since "experience concludeth nothing universally." Thus, although the more experience we have, the more likely our conjectures are, "the taking of signs by *experience*, is that wherein men do ordinarily think, the difference stands between man and man in *wisdom*, by which they commonly understand a man's whole ability or *power cognitive*; but this is an *error*; for the signs are but conjectural; and according as they have often or seldom failed, so their assurance is more or less; but *never full* and *evident*."[48]

For John Locke, whose *Essay concerning Human Understanding*[49] appeared the year before Bentley's *Epistula ad Millium*,[50] our knowledge of what might generally be called historical events, that is, matters of fact that are not immediately present to the senses, is always to some degree conjectural. Locke defines probability as "likeness to be true"; that is, verisimilitude. The mind's acceptance of probable propositions is referred to as assent. Thus, corresponding to degrees of probability, there are degrees of assent, which range "from full *Assurance* and Confidence, quite down to *Conjecture, Doubt,* and *Distrust*."[51] While knowledge depends on immediate intuition of a connection between ideas, probability exists to supplement the considerable limitations under which human knowledge labors.

The Port-Royal *Logic* explains how we take account of "the conformity of any thing with our own knowledge, observation, and experience" in the granting of assent to a probability by using examples drawn from textual criticism.[52] The authors of the *Logic* note that while many things can be ascertained by reason alone, many other facts can only be

48. Hobbes 1840, 17–18.
49. Locke 1975.
50. Paul Maas called this "the incunabulum of conjectural criticism" (1958, 34).
51. Locke 1975, 4.15.3.
52. Arnauld and Nicole 1996, 260–273 (4.12–15).

accepted on the basis of authority;[53] they then ask what criteria might determine when we should assent to facts given on the authority of humans. Historical events, which require our belief because we did not actually witness them, fall into this category. In considering historical testimony, the authors write, it is good to take into account not just the believability of the event alone, but also the circumstances that surround it. (These are the external and internal circumstances I discussed in the introduction to part 2.) Evaluating the likelihood of an event on the basis of external circumstances depends, for the *Logic,* on the frequent coincidence of certain events. Events that go together frequently are called "common circumstances"; these "are encountered in many facts and they are found more often than not joined to truth than to falsehood."[54] Only the words have changed from Hobbes's discussion of conjecture from signs: a sign is very little more than a common circumstance to an event. And as with Hobbes, for whom such conjectures are probable and not certain, the assent we are to give in the Port-Royal *Logic* is a matter of probability, not of certainty: "If they are not counterbalanced by other particular circumstances that weaken or destroy in the mind the grounds for belief that the mind derives from these common circumstances, we are right to believe in these events, if not with certainty, at least with high probability."[55] Primary examples for the authors are the debunking of ancient texts as forgeries.

The *Logic* makes a rigid distinction between the act of inscription, which is the event in which an author puts pen to paper, and all the witnesses to that act, that is, all texts deriving from that event, including the first text that emerges from the act of inscription, the author's manuscript or autograph. It is curious, but not at all unimportant, that even when we are faced with an autograph, we are only licensed to conclude that it was written by that author with a high degree of *probability* and not with certainty: once the event is over, its trace is no longer part of it, but only the first witness to it. This is counterintuitive, but it cannot be belied. As long as the object of philological research is the act of inscription, *no* witness, not even the best—that is, the autograph—will provide us with *certain proof* of the substance of that act, only with a demonstration more or less credible. Likewise, if we aim to gain knowledge of the act of inscription through a reconstruction of the autograph, it follows

53. Ibid., 260 (4.12).
54. Ibid., 270 (4.15).
55. Ibid., 270. Thomas Hearne, writing of historiography in 1698, concurs, noting that the historian's field is one of probability, not certainty, and derives from conjectures from signs (Hearne 1698, 14).

from the canons of the Port-Royal *Logic* that even if we could reconstruct that text perfectly we could not deduce from our reconstruction *with certainty* what the author was writing during the act of inscription: strictly speaking we could only do so with a very high degree of probability. While the study of manuscripts may be aimed at the discovery of the original, conjecture aims to leap from there back to the event, and we must interpret this leap in terms of probability and not of certainty.

Textual critics have been consistently aware of the probabilistic nature of their conjectural undertakings. Gaspar Schoppe entitled his 1662 book of corrections *Verisimilium*, "[books of] likenesses to truth," and commented, "Now at the beginning it pleased me to give the name of VERISIMILITUDES to these books; I could have called the same work *suspicions, guesses, conjectures,* titles which others use."[56] The short work of theory on the subject of textual criticism he published the same year, *Small Commentary on the Critical Art, and especially on the other part of it, associated with emendation, what method ought to be observed in emending Latin writers with the use of ingenium,*[57] is a list of the kinds of circumstances that should lead a critic to suspect a corruption in a manuscript, and that can only lead to possible conjectures. Schoppe notes that many critics make emendations to ancient texts without having access to manuscripts: his goal is to provide such critics, who by necessity must rely on *ingenium* alone, with a list of the kinds of errors likely to be in these manuscripts, so that their conjectures might less resemble *aegrotorum somnia,* "the dreams of sick men."[58] A better knowledge of the kinds of errors committed by scribes, suggests Schoppe, will prevent critics from creating such unlikely constructions in their editions. Clearly *ingenium* is the predecessor of Housman's "thought," the core of the text-critical resistance to theory. As we will see in the cases of Page and Diggle, to the degree that text-criticism is a resistance to theory, the expression of this resistance is a theory of indetermination or probability.

The fact that conjecture cannot make claims about the *certainty* of a critical emendation causes critics some methodological anxiety. We never know *for sure* that we are restoring the words of the original: we

56. "Principio dum VERISIMILIUM nomen his facere libris placuit: eadem opera Suspiciones, Divinationes, Conjectanea, quibus alii utuntur indicibus, inscribere potuissem" (Schoppe 1662b).

57. Schoppe 1662a.

58. Ibid. The reference to Horace is instructive: Horace had used the simile to describe books in which empty figures are created out of components that do not go together (*Ars poetica* 7–9), as when a painter places a dolphin in the woods or a boar in the waves (30)—when, a reader of the Port-Royal *Logic* might take it, circumstances that do not normally go together are placed together in an incredible manner.

may just as easily be correcting as corrupting. In a *Satyra Menippaea* on the subject of criticism, Lipsius relates a dream in which he is transported to the "Senate of the Republic of Letters." Cicero has convened a session to address the serious issue of the "correctors" who, he complains, have taken great liberties with the ancient texts and inflicted great wounds on them. Lipsius, who considers himself among the company of correctors, is struck with great fear at these charges:

> He seemed to cast his eyes at our seat, openly, as though to point towards us. "A freezing terror shook my limbs, and my blood ran cold with fear:" and I said with trepidation to Duza, "touch me, brother, I am colder than Gallic snow. We perish, we have entered the Cyclop's cave, what Pallas will rescue us from the middle of death?" Duza said nothing to this, but himself sat anxiously, his head down. . . . I was now awaiting a lictor who would lead us away, and "Oh," I said to myself, "if only that sword was in my hand, that I laid aside at the threshold of the Curia!"[59]

Varro speaks in defense of modern criticism, and carries the day: a senatorial decree is drawn up, condoning the work of the correctors, though with considerable reservations. It is an ambiguous victory; modern editors are not praised so much as tolerated.

The *Satyra* appears near the end of the first volume of Lipsius's collected works, after nearly one thousand pages of corrections to the texts of ancient literature. Although it presents itself as a Menippean Satire, the fact that the satire is cast in the form of a dream makes it hard not to see in this work an echo or an answer to the dream of Scipio at the end of Cicero's *De re publica*: Lipsius's emendations are themselves contributions, as it were, to the substance of the republic of letters, and in the ordering of the collected works his dream becomes the concluding vision of the rules and value of citizenship therein.[60] Compared to Scipio's optimistic vision of the fate of the Roman patriot, the civic fate of the corrector is set in considerably darker shades.

The anxiety has not lessened with the passage of time. Paul Maas asks, "What degree of certainty can we hope to attain in the *examinatio*, particularly in conjecture?" His answer is generally pessimistic:

59. "Visus mihi aperte signateque oculos conjicere ad subsellia nostra. *Mihi frigidus horror / Membra quatit, gelidusque coit formidine sanguis*: et trepide ad Duzam, tange me frater, inquam, frigidior nive Gallica sum. Periimus, in Cyclopis antrum devenimus, quae Pallas eripiet nos e media morte? Nihil ad eas voces Duza; sed et ipse sedebat anxius, capite demisso. . . . Itaque ego iam lictorem exspectabam qui nos duceret, et o saltem (aiebam mecum) gladius ille ad manum fuisset, quem ad limen Curiae posui!" (Lipsius 1675, 982).

60. On the role of textual criticism in the republic of letters, see chapter 4.

> The surprises sprung on us by almost every papyrus find, and still more the radical discrepancies in the standard editions where the tradition itself remains unchanged, do not indicate that examination has brought the texts in general to a very high degree of certainty. All too often, even in the most widely read classical texts, the best-qualified critics had overlooked a corruption, wrongly cast suspicion on a sound tradition, treated a wrong conjecture as a certain restoration of the original, or rejected a correct emendation. The question is whether these mistakes are due merely to insufficient concentration on the individual case (which might be excused in view of the vast extent of the material) or whether we are faced with faults in *method.* My general impression is that on the one hand too many conjectures have been accepted of a kind which assumes a violent (that is, really irredeemable) mutilation of the text, while on the other hand scholars have been too ready to overlook corruption in the tradition or the vulgate text simply because no convincing solution has yet been offered. Both these faults spring from a reprehensible fear of admitting that he has not reached an entirely satisfying solution; for to present what is doubtful as certain is to remain farther from the goal than if one were to confess one's doubt. Admittedly the former procedure takes fewer words, but this is a misleading brevity; it easily tempts others to assert the opposite with equal brevity, and only a third mode of presentation will do justice to the true position (i.e. that the case is doubtful). Of course this is true of all fields of research, and an over-conscientious weighing of probabilities is liable eventually to stifle the germ of progress. But texts are the foundation of all philological investigation and should be so treated that the least possible doubt prevails as to how far they are reliable.[61]

The anxiety of Lipsius and Maas arises from their awareness of the probabilistic status of the critical conjecture. Since a conjecture can only be probable, some other guess might be correct: indeed, the mere probability of a conjecture almost seems to invite other solutions. The result is variant versions of a classical text. These variations might seem scandalous to an observer of a more positivistic bent; the history of criticism has been marked by the kinds of false starts, vacillations, and absence of unanimity that according to Kant characterized courses of study not yet firmly grounded as science.[62]

But the probabilistic nature of critical conjecture has provided the methodological basis for a new kind of text-critical systematicity. This

61. Maas 1958, 16–17.

62. "If after many preliminaries and preparations are made, a science gets stuck as soon as it approaches its end, or if in order to reach this end it must often go back and set out on a new path; or likewise if it proves impossible for the different co-workers to achieve unanimity as to the way in which they should persue their common aim; then we may be sure that such a study is merely groping about, that it is still far from having entered upon the secure course of a science" (Kant 1998 B vii [106]).

represents the last significant approach to the play and provides the groundwork for my study. I refer to the approach represented in the Oxford text of James Diggle, which covers ground cleared in 1934 by Denys Page and gestured toward in Maas's endorsement of an explicit language of uncertainty in the passage cited above.[63] We may not be certain about a text's original form, says Maas, but we should be certain about our *uncertainty*.

Diggle believes that the play was not finished by Euripides, and the text that came down to us was incrementally altered by many hands. But the genuine and the interpolated lines are tangled in a knot that cannot be untied.[64] Responding to this complex situation, he nuances his text with a fourfold system of sigla designating the probability that each line was written by Euripides. Passages he confidently attributes to later hands he marks with a black circle (●); those he attributes less confidently to later hands he marks with a circle with an "x" inside (⊗); those he attributes to Euripides but not confidently he marks with a circle with a single bar inside (⊖) and those he suspects to be Euripides he marks with an empty circle (○). To a reader who wants simply to work with *the* text of the *Iphigenia at Aulis*, these markers present a distressing problem: How is one to read a text that is now not just a theory of the original form of the text, but has a fourfold canon of probability woven into it, so that it represents the critic's own responses to the textual tradition? One seems no longer to be reading Euripides, but rather to be reading Diggle in dialogue with the textual tradition. I propose below that a text like this actually assists in achieving the proposed goal of this study, namely, a reading of *Iphigenias at Aulis* as singular plural, and getting the sense of the classical text. In the sense proposed by Kant (see chapter 3), Diggle's edition gives the *Iphigenia at Aulis* as a singular idea.

Diggle's work on the *Iphigenia at Aulis* is significantly foreshadowed by Denys Page's experiments with modalized judgments in *Actors' Interpolations in Greek Tragedy*.[65] For Page the "original text" of this play has

63. The procedure was also endorsed by Wilkins 1985.

64. Euripides 1994 (ed. Diggle), 1:iv.

65. Page 1934. An important (and particularly lucid) statement concerning the text-critical codification of probability is contained in Langland (Kane and Donaldson, eds.) 1988. "We do not know of any other method of classification which would answer as well as [recension] to the circumstances of manuscript transmission; nevertheless we must, before presenting our results, insist on its limitations. The first is human: because the method requires exercise of judgment at every stage...it implies successive possibilities of error. The second limitation is set by the almost always conflicting, often obscure quality of the evidence and the problem of interpretation by assessing relative probabilities that this poses" (19). What Kane and Donaldson describe as "total scepticism" (18) about their methods leads to an explicit canon of probability not at all unlike those of Page or Diggle.

lost its function as a first cause in the textual tradition, since it was left unfinished by the author at his death and finished by others:

> And then he died. His play was finished by a second hand, possibly that of his son, who produced it on the stage soon after 406 B.C. The task of the producer was this. He must add at least a few lines to the Parodos; introduce and write a messenger's speech, after v. 403; finish with more detail the reconciliation of the brothers, from v. 506 onwards; introduce and describe the arrival of Klutaimestra, Iphigeneia, and Orestes, after v. 589; finish the next scene, after v. 745; give Achilleus a reply to Klutaimestra, after 918, and round the scene off at the end...; give Achilleus a reply to Iphigeneia, from v. 1404, and send him off the stage; write a choral interlude after v. 1509, to allow a little time to pass; then append a conclusion to the whole play, either by bringing in a Messenger to narrate the scene at the altar, or merely by causing Artemis to appear *ex machina* and console Klutaimestra. He would be likely also to add and alter lines here and there throughout Euripides' manuscript, and to fill up a few smaller gaps.
>
> When I say that Euripides left a certain passage out and the producer had to supply it, I am ignoring an obvious possibility: perhaps the producer cut out a passage written by Euripides and inserted his own.... Or perhaps both methods were used: the producer had some gaps to fill, but he also cut some passages and inserted his own supplement.[66]

This narrative makes the origin into a complex dialogic space, a space already replete with a multiplicity of hands and possibilities. Further this deconstructed origin can not be spoken of simply as an unconditioned first cause of the ensuing tradition, since in Page's theory a continuing process of alteration and interpolation affects the text in ways not predictable from its beginning—the "actors' interpolations" of his title.

This history of the text's alterations in antiquity begins with the observation that the lines of Aelian cannot be Euripides.[67] The use of the future tense in the fragment implies that Artemis speaks before the messenger arrives on the scene; but then there is a question why Artemis needs to speak at all. Therefore Aelian's verses and the

"We have divided our conjectures into three groups, those in which we have as much confidence as editorial experience allows, those which we judge at least likely restorations of a corrupted original, and those where, while we have no doubt of the archetypal corruption, we cannot rate our emendation higher than as possibly original" (192).

66. Page 1934, 208–209.

67. "(*a*) there are only two parallels to *σήν* prospective at the end of an iambic in Eur., Alk658, Hik1010 (communicated to me by Mr. E. Harrison); in each of these two the sequent noun follows immediately at the beginning of the next verse; no word intervenes as here. There is no instance at all in the later plays like IA. (*b*) Future of *αὐχέω* is not found in fifth- or fourth-century Greek. (*c*) *φίλαις* is the adjective of a much inferior poet. (*d*) *Ἀχαιῶν χερσίν* is an inaccuracy better attributed to a careless writer" (Page 1934, 200).

messenger speech currently extant never shared space in the same text. Thus there were at least two endings in antiquity, which Page speculates were in circulation between 360 and 200 BCE. To this he adds an additional, earlier ending, on the basis of pictorial evidence. One tradition of vase representations of Iphigenia's death is consistent with our text up to 1532; a second tradition is consistent with what is now contained from there to the end of the text. There might therefore have been three endings, none by Euripides: (1) the text we have, based on the painting by Timanthes;[68] (2) the ending read by Aelian; (3) an old conclusion, inconsistent with that of Aelian, which was replaced by the extant text. Aristophanes of Byzantium knew Aelian's ending and the ending that is now extant and may have transcribed both, allowing later booksellers to choose which they preferred. Didymus had the choice of both and chose the one that was to become our text. The other ending became recondite, then disappeared.[69]

We thus have a proliferation of possible endings in antiquity, between two of which it seems copyists and booksellers were able to choose. Page describes a similar situation for the play's opening. Euripides wrote the iambics, "a good early writer" wrote the anapests, and someone else combined them (badly) and wrote a few verses (verses 106–114) to join the iambics to the last half of the anapests (verses 139–140). Thus with the opening we have a multiplying of alternatives in antiquity; an original iambic prologue by Euripides is supplemented by a later anapestic dialogue. In contrast to the ending, where a choice was made of one version at the expense of another, here the solution to the problematic multiplicity of texts was to splice them together. Page describes the history of criticism in a manner that exactly mirrors the proliferation of variants in antiquity:

> Since the purpose of the investigation was to determine which verses Euripides wrote and which he did not write, there was great room for difference of opinion about the number and position of interpolations, and this rapidly became an infinite chaos of more or less widely divergent estimates. At last the problem was abandoned, not because it was solved, but because it seemed insoluble. And insoluble indeed it is, if its only end is unanimous consent about the number and position of interpolations. There will be general agreement that this or that passage is largely spurious; but whether these are wholly spurious, and whether other passages and lines are at all spurious, are questions which will never be answered unanimously. There

68. See chapter 1.
69. Page 1934, 200–204.

has been a curious reluctance to accept this—to distinguish between parts certainly interpolated and parts probably or possibly interpolated—and to acquiesce in the result.[70]

Just as antiquity saw a plurality of variant versions of the tragedy, so also has modern criticism produced a rich spectrum of conjectures.

Page adds a second echo between the ancient and the modern lives of the text. *Iphigenia at Aulis* began as a fragment (Euripides died without finishing it); it ends in Page's analysis as a fragment. He concludes his commentary by arguing that the extant ending of the play, in which he sees numerous unforgivable glitches and irregularities, is the result of an incompetent late scribe supplementing a mutilated manuscript. Page reconstructs that fragment (see chapter 4, fig. 3) and, as with the critical fragments of Hartung and Hermann, here the fragmentary text is an image of textual flux, a figure for the essential plurality of *Iphigenia at Aulis.* Fragment and plurality, here as elsewhere, come together in a close symbolic relationship.

In a discussion of Euripides' *Phoenissae,* Page endorses an explicit probabilism that is the precursor of Diggle's practice in the *Iphigenia at Aulis.* By acknowledging that conjectures are not certain, and by working within this acknowledgment, critics can escape from the old "chaos of more or less widely divergent solutions." The student of interpolations, he writes, develops with respect to certain passages an overwhelming *feeling,* despite or in addition to the reasoned arguments and visible facts:

> And this is because of the part played by his own judgment, his *Stilgefühl.* . . . "Est enim," as Kuiper once wrote, "est enim quaedam in nostra quoque doctrina αἴσθησις, quae aliam quidem via ingressa quam dialectica illa ars quae per argumenta disputando pergit, vix tamen minus certa ac probata dici potest. Siquis vir doctus, in poetis tragicis versatissimus, litterarum, artis rhythmicae peritissimus, poetae cuidam graeco opus quoddam sive deneget sive tribuat, ratio mihi videtur habenda eius iudicii, etiamsi alia argumenta, praeter ea quae ex "intimo illu sensu" petuntur, desint." [For there is a certain *aesthesis* in our discipline also, which, though having entered by a route different from that dialectical art that works out its disputes in argument, is nevertheless hardly less certain and can be spoken of with approval. If some learned man, very familiar with the tragic poets, very learned in letters and metrics, denies or attributes a work to some Greek poet, it seems to me we must consider his judgment seriously, even if all the other arguments, except those that pertain to "that inner sense"

70. Ibid., x.

> are absent.] Yet we must not exaggerate the importance of this αἴσθησις. It is rarely strong enough to justify immediate deletion. As a rule, the most it tells us is that we should suspect a passage. We must cherish a special category of Suspected Verses. We ought not to bracket verses, or to write about base and stupid interpolators, unless our αἴσθησις brings overwhelming conviction to us, and, I would say, to some others too. Meantime, ἦ φρονεῖν δεῖ ἔλασσον ἢ μεῖζον δύνασθαι. And this must be said not as being highly original, but to condemn a detestable habit that translates a hasty subjective feeling into an intuitive certainty, and mistakes possibility for truth.[71]

To this epistemology Page adds a methodology. He proposes that four categories be used in the analysis of a tragic text: (1) lines certainly interpolated, probably by actors; (2) lines more or less probably interpolated; (3) where the case for interpolation is not yet strong enough; (4) where interpolation is more or less certain, but not histrionic.[72]

The appearance of such an attempt to formalize the probability of critical conjecture may participate in a recuperation of rigor which had occurred in vastly different intellectual fields only shortly before. The late nineteenth century saw new developments in the mathematics of probability and in their philosophical interpretation.[73] For Henri Poincaré, empirical science required a calculus of probabilities, a formalization of "that obscure instinct, which we may call good sense, and to which we are wont to appeal to legitimize our conventions."[74] Every time, says Poincaré, a scientist reasons by induction, he requires the calculus of probabilities, and to condemn it "would be to condemn the whole of science."[75] This "good sense" with which scientists work when they proceed inductively may very well be the same as what Page calls αἴσθησις; its existence implies some mathematics of probabilities. Poincaré imagines a gambler who wants to make a bet in a game of dice. A mathematician could give the gambler advice, but this advice will not guarantee success. Poincaré calls the gambler's experience *subjective probability*. But someone watching the game and keeping track of it might later go back over all the rolls of the dice and discover that the outcomes were in conformity with the laws of probability. This Poincaré calls *objective probability*. Nothing can change the fact that the gambler is gambling, that his bet about where the dice may fall could be wrong (the role of the dice, after all, cannot abolish chance). The equivalent of a

71. Ibid., 59–60.
72. Ibid., 24–29.
73. See Cassirer 1956; Hacking 1975.
74. Poincaré 1913, 156–157.
75. Ibid., 157.

gambler's bet in textual criticism would be the risk a critic takes with a conjecture or an attribution that, in the light (for example) of unforeseen papyrological evidence, may turn out to be incorrect. Objectivity is only possible when someone else is playing and a scientist canonizes the results in mathematically expressible formulae. Page's division of interpolations according to probability represents just such a withdrawal from the game: in *Actors' Interpolations* it is not a question of betting against the chance that a conjecture might be incorrect, but of trying to formulate the conditions under which our conjectures take place. Textual criticism is no longer a practical art but a rigorous theoretical undertaking; its methods do not provide us with certainty about facts, only with outlines of the possibility of our being correct.[76]

It is worth asking at this point whether the abhorrence of the category of the "suspected verse" in the critics Page attacks, and the tendency to cherish subjective feeling, which led to massive disagreement among those competent to judge, was not in fact the primary engine of the history of difference and disagreement Page summarizes in his introduction. Does the contrary tendency—an emphasis and a full awareness of the mere possibility of our conjectures and our suspicions—lead to an end of history, so to speak? Does the condition of the gambler emblematize the condition of the subject in history, who is going to win or lose again next time, while the condition of the probabilist carefully recording the results of each game and exploring their conformity to the laws of probability represents that of someone who has somehow stepped outside of the vicissitudes of history? The answer to this must be both yes and no. Insofar as history is only chronological progression, in which there will be more rolls of the dice, there is no way in which any text could escape it. But to the degree that we are both subject to history and its active producers, perhaps the canonization of textual probability pioneered by Page represents an opportunity to end. How we see something affects how it is, especially in matters of human creation. When we see the text as essentially plural, our subjection to its history changes. At this point the tables may be reversed: we see the history of the text as *subject to us*.

Diggle's *Iphigenia at Aulis* executes systematically what is prepared for in the arguments of Page. Faced with the difficulties of a posthumous text, Diggle chooses to make a record of his struggles with it, placing

76. It may be coincidence that for Poincaré one of the things that makes the theory of probabilities necessary is "the problem of interpolation, in which, knowing a certain number of values of a function, we seek to define the intermediate values" (ibid., 157).

to the left of the column of text a new apparatus of markers designed to indicate his judgment concerning the attribution of individual passages. The language he uses in the preface to the edition to describe this new apparatus is important. His four circles mean, in turn, *fidenter* (○), *minus fidenter* (⊖), *omnem citra fidentiam* (⊗), and *suspicor* (●) ("faithfully" [attributed to Euripides], "less faithfully," "without any faith," and "I suspect") (fig. 4): not the language of certainty, but the language of probability. A second explanation of the new textual operators appears at the beginning of the play: here he explains his black circles to be *non Euripidei* (not Euripides'), with no sign of hesitancy. But remarkably he explains the clear circles as *fortasse Euripidei*, "perhaps Euripides.'" Trust in the legibility of any of the author's traces has evaporated; the only thing that is sure is the fact that the text has been interpolated. To this radical uncertainty about the form of the historically original text is linked a new form of rigorous certainty, defined not in terms of historical objects but in terms of the critic's own dialogue with the tradition, and expressed in terms of a fourfold canon of probability.

This represents the kind of revolution in method and perspective that Kant argued must happen in any field for it to become a firmly grounded science. Kant's proposal for the critical reform of metaphysics was to treat objects as informed—that is, actively determined—by thought, and not vice versa. According to Kant the revolutionary insight that grounded mathematics and natural science consisted in making thought consider its objects not as active stimuli of a passive representational capacity, but rather as representations whose content is actively determined by the intellect. The invention of mathematics is said by Kant to have been based not on the interpretation of already-existing geometric figures (stones in triangular shapes, for example), but rather on their construction according to principles known a priori. In this way mathematical objects were not conceived as "given" for analysis, but were instead constructed synthetically. Similarly the scientific revolution is said to have been brought about through an active approach that elicited a response from nature by invasive procedures of experimentation, changing nature to discover what it was. These reversals of perspective produced what Kant called "Copernican revolutions."[77] I claim that a similar revolution took place in Diggle's attempt to systematize not only the style and language of the *Iphigenia at Aulis*, but also the probability of his critical judgments: what we read in this case is not a theory of the

77. Kant 1998, B xvi–xviii (110–111).

Αγ.	πόλλ' ἀνδρὶ βαςιλεῖ καὶ ςτρατηλάτηι μέλει.		645
Ιφ.	παρ' ἐμοὶ γενοῦ νῦν, μὴ 'πὶ φροντίδας τρέπου.		
Αγ.	ἀλλ' εἰμὶ παρὰ coὶ νῦν ἅπας κοὐκ ἄλλοθι.		
Ιφ.	μέθες νυν ὀφρὺν ὄμμα τ' ἔκτεινον φίλον.		
Αγ.	ἰδού, γέγηθά c' ὡς γέγηθ' ὁρῶν, τέκνον.		
Ιφ.	κἄπειτα λείβεις δάκρυ' ἀπ' ὀμμάτων ςέθεν;		650
Αγ.	μακρὰ γὰρ ἡμῖν ἡ 'πιοῦς' ἀπουςία.	○	
Ιφ.	οὐκ οἶδ' ὅτι φήις, οὐκ οἶδα, φίλτατ' ἐμοὶ πάτερ.	●	652
	ποῦ τοὺς Φρύγας λέγουςιν ὠικίςθαι, πάτερ;	○	662
Αγ.	οὗ μήποτ' οἰκεῖν ὤφελ' ὁ Πριάμου Πάρις.		663
Ιφ.	μακρὰν ἀπαίρεις, ὦ πάτερ, λιπὼν ἐμέ.	○	664
Αγ.	ἐς ταὐτόν, ὦ θύγατερ, ἥξεις ςῶι πατρί.	●	665
	ςυνετὰ λέγουςα μᾶλλον εἰς οἶκτόν μ' ἄγεις.	○	653
Ιφ.	ἀςύνετά νυν ἐροῦμεν, εἰ cέ γ' εὐφρανῶ.		
Αγ.	παπαῖ· τὸ ςιγᾶν οὐ ςθένω, cὲ δ' ἤινεςα.		655
Ιφ.	μέν', ὦ πάτερ, κατ' οἶκον ἐπὶ τέκνοις ςέθεν.		
Αγ.	θέλω γε, τὸ †θέλειν† δ' οὐκ ἔχων ἀλγύνομαι.		
Ιφ.	ὄλοιντο λόγχαι καὶ τὰ Μενέλεω κακά.		
Αγ.	ἄλλους ὀλεῖ πρόςθ' ἁμὲ διολέςαντ' ἔχει.		
Ιφ.	ὡς πολὺν ἀπῆςθα χρόνον ἐν Αὐλίδος μυχοῖς.		660
Αγ.	καὶ νῦν γέ μ' ἴςχει δή τι μὴ ςτέλλειν ςτρατόν.		661
Ιφ.	φεῦ·		
	εἴθ' ἦν καλόν †μοι ςοί τ' ἄγειν ςύμπλουν ἐμέ†.		666
Αγ.	ἔτ' ἔςτι καὶ ςοὶ πλοῦς, ἵνα †μνήςηι† πατρός.		
Ιφ.	ςὺν μητρὶ πλεύςας' ἢ μόνη πορεύςομαι;		
Αγ.	μόνη, μονωθεῖς' ἀπὸ πατρὸς καὶ μητέρος.		
Ιφ.	οὔ πού μ' ἐς ἄλλα δώματ' οἰκίζεις, πάτερ;		670

645 ςτρατηλάτη P^2: -τει L   646 μὴ Barnes: καὶ μὴ L   647 εἰμί P^2: εἶμι L   649 γέγηθά c' ὡς γέγηθ' Musgrave: γέγηθ' ἕως γέγηθά c' L   662–5 post 652 trai. Jackson, deletis 652 et 665   662 ὠικίςθαι Porson: ᾠκῆςθαι L   664 ἀπαρεῖς Wecklein   665 ἥξεις Jackson, praeeunte Bothe (1825): ἥκεις L   653 εἰς οἶκτον μ' Tr^2: μ' εἰς οἶ- ⟨L⟩P   657 τελεῖν Markland, μένειν Diggle (praeeunte England)   659 πρόςθ' ἁμὲ Porson: -θ' ἅ με L: -θεν ἅ με Tr^2 661 γέ μ' Aldina: γ' ἔμ' L   666 ςε κἀμέ ςοι ςύμπλουν ἄγειν Hermann, ςοι κἄμ' ἄγειν ςύμπλουν ὁμοῦ Diggle   667 ἔτ' ἔςτι Porson: αἰτεῖς τί; L   ἵν' οὐ μνήςηι Musgrave, ἵν' ἀμνηςτῆις Diggle   670 ἐς Tr$^{2/3}$: εἰς ⟨L⟩P   οἰκιεῖς Wecklein

384

Αγ.	ἐατέ· οὐ χρὴ τοιάδ' εἰδέναι κόρας.		
Ιφ.	ςπεῦδ' ἐκ Φρυγῶν μοι, θέμενος εὖ τἀκεῖ, πάτερ.		
Αγ.	θῦςαί με θυςίαν πρῶτα δεῖ τιν' ἐνθάδε.	○	
Ιφ.	ἀλλὰ ξὺν ἱεροῖς χρὴ τό γ' εὐςεβὲς ςκοπεῖν.	⊖	
Αγ.	εἴςηι ςύ· χερνίβων γὰρ ἑςτήξεις πέλας.	⊖	675
Ιφ.	ςτήςομεν ἄρ' ἀμφὶ βωμόν, ὦ πάτερ, χορούς;	○	
Αγ.	ζηλῶ ςὲ μᾶλλον ἢ 'μὲ τοῦ μηδὲν φρονεῖν.		
	χώρει δὲ μελάθρων ἐντός—ὀφθῆναι κόραις		
	πικρόν—φίλημα δοῦςα δεξιάν τέ μοι,		
	μέλλουςα δαρὸν πατρὸς ἀποικήςειν χρόνον.	○	680
	ὦ ςτέρνα καὶ παρῆιδες, ὦ ξανθαὶ κόμαι,	⊖	
	ὡς ἄχθος ἡμῖν ἐγένεθ' ἡ Φρυγῶν πόλις		
	Ἑλένη τε. παύω τοὺς λόγους· ταχεῖα γὰρ		
	νοτὶς διώκει μ' ὀμμάτων ψαύςαντά ςου.		
	ἴθ' ἐς μέλαθρα. ςὲ δὲ παραιτοῦμαι τάδε,		685
	Λήδας γένεθλον, εἰ κατωικτίςθην ἄγαν,		
	μέλλων Ἀχιλλεῖ θυγατέρ' ἐκδώςειν ἐμήν.		
	ἀποςτολαὶ γὰρ μακάριαι μέν, ἀλλ' ὅμως		
	δάκνουςι τοὺς τεκόντας, ὅταν ἄλλοις δόμοις		
	παῖδας παραδιδῶι πολλὰ μοχθήςας πατήρ.		690
Κλ.	οὐχ ὧδ' ἀςύνετός εἰμι, πείςεςθαι δέ με		
	καὐτὴν δόκει τάδ', ὥςτε μή ςε νουθετεῖν,		
	ὅταν ςὺν ὑμεναίοιςιν ἐξάγω κόρην·	⊖	
	ἀλλ' ὁ νόμος αὐτὰ τῶι χρόνωι ςυνιςχνανεῖ.	⊗	
	τοὔνομα μὲν οὖν παῖδ' οἶδ' ὅτωι κατήινεςας,	○	695
	γένους δὲ ποίου χὠπόθεν μαθεῖν θέλω.		
Αγ.	Αἴγινα θυγάτηρ ἐγένετ' Ἀςωποῦ πατρός.		
Κλ.	ταύτην δὲ θνητῶν ἢ θεῶν ἔζευξε τίς;		

671 ἐατέ' Stadtmüller: ἔα γε L   τοιάδ' Markland: τοι τάδ' L   674 si Euripideus, fort. corruptus   675 ἑςτήξεις Elmsley: -ξη L   677 ςὲ Matthiae: ςε L   ἢ 'μὲ P^2: ἤ με L   678–9 dist. England   679 τέ μοι Matthiae: τ' ἐμοί L   682 ὑμῖν Musgrave   684 διαίνει Herwerden   685 τόδε England   688 μακάριον Murray   691 δ' ἐμὲ Matthiae   694 ςυνιςχνανεῖ Musgrave: ςυνανίςχει L: ςυνιςχάνει P^2, -χανεῖ Heath   696 δ' ὁποίου Porson, sed uide IT 256–7, Ion 785–6   698 ἔζευξε τίς Lenting: -έ τις L

385

FIG. 4. Euripides 1994 (ed. Diggle), *Iphigenia at Aulis* vv. 645–696. Diggle's sigla of probability are placed to the right of the column of text. Reprinted by permission of Oxford University Press.

object "in itself," but rather a representation in which the object is shown conforming to the expectations and judgments of the critic. Just as in the revolutions described by Kant, the objects are made to conform to the thought of the inquirer, so here is the text made to represent and bear on its surface the judgment of the critic.

This has a paradoxical effect: on the one hand, explicitly using probabilistic sigla produces the impression that the critic is quarantining his judgment in the margins, downplaying his ability to reconstruct any original form. But at the same time, the ubiquitous presence of such signs infuses the text with a modality that redirects its signification. The text no longer presents itself as a continuation of the tradition; now it presents itself as a critical theater in which every line has undergone review, and even those lines that pass with a minimum of suspicion bear the mark of the process. There is in this procedure, in other words, both an admission of the weakness of text-critical judgment and a tangible record of its pervasive expansion throughout the entire fabric of the text.

Such a combination of restriction and expansion produces a textual practice of heightened rigor. A text produced in this way has the objectivity and the logical immaculateness of a conditional statement: "if I investigated the text to the best of my abilities, this would be the record of my investigations." But at the same time this rigorous self-critical practice produces a situation very much like that imagined by Kant for metaphysics after critical philosophy. A major result of the investigations of the first *Critique* is that it is no longer possible to *cognize* the unconditioned object (in the case of textual criticism, the "original work") in a systematic, theoretical fashion. It is possible to *think* it to ourselves, though when we think it in this manner we do not think it as some external conditioning thing (the "first cause" of the textual tradition). Rather we think it as the condition of our own representations, the cause not of the tradition but rather of our contemplation of the tradition. For textual criticism, this means that the "original form of the work" ceases to be a first cause and becomes a grounding condition of possibility for the representation of the text. After this change of perspective, textual criticism becomes a rigorous science *at the expense* of its archaeological or "reconstructive" function.

This position is neutral with regard to the actual existence of a Euripidean original. It may well have existed; it may even be ethically and practically expedient to hold that it must exist. But it cannot be *known*, only thought. The authoritative original takes on the status of concepts like God and Freedom in Kant's critical philosophy: though they cannot be cognized, they continue to haunt and to control thought as a whole. Thus a critic like Diggle may believe in the existence of the original text of the *Iphigenia at Aulis* (even in fragmentary, inchoate form) without arrogating to himself the ability to reconstruct it. It might also be possible for other critics to believe that they can grasp the original text scientifically. But this belief (under the terms of the Copernican revolution accomplished in Diggle's text), while it may have some practical expediency, has no theoretical basis.

If Diggle's is to be a rigorous presentation in a new mode, we must ask how and under what conditions this rigor presents itself. In other words if, as I have claimed, the innovation of Page and Diggle is to reconceive the classical text in terms of the conditions of possibility for our representation of the text, how are we, as readers of these texts, to conceive this reconception; how are we to read a text produced after such a reconception? If we are to take the new sigla in Diggle's *Iphigenia at Aulis* seriously, it becomes a pressing question how any reader is to respond to a text in which one line is given a value of *fidenter* (confidently), and another is given a different value, *minus fidenter* (less confidently), for example. Not only must one respond to each line in terms of its own particular probabilistic value, but one must also try to read the text as a whole. How can a single text contain parts that are of various degrees of actuality?

Diggle's text can be explained using Saul Kripke's possible-world semantics of modal notions.[78] According to Kripke, possibility is measured by quantifying over possible worlds. The possibility of a notion is its truth in at least one possible world. Thus, for example, the statement "Euripides spoke modern English," while false in this (the "actual") world, is possible if it could be true in some world other than this one. We accordingly say that "it is possible that Euripides spoke modern English" is true if the statement "Euripides spoke modern English" is true in some possible world. If, on the other hand, we believe that it is impossible that Euripides could have spoken English, then we would have to say that Euripides did not speak modern English in any possible world. We may speak, accordingly, of an increase in possibility as an increase in the number of possible worlds in which some statement is true: if it is true in none, it is impossible; if in all, necessary; if in x number of worlds, possible; if in $x+n$ number of worlds, more possible. By "true" here we can understand that the fact or event designated by a statement *occurs* or is the case. Thus we may say that a statement is

78. Kripke 1971.

possible if the fact or event it designates is the case or occurs in some number of possible worlds.[79]

Accordingly I interpret Diggle's sigla as a system of probability that says that certain lines may have been written by Euripides *in some number of possible worlds.* Each degree of probability may be interpreted as quantifiable over an increasing number of possible worlds. In other words we can unpack Diggle's sigla as follows, according to the semantics of modal logic:

(○) = "lines written by Euripides in x possible worlds"
(⊖) = "lines written by Euripides in y possible worlds"
(⊗) = "lines written by Euripides in n possible worlds"
(●) = "lines written by Euripides in m possible worlds"

where

$$x > y > n > m$$

To make rigorous sense of Diggle's probabilistic markers, in other words, we must imagine Euripides' *Iphigenia at Aulis* existing in different states in some number of possible worlds, some number of possible *Iphigenias at Aulis.* Each passage, according to its marker, has a "weight," that is, it can be imagined to have been in Euripides' text in some subset of possible worlds. Each passage, by virtue of its probabilistic value, is *implicitly plural.*

Diggle's text is not a stratified theory of interpolation: that is, its fourfold canon of probability does not designate four different hands at work in the text, and thus there is no reason to imagine that all lines of equal probability occur in the *same* possible worlds: indeed, verses 590–597 and verse 634, both weighted (⊗) ("*omnia citra fidenter*" or "*vix Euripidei*") might be completely incompatible with each other and thus might be said to coincide in *no single possible world,* though each occurs in n possible worlds, none of which overlap. We are thus dealing with a very large number of possible worlds in the semantics of Diggle's new probabilistic sigla. While it might be conceivable that the set of possible worlds over which Diggle's text quantifies could contain one or more of the historical versions that we have discussed, this is not by any means necessary: Diggle's probabilistic sigla do not refer to the history

79. For further discussion of possible worlds and modal semantics, see Plantinga 1974; Kripke 1980; Lewis 1986; Margolin 1990; Dolezel 1998.

of textual criticism any more than they refer to any stratification of interpolation in the textual tradition itself. As a whole this text is a text of texts, a text that takes the measure of a plethora of possible texts, a singular edition not of *the Iphigenia,* but of *Iphigenias.*

Diggle's appendix entitled "Who First Condemned Which Line First, and When" (*quem quis quando versum primus damnaverunt*)[80] condenses the history of textual criticism on the play into two and one-half pages, revealing in the process that all but 165 lines have been doubted by some critic since 1762. We can read this appendix as a kind of negative archive, an archive of erasures where *Iphigenia at Aulis* reveals its scars. It is a log of offense—not a list of those places where the tragedy is so offensive that an excision must be made, but a record of those who have taken offense and the occasions for their offense. But like the probabilistic operators, this historical condensation of criticism reveals nothing about the original form of the text, or about the history of critical editions. Critics are registered only when their excision is first: repetitions are not recorded, nor are the contours of each individual edition. Nor, indeed, do the 165 lines that have escaped the critical knife step forward as trustworthy: Diggle's text marks many of them with barred or crossed circles. Thus the appendix provides a historical vision of the text that is complementary to the probabilistic vision presented in the text itself: it contains and condenses within itself a very large number of extant editions. So Diggle's text contains one multiplicity of possible texts and a different multiplicity of historical texts.

Two axes of plurality are contained here. The probabilistic text collects within itself a full range of critical possibilities, possible variant versions according to the judgment of the critic. The historical appendix, in turn, condenses a full range of traditional variants, that is, according to the historical researches of the scholar. What is summed up in this text, in other words, are the twin axes of *codices et conjectura* upon which all textual criticism relies. Diggle's *Iphigenia at Aulis* is a complete systematization of the text-critical adventure.

An archive of erasure and a record of excisions that offers the body fragmented and cries out for a postmortem, Diggle's text is a call to scholarship, not to a text-critical philology, but to a philology of critical texts. Such a philology—call it radical—should be attentive to the rich plurality of textual versions possible and extant, not as a catalogue of hypotheses to be tested and rejected in the name of a new version, but as a plurality as such, a universe of human endeavor and creative

80. Euripides 1994 (ed. Diggle), 423–425.

work. Those philologists whom Diggle invites us to study are no longer individuals who failed to recover what was lost, chapters in a history of catastrophe, but rather voices in a polyphonic chorus. Diggle's text is the screen through which this chaos of attempts takes place as a symphony of multiple voices.

Afterword to Part 2

Diggle's text is singular plural.

> Events are produced in a Chaos, in a Chaotic multiplicity, but only under the condition that a sort of screen intervenes. Chaos does not exist; it is an abstraction because it is inseparable from a screen that makes something—something rather than nothing—emerge from it. Chaos would be a pure *Many*, a purely disjunctive diversity, while the something is a *One*, not a pregiven unity, but instead the indefinite article that designates a certain singularity. How can the many be the One? A great screen must be placed in between them. Like a formless elastic membrane, an electromagnetic field, or the receptacle of the *Timaeus*, the screen makes something issue from chaos, and *even if this something differs only slightly*.[1]

Singularity, referred to in this passage by Deleuze as the manner in which multiplicity is brought together without being reduced to a "pregiven unity," is of crucial importance in contemporary social and philosophical thought.[2] It can be usefully encapsulated with reference to Kant, for whom the primary examples of singularities are the ideas of space and time. These are described as pure intuitions according to which we coordinate and organize sensible objects. They exist prior to any spatial

1. Deleuze 1993, 76.
2. See Agamben 1993; Nancy 2000.

or temporal coordinate, and they govern the production of coordinates for sensible things.[3]

The singularity serves as a principle according to which the phenomenal manifold is representable. Within and according to it, the multiplicity of sensible intuitions, themselves inexhaustible, are organized into a cognizable whole. Note that the singularities space and time organize the manifold and not vice versa: they are not mental representations *abstracted* from sensible experience, nor actualities existent in independent realities, but the *form* of experience provided by the cognitive needs and capacities of the mind itself. Similarly Diggle's text organizes a textual multiplicity within its space. It does not represent an "original text" from which all variants are derived as imperfect copies or descendents, but rather serves as a singular container for a multiplicity of critical texts.

It is within a text such as Diggle's that the singular plurality of *Iphigenia at Aulis* becomes legible: that is, a text like this contains the multiplicity of *Iphigenias at Aulis* within a single presentation. And within this singularity the shattered state of the text can be redeemed. To bring the scattered remnants of history together into a plural singularity is to perform in the present a philological redemption, to bring about what Benjamin called a Messianic time: "The present, . . . as a model of Messianic time, comprises the entire history of mankind in an enormous abridgement."[4] This present, this enormous abridgment of history, is the singularity that constitutes another kind of origin, not one that is unique and unconditioned but origins that are plural and unending, an infinite dissemination of origins:

> Origin is an eddy in the stream of becoming, and in its current it swallows the material involved in the process of genesis. That which is original is never revealed in the naked and manifest existence of the factual; its rhythm is apparent only to a dual insight. On the one hand it needs to be recognized as a process of restoration and reestablishment, but, on the other hand, and precisely because of this, as something imperfect and incomplete. There takes place in every original phenomenon a determination of the form in which an idea will constantly confront the world, until it is revealed fulfilled, in the totality of its history. Origin is not, therefore, discovered by the examination of actual findings, but it is related to their pre-history and their afterhistory.[5]

3. "Conceptus Spatii est singularis repraesentatio omnia *in se* comprehendens, non *sub se* continens notio abstracta et communis" (Kant 1922, 15.B). See chapter 3.

4. Benjamin 1968, 263.

5. Ibid., 45–46, translation slightly modified.

Within the space of Diggle's edition, the intervention of the critic polarizes the text so that both its prehistory and its afterhistory become legible; but at the same time both prehistory and afterhistory are, as Benjamin would desire, blasted out of the continuum of chronological history.[6] Prehistory does not refer to the moment of inscription (genesis), since that is only indicated probabilistically, and posthistory does not mean merely the continued and continuing tradition of critical editions, but rather a crystalized field in which the entire tradition resonates with tensions and influences, a contracted time in which past and present coalesce into a constellation.[7]

That is to say, in fact, that Diggle's text does mark the closure of a certain historical period in textual criticism, though not its end. Textual criticism continues—Diggle's was not the last text, nor was it intended to be ("The historical evidence polarizes itself into fore- and after-history always anew, never in the same way. And it does so at a distance from its own existence, in the present instant itself").[8] But Diggle's text inaugurates a systematic procedure for the representation of classical texts which is lifted out of a merely chronological progression of variance. This could transform the text critical devil into an angel.

Within Diggle's singularity, an essential plurality of texts and possibilities takes place. In enacting the absence of origin (understood as a first cause), it discloses the plurality of multiple origins, the plurality of extant and possible texts each of which is its own originary moment. This plurality of origins is the "eddy in the stream of becoming" referred to by Benjamin; by being originary in this latter sense, Diggle's text becomes a meaningful text. But the meaning of his text only comes about through an emptying of meaning. There is no longer a unique, original text from which or with which any meaning or range of meanings could be identified. Rather there is a plurality of texts between which and in which meaning ceaselessly occurs; each text its own meaning, each text in meaning with the other texts. Polysemy is replaced with dissemination. Through Diggle, the multiplicity of texts announces itself to us, using the words, perhaps, of Jean-Luc Nancy: "We do not 'have' meaning anymore, because we ourselves are meaning—entirely, without reserve, infinitely, with no meaning other than 'us.'"[9] It is this call, the call of what Nancy would call the singular plural, that we must answer. We already know

6. The historical materialist "remains in control of his powers, man enough to blast open the continuum of history" (Benjamin 1968, 262).

7. Benjamin 1999, N 10a, 3.

8. Ibid., N 7a, 1.

9. Nancy 2000, 1.

how to answer it: by a return to what speaks through Diggle, to the texts, the plurality of *Iphigenias at Aulis.* Not by "a reading" of "the text"—that would be to present a unique origin, a first principle that would negate the meaning of Diggle's text. To "read" in this fashion would be to run our hands not over the concrete materiality of the texts, but rather over a thick mediating film that conceals them from us: not a return to the texts, but a return to a Greece unquestioned and unquestionable. A Greece without thought and an origin without meaning. According to Nancy, it is the one origin that is meaningless: "that relation in which one unique Origin would be related to everything else as having been originated would be a relation of saturated meaning: not really a relation, then, but a pure consistency; not really a meaning, but its sealing off, the *annulment* of meaning and the end of the origin."[10]

By contrast, philology must always comprise a due and sensitive attentiveness to the irregularities of being, to the cracks and fissures and flaws and glitches that make every object unique, every origin singular. Our hands and eyes were made for this work. Philology never cared for any "first" text, any "original" Athens, or any "original" Greece. Those are metaphysical, speculative notions not suited to the loving caretakers of the word. Philology cares for—can only care for, will always care for—the naked rubble of history, the grain of language, and the sharp edge of the concrete.

10. Ibid., 84.

Appendix

Because my argument depends to some degree on the observation that Kovacs's identification of a "public prophecy" theme is based on probable inference, I will pause here to discuss each of the instances of the "public prophecy motif." I take it that Kovacs's interpretation rests on probable inference and not intuitive certainty if another interpretation can be adduced that is as possible as his. It is important that I not be perceived as arguing that Kovacs is wrong: all that is needed from my perspective is that he is not necessarily right.

87–91

"Lines 87–91 clearly imply that *ἀπορίᾳ κεχρημένοις* refers to the Greek army as a whole: 'For with the army mustered and gathered together we sit at Aulis with unfavorable sailing weather. To us in our perplexity Calchas the prophet responded that we must sacrifice Iphigenia, my daughter, to Artemis who dwells in this region'. Likewise Agamemnon's public proclamation to disband the army implies, surely, that they can understand the reason he gives in 96" (Kovacs 2003, 78–79).

The assumption is that *κεχρημένοις* designates all the Greeks. But this *is* an *assumption*; and Willink 1971, 348 offers a third possibility (rejected by Kovacs, but without argument), that the prophecy could have been delivered to a council of generals separate from the host. This possibility alone indicates that Kovacs's inference from 87–91 is not certain. The Greek at 94–95 does not actually mean that the herald Talthybius *dismisses* the army, only that Agamemnon commands him to do so. Menelaus could have prevented the order from being fulfilled before the announcement was made (just as he intercepts Agamemnon's second letter to Argos), in which case there would be no reason for the army as a whole to know of the prophecy.

324

"In 324 Menelaus threatens to show Agamemnon's letter to *all* the Greeks, which would make sense only if they all knew Calchas's prophecy" (Kovacs 2003, 79).

But the revelation of the plot and the announcement of the letter could happen at the same time. The main point of Menelaus's denunciation, Agamemnon's failure to do his duty as generalissimo, would be the same.

538–540

"Agamemnon asks Menelaus to go round the whole army and make sure they do not reveal the truth prematurely to Clytemnestra. This implies that they can" (Kovacs 2003, 79).

The passage reads as follows (in Kovacs's text):

> ἕν μοι φύλαξόν, Μενέλεως, ἀνὰ στρατὸν
> ἐλθών, ὅπως ἂν μὴ Κλυταιμήστρα τάδε
> μάθῃ, πρὶν Ἅιδῃ παῖδ' ἐμὴν προσθῶ λαβών,
> ὡς ἐπ' ἐλαχίστοις δακρύοις πράσσω κακῶς.
> ὑμεῖς δὲ σιγήν, ὦ ξέναι, φυλάσσετε.

> Take care of this one thing, Menelaus: go through the army so that Clytemnestra does not learn these things until I take my daughter and send her to Hades. This way I will act badly with the least number of tears. And you, friends, guard silence.

The text does not explicitly have Agamemnon sending Menelaus to the army to silence them. Expressed is only the *result* of Menelaus's going to the army: that Clytemnestra will not hear of the plot, and that

Agamemnon can get through his heinous deed with a minimum of tears. The cause is not explicitly named, beyond the fact that it involves dismissing Menelaus. At least one other interpretation is likely: Agamemnon is sending Menelaus away because Menelaus has lost his resolve to kill Iphigenia (he has just been advising Agamemnon to call off the sacrifice, 473–537) and his mournful visage could give the plan away. The *result*, which is all that is expressed in the text, would be the same.

In fact, Kovacs brackets 473–537 (in which Menelaus decides to oppose the sacrifice) as spurious. But if, as Kovacs claims, it is the "private prophecy motif" that decisively reveals the interpolator's hand and serves as the basis for all of Kovacs's subsequent excisions, then it would be circular to excise a major portion of text to support the methodological basis of major excisions.

814–818

"In 814–818 Achilles reports the Myrmidons' complaint that the Atridae are slow to act. Since the winds are against them, it is clear that they are complaining of Agamemnon's slowness in carrying out Calchas's advice. Achilles, furthermore, nowhere implies that the coming sacrifice of Iphigenia is news to him" (Kovacs 2003, 79).

It could just as easily be supposed that the Myrmidons want *something* to be done. Hearing in 817 δρᾶ <δ'>, εἴ τι δράσεις (act, if you are going to act), a reference to the sacrifice of Iphigenia made vague because of Clytemnestra's presence, while possible, will not serve as evidence for any matter of fact. Achilles' failure to deny that he knew anything about the sacrifice has the strength of any *argumentum ex silentio.*

1259–1275, 1345–1357

"At 1259–1275 and 1345–1357 it is plain that the soldiers all know about the sacrifice, yet there has been no indication that anyone has revealed the truth to them subsequent to the beginning of the play."

That the Greeks now call for Iphigenia's death means only that they have been informed at some time: there is no evidence in the text *when* they were informed, but several possibilities are raised. At 524–525 it is suggested that they could be told by Odysseus, and at 518, that Calchas could do so. Kovacs would cut these passages, thus doing away with the strongest counterargument. See my remark on 538–540, above.

Works Cited

Ackermann, H. C., and J.-R. Gisler, eds. 1981. *Lexicon Iconographicum Mythologiae Classicae (LIMC)*. Zürich: Artemis.

Aelian (A. F. Scholfield, ed. and trans.). 1971. *On the Characteristics of Animals*. Cambridge: Harvard University Press.

Aeschylus (E. Fraenkel, ed.). 1950. *Agamemnon*. Oxford: Clarendon.

—— (D. L. Page and J. Denniston, eds.). 1957. *Agamemnon*. Oxford: Clarendon.

—— (D. L. Page, ed.). 1972. *Septem Quae Supersunt Tragoedias*. Oxford: Clarendon.

—— (S. Radt, ed.). 1985. *Tragicorum Graecorum Fragmenta Volume III*. Göttingen: Vandenhoeck & Ruprecht.

—— (M. L. West, ed.). 1990. *Tragoediae*. Stuttgart: Teubner.

Agamben, G. 1993. *The Coming Community*. Translated by M. Hardt. Minneapolis: University of Minnesota Press.

Arnauld, A., and P. Nicole. 1996. *Logic or the Art of Thinking*. Translated by J. V. Buroker. Cambridge: Cambridge University Press.

Asensi, M., and J. H. Miller. 1999. *J. Hillis Miller, or, Boustrophedonic Reading*. Stanford: Stanford University Press.

Bain, D. 1977. "The Prologues of Euripides' *Iphigenia in Aulis*." *Classical Quarterly* 27: 10–26.

Bang, J. P. 1867. *De auctore "Iphigeniae Aulidensis" disputatio*. Copenhagen: Bianci Luni.

Barkan, L. 1999. *Unearthing the Past: Archaeology and Aesthetics in the Making of Renaissance Culture*. New Haven: Yale University Press.

Barthes, R. 1975. *S/Z*. Translated by R. Miller. London: Jonathan Cape.

Barthes, R. 1982. "The Reality Effect." In *French Literary Theory Today*, edited by T. Todorov and translated by R. Carter, 11–17. Cambridge: Cambridge University Press.

Baumgarten, A. G. (H. R. Schweizer, ed.). 1983. *Theoretische Ästhetik.* Hamburg: F. Meiner.
Bayle, P. 1734–1738. *The Dictionary Historical and Critical of Mr. Peter Bayle.* 5 vols. London: J. J. and P. Knapton.
Bayle, P. 1740. *Dictionaire historique et critique.* Amsterdam: P. Brunel.
Benjamin, W. 1968. "Theses on the Philosophy of History." In *Illuminations,* edited by H. Arendt, 253–264. New York: Schocken.
——1998. *The Origin of German Tragic Drama.* Translated by J. Osborne. London: Verso.
——1999. *The Arcades Project.* Translated by K. McLaughlin. Cambridge: Harvard University Press.
Blomfield, J. 1814. "Animadversiones Quaedam in Euripidis *Supplices* et *Iphigenias*. . . ." *Museum Criticum* 2: 181–193.
Boeckh, A. 1808. *Graecae tragoediae principum, Aeschyli, Sophoclis, Euripidis, num ea, quae supersunt, et geniuna omnia sint, et forma primitiva servata, an eorum familiis aliquid debeat ex iis tribui.* Heidelberg: Mohrii and Zimmeri.
Boeckh, A. 1886. *Encyclopädie und Methodologie der philologischen Wissenschaften.* Edited by E. Bratuscheck. Leipzig: Teubner.
Boeckh, A. 1968. *On Interpretation & Criticism.* Translated by J. P. Pritchard. Norman: University of Oklahoma Press.
Bolgar, R. R. 1954. *The Classical Heritage and Its Beneficiaries.* Cambridge: Cambridge University Press.
Bollack, J. 1990. *L'"Oedipe Roi" de Sophocle: Le texte et ses interprétations.* 4 vols. Lille: Presses universitaires de Lille.
Bots, H., and F. Waquet. 1997. *La république des lettres.* Paris: De Boeckh.
Bremi, J. H. 1819. "Über zwei Ausgaben der *Iphigenia in Aulis,* den Anfang und das Ende dieses Dramas." *Beiträge aus der Schweiz* 1: 143–155, 211–243.
Brink, C. O. 1986. *English Classical Scholarship: Historical Reflections on Bentley, Porson, and Housman.* Oxford: Oxford University Press.
Callimachus (R. Bentley and A. Ernestus, eds.). 1761. *Fragmenta.* Leiden: Luchtmans.
Cassirer, E. 1956. *Determinism and Indeterminism in Modern Physics: Historical and Systematic Studies of the Problem of Causality.* Translated by O. T. Benfey. New Haven: Yale University Press.
Cerquiglini, B. 1999. *In Praise of the Variant: a Critical History of Philology.* Translated by B. Wing. Baltimore: Johns Hopkins University Press.
Chant, D. 1986. "Role Reversal and Its Function in the *Iphigenia at Aulis.*" *Ramus* 15: 83–92.
de Campos, A. 1970. "Pilot Plan for Concrete Poetry." In *Concrete Poetry: A World View,* edited by M. E. Scott, 71–72. Bloomington: Indiana University Press.
Deleuze, G. 1992. *Cinema 1: The Movement Image.* Translated by B. Habberjam. London: Athlone.
——1993. *The Fold: Leibniz and the Baroque.* Translated by T. Conley. Minneapolis: University of Minnesota Press.
——1994. *Difference and Repetition.* Translated by P. Patton. New York: Columbia University Press.
Deleuze, G., and F. Guattari. 1986. *Kafka: Toward a Minor Literature.* Translated by D. Polan. Minneapolis: University of Minnesota Press.
De Man, P. 1986. *The Resistance to Theory.* Minneapolis: University of Minnesota Press.

Derrida, J. 1976. *Of Grammatology*. Translated by G. Spivak. Baltimore: Johns Hopkins University Press.
——1977a. "Limited Inc. abc." *Glyph* 2: 162–254.
——1977b. "Limited, Inc." *Glyph* 2: Supplement.
——1978. *Writing and Difference*. Translated by A. Bass. Chicago: University of Chicago Press.
——1981. *Dissemination*. Translated by B. Johnson. Chicago: University of Chicago Press.
——1982. *Margins of Philosophy*. Translated by A. Bass. Chicago: University of Chicago Press.
——1994. *Specters of Marx: The State of the Debt, the Work of Mourning, and the New International*. Translated by P. Kamuf. New York: Routledge.
Diderot, D. 1994. *Selected Writings on Art and Literature*. Translated by G. Bremmer. London: Penguin.
Dolezel, L. 1998. *Heterocosmica: Fiction and Possible Worlds*. Baltimore: Johns Hopkins University Press.
Duclos, C. P. 1769. *Considérations sur les moeurs de ce siècle*. London: Dodsley.
Eichstaedt, H. K. A. 1793. *De dramate Graecorvm*. Leipzig: Muilleria.
Eisenstein, E. L. 1979. *The Printing Press as an Agent of Change: Communications and Cultural Transformations in Early Modern Europe*. Cambridge: Cambridge University Press.
——1993. *The Printing Revolution in Early Modern Europe*. Cambridge: Cambridge University Press.
Erasmus, D. 1906–1958. *Opus Epistolarum Desiderius Erasmi Roterdami*. Edited by P. S. Allen. Oxford: Oxford University Press.
——1969. "Euripidis *Iphigenia in Aulide*." In *Opera omnia Desiderii Erasmi Rotterdami*, edited by L. Waszinck. 193–359. Amsterdam: North-Holland.
Erasmus, D. 1975. *The Correspondance of Erasmus, Letters 142–279 (1501–1514)*. Translated by R. A. B. Mynors and D. F. S. Thomson. Toronto: University of Toronto Press.
Erp Taalman Kip, A. M. 1990. *Reader and Spectator: Problems in the Interpretation of Greek Tragedy*. Amsterdam: J. C. Gieben.
Euripides. 1503. *Tragoediae Septendecim*. Venice: Aldus Manutius.
——1550. *Tragoediae XVIII*. Translated by D. Camillus. Basil: Apiarius.
——1562. *Tragoediae quae hodie extant*. Translated by P. Melanchthon. Frankfurt: Lodovium Lucium.
——(W. Canter, ed. and trans.). 1602. *Tragoediae quae extant*. Geneva: P. Stephanus.
——(J. Barnes, ed. and trans.). 1694. *Euripidis Quae Extant Omnia*. Cambridge: John Hayes.
——(J. Markland, ed.). 1771. *"Iphigenia in Aulide" et "Iphigenia in Tauris."* London: Bower and Nichols.
——1783. *"Iphigenia in Aulide" et "Iphigenia in Tauris" editio altera*. London: Bower and Nichols.
——(R. Porson, ed.). 1802. *Hekabe*. Cambridge: J. Burges.
——(A. H. Matthiae, ed.). 1813–1837. *Tragoediae et Fragmenta*. 10 vols. Leipzig: I. A. G. Weigel.
——1821. *Opera Omnia*. Translated by S. Musgrave. Glasgow: A. and J. M. Duncan.
——(G. Hermann, ed.). 1831. *Tragoediae*. Leipzig: Weidmann.
——(J. A. Hartung, ed.). 1837. *Iphigenia in Aulide*. Erlangen: J. J. Palmii and E. Enkii.

—— (F. Vaterus, ed.). 1845. "*Iphigenia in Aulide,*" *ex recensione minoris Euripidis.* Moscow: Typis Universitatis Caesareae.
—— (J. A. Hartung, ed. and trans.). 1852. *Iphigenia in Aulis.* Leipzig: Englemann.
—— (J. H. Monk, ed.). 1857. *Fabulae Quatuor.* Cambridge: Deigton, Bell, et soc.
—— (H. Weil, ed.). 1868. *Sept tragédies.* Paris: Hachette.
—— (F. A. Paley, ed.). 1872. *Euripides.* London: Whittaker.
—— (E. B. England, ed.). 1891. *The "Iphigenia at Aulis."* London: Macmillan.
—— (N. Wecklein and N. Prinz, ed.). 1899. *Fabulae.* Leipzig: Teubner.
—— 1909. *Iphigenia at Aulis.* Translated by J. L. Lumley. London: Malone Society Reprints.
—— (G. Murray, ed.). 1913. *Fabulae.* Oxford: Oxford University Press.
—— (H. C. Günther, ed.). 1988. *Iphigenia Aulidensis.* Leipzig: Teubner.
—— (W. Stockert, ed.). 1992. *Iphigenie in Aulis.* Vienna: Österreichische Akademie der Wissenschaften.
—— (J. Diggle, ed.). 1994. *Fabulae.* 3 vols. Oxford: Clarendon.
—— (D. Kovacs, ed. and trans.). 2003. *Bacchae, Iphigenia at Aulis, Rhesus.* Cambridge: Harvard University Press.
Ferris, D. 2000. *Silent Urns: Romanticism, Hellenism, Modernity.* Stanford: Stanford University Press.
Finley, M. 1983. *Politics in the Ancient World.* Cambridge: Cambridge University Press.
Fish, S. E. 1980. *Is There a Text in This Class? The Authority of Interpretive Communities.* Cambridge: Harvard University Press.
Fletcher, J. 1999. "Exchanging Glances." *Helios* 26: 11–34.
Fontenelle, B. 1990. *Oeuvres complètes.* 9 vols. Paris: Fayard.
Forshall, J. 1839. *Description of the Greek Papyri in the British Museum.* London: British Museum.
Foucault, M. 1972. *Archaeology of Knowledge.* Translated by A. M. S. Smith. New York: Pantheon.
—— 1988. "On the Archaeology of the Sciences." In *Aesthetics, Method, and Epistemology,* edited by J. D. Faubion and translated by R. Hurley, 297–333. New York: The New Press.
Frank, P. 1998. *The Law of Causality and Its Limits.* Translated by R. S. Cohen and M. Neurath. Dordrecht: Kluwer.
Franklin, J. 2001. *The Science of Conjecture: Evidence and Probability before Pascal.* Baltimore: Johns Hopkins University Press.
Freud, S. 1958 (1914). "Remembering, Repeating, and Working Through." In *The Standard Edition of the Complete Psychological Works of Sigmund Freud,* translated by J. Strachey, 12: 145–156. London: Hogarth Press.
Gallo, I. 1986. *Greek and Latin Papyrology.* Translated by M. R. Falivene and J. R. March. London: Institute of Classical Studies.
Gasché, R. 1991. "Foreward: Ideality in Fragmentation." In *F. Schlegel: Philosophical Fragments,* translated by P. Firchow, vii–xxxii. Minneapolis: University of Minnesota Press.
Gentili, B. 1988. *Poetry and Its Public in Ancient Greece.* Baltimore: Johns Hopkins University Press.
Gibert, J. C. 1995. *Change of Mind in Greek Tragedy.* Göttingen: Vandenhoeck & Ruprecht.
Goldhill, S. 1986a. *Reading Greek Tragedy.* Cambridge: Cambridge University Press.

——1986b. "Rhetoric and Relevance: Interpolation at Euripides' *Electra* 367–400." *GRBS* 27: 157–171.
——1987. "The Great Dionysia and Civic Ideology." *Journal of Hellenic Studies* 107: 58–76.
——1999. "Literary History without Literature." *Sub-Stance* 88: 57–89.
——2000. "Civic Ideology and the Problem of Difference." *Journal of Hellenic Studies* 120: 34–56.
——2002. *Who Needs Greek? Contests in the Cultural History of Hellenism.* Cambridge: Cambridge University Press.
Goldstein, L. 1977. *Ruins and Empire: The Evolution of a Theme in Augustan and Romantic Literature.* Pittsburgh: University of Pittsburgh Press.
Gomringer, E. 1970. "From Lines to Constellations." In *Concrete Poetry: A World View,* edited by M. E. Scott, 67. Bloomington: Indiana University Press.
Goodman, N. 1976. *Languages of Art: An Approach to a Theory of Symbols.* Indianapolis: Hackett.
Grafton, A. 1983. *Joseph Scaliger: A Study in the History of Classical Scholarship.* Oxford: Clarendon Press.
——1991. *Defenders of the Text: The Traditions of Scholarship in an Age of Science, 1450–1800.* Cambridge: Harvard University Press.
Greg, W. W. 1927. *The Calculus of Variants: An Essay in Textual Criticism.* Oxford: Clarendon.
Grésillon, A. 1994. *Eléments de critique génétique: Lire les manuscrits modernes.* Paris: Presses universitaires de France.
Grigely, J. 1991. "The Textual Event." In *Devils and Angels: Textual Editing and Literary Theory,* edited by P. Cohen, 167–194. Charlottesville: University Press of Virginia.
Gruppe, O. F. 1834. *Ariadne.* Berlin: G. Reimer.
Gumbrecht, H. U. 1998. "Play Your Roles Tactfully! About the Pragmatics of Text-Editing, the Desire for Identification, and the Resistance to Theory," in *Editing Texts/Texte edieren,* edited by G. W. Most, 237–250. Göttingen: Vandenhoeck & Ruprecht.
——2003. *The Powers of Philology: Dynamics of Textual Scholarship.* Urbana: University of Illinois Press.
Hacking, I. 1975. *The Emergence of Probability.* Cambridge: Cambridge University Press.
Hartung, J. A. 1844. *Euripides restitutus sive scriptorum Euripidis ingeniique censura.* Hamburg: Freiderich Perthes.
Hay, L. 1988. "Does 'Text' Exist?" *Studies in Bibliography* 41: 64–76.
Hearne, T. 1698. *Ductor Historicus; or, A Short System of Universal History, and An Introduction to the Study of That Science.* London: Tim Childe.
Heath, B. 1762. *Notae sive lectiones ad tragicorum Graecorum veterum Aeschyli, Sophoclis, Euripidis, quae supersunt dramata deperditorumque reliquias.* Oxford: Clarendon.
Heidegger, M. 1996. *Hölderlin's Hymn "The Ister."* Translated by J. Davis. Bloomington: Indiana University Press.
——2000. *Introduction to Metaphysics.* Translated by G. Fried and R. Polt. New Haven: Yale University Press.
Hennig, H. 1870. *De "Iphigeniae Aulidensis" forma ac condicione.* Berlin: Weidmann.
Henry, A. C. 2000. "The Re-Mark-Able Rise of '...': Reading Ellipsis Marks in Literary Texts." In *Ma(r)king the Text: The Presentation of Meaning on the Literary Page,* edited by J. Bray, M. Handley, and A. C. Henry, 120–143. Burlington: Ashgate.

Hermann, G. 1816. *Elementa doctrinae metricae.* Leipzig: Fleischer.

——1877. "De interpolationibus Euripideae *Iphigeniae in Aulide* dissertatio (1847–1848)." In *Opuscula,* edited by T. Fritzsche, 218–242. Leipzig: Fleischer.

Heumann, C. A. 1718. *Conspectus reipublicae literariae sive via Ad historiam literariam iuventuti studiosae.* Hanover: Foerster.

Hobbes, T. 1840. "Tripos: in Three Discourses." In *The English Works of Thomas Hobbes,* edited by W. Molesworth, 1–278. London: John Bohm.

Hodgson-Wright, S. 1998. "Jane Lumley's *Iphigenia at Aulis*: *Multum in parvo*; or, Less Is More." In *Readings in Renaissance Women's Drama: Criticism, History and Performance 1594–1998,* edited by M. Wynne-Davies, 129–141. London: Routledge.

Horace (R. Bentley, ed.). 1711. *Q. Horatius Flaccus.* Cambridge: Cambridge University Press.

——1725. *The "Odes", "Epodes", and "Carmen Seculare" of Horace, in Latin and English: With a translation of Dr. Bentley's notes, to which are added notes upon notes, in 24 parts complete.* London: Bernard Lintott.

Horstmann, A. E. A. 1992. *Antike Theoria und moderne Wissenshaft: August Boeckhs Konzeption der Philologie.* Frankfurt am Main: Peter Lang.

Housman, A. E. 1972. "The Application of Thought to Textual Criticism." In *The Classical Papers of A. E. Housman,* edited by J. Diggle and F. R. D. Goodyear, 1058–1069. Cambridge: Cambridge University Press.

Hummel, P. 1999. *L'Épithète pindarique: Étude historique et philologique.* Bern: Peter Lang.

——2000. *Histoire de l'histoire de la philologie: Étude d'un genre épistémologique et bibliographique.* Geneva: Droz.

Hurlebusch, K. 2000. "Understanding the Author's Compositional Method: Prolegomenon to a Hermeneutics of Genetic Writing." *Text* 13: 55–101.

Irailh, A. S. 1761. *Querelles littéraires; Ou, mémoires pour servir à l'histoire de révolutions de la république des lettres, depuis Homère jusqu'à nos jours.* Paris: Durand.

Iser, W. 1978. *The Act of Reading: A Theory of Aesthetic Response.* Baltimore: Johns Hopkins University Press.

——1993. *The Fictive and the Imaginary: Charting Literary Anthropology.* Baltimore: Johns Hopkins University Press.

Janowitz, A. 1990. *England's Ruins: Poetic Purpose and National Landscape.* Cambridge: Blackwell.

Jaumann, H. 2001. "*Respublica litteraria*/Republic of Letters. Concept and Perspectives of Research." In *Die europäische Gelehrtenrepublik im Zeitalter des Konfessionalismus/The European Republic of Letters in the Age of Confessionalism,* edited by H. Jaumann, 11–20. Wiesbaden: Harrassowitz.

Jauss, H. R. 1982. *Toward an Aesthetic of Reception.* Translated by T. Bahti. Minneapolis: University of Minnesota Press.

Kant, I. 1922. "*De mundi sensibilis atque intellibilis forma et principiis.*" In *Werke,* edited by E. Cassirer, 401–436. Berlin: Bruno Cassirer.

——1979. *The Conflict of the Faculties.* Translated by M. J. Gregor. New York: Abaris.

——1998. *Critique of Pure Reason.* Translated by P. Guyer and A. Wood. Cambridge: Cambridge University Press.

Kenney, E. J. 1974. *The Classical Text: Aspects of Editing in the Age of the Printed Book.* Berkeley: University of California Press.

Knowles, D. 1963. *Great Historical Enterprises.* London: Nelson.

Knox, B. M. W. 1966. "Second Thoughts in Greek Tragedy." *Greek, Roman, and Byzantine Studies* 7: 213–232.
——1972. "Euripides' *Iphigenia in Aulide* 1–163 (in that order)." *Yale Studies in Classical Philology* 22: 239–261.
Kovacs, D. 1986. "Castor in Euripides' *Electra* (*Electra* 307–313 and 1292–1307)." *Classical Quarterly* 35: 306–314.
——1987. "Treading the Circle Warily: Literary Criticism and the Text of Euripides." *Transactions of the American Philological Association* 117: 257–270.
——1990. "De Cephisophonte Verna, ut Perhibent, Euripidis." *Zeitschrift für Papyrologie and Epigraphik* 84: 15–18.
——2003. "Towards a Reconstruction of the *Iphigenia Aulidensis*." *Journal of Hellenic Studies* 123: 77–103.
Kripke, S. 1971. "Semantical Considerations on Modal Logic." In *Reference and Modality*, edited by L. Linsky, 62–72. Oxford: Oxford University Press.
Kripke, S. A. 1980. *Naming and Necessity*. Cambridge: Harvard University Press.
Lacoue-Labarthe, P., and J.-L. Nancy. 1988. *The Literary Absolute: The Theory of Literature in German Romanticism*. Translated by P. Bernard and C. Lester. Albany: SUNY Press.
Langland, E. (G. Kane and E. Talbot Donaldson, eds.). 1988. *Piers Plowman: The B Version*. Rev. ed. London: Athlone.
Laurence, S. E. 1988. "*Iphigenia at Aulis*: Characterization and Psychology in Euripides." *Ramus* 17: 91–109.
Lebrave, J.-L. 1986. "L'Écriture interrompue: Quelques problèmes théoriques." In *Le manuscript inachevé: Écriture, création, communication*, edited by L. Hay, 127–160. Paris: CNRS.
Le Clerc, J. 1778 (1712). *Ars critica*. 3 vols. Leiden: Luchtmans.
Leibniz, G. W. 1951. *The Monadology and Other Philosophical Writings*. Translated by R. Latta. London: Oxford University Press.
Levinson, M. 1986. *The Romantic Fragment Poem*. Chapel Hill: University of North Carolina Press.
Lewis, D. K. 1986. *On the Plurality of Worlds*. Oxford: B. Blackwell.
Lipsius, J. 1675. "Satyra Menippaea: Somnium; Lusus in nostri aevi criticos." In *Opera Omnia*, 975–990. Wesel: Andræam ab Hoogenhysen.
Lloyd-Jones, H. 1992. "Review of Jean Bollack, *L'Oedipe-Roi* de Sophocle (Lille: Presses universitaires de Lille, 1990)." *Classical Review* 42: 429–430.
Locke, J. 1975. *An Essay concerning Human Understanding*. Edited by P. H. Nidditch. Oxford: Oxford University Press.
Lushnig, C. A. E. 1988. *Tragic Aporia: A Study of Euripides' "Iphigenia at Aulis."* Berwick, Victoria: Aureal.
Maas, P. 1958. *Textual Criticism*. Translated by B. Flower. Oxford: Clarendon.
Mabillon, J. 1687. *Museum Italicum*. Paris: Edmund Martin, J. Boudot, Stephanum Martin.
——1704. *De re diplomatica*. Paris: C. Robustel.
MacIntyre, A. 1981. *After Virtue: A Study in Moral Theory*. Notre Dame: University of Notre Dame Press.
Maffei, S. 1727. *Istoria diplomatica*. Mantua: Alberto Tumermani.
——1749. *Museum Veronense*. Verona: Typis Seminarii.
——1977 (1732). *Verona illustrata*. Rome: Multigraphica.

Mallarmé, S. 1998. *Oeuvres complètes*. Edited by B. Marchal. Paris: Gallimard.
Manilius (A. E. Housman, ed.). 1937. *Astronomicon*. 2nd ed. Cambridge: Cambridge University Press.
Marchand, S. L. 1996. *Down from Olympus: Archaeology and Philhellenism in Germany, 1750–1970*. Princeton: Princeton University Press.
Margolin, U. 1990. "Individuals in Narrative Worlds: An Ontological Perspective." *Poetics Today* 11: 843–871.
Marino, A. 1990. "Literature and Ideology in the Republic of Letters." In *Aesthetics and the Literature of Ideas*, edited by F. Jost, 124–224. Newark: University of Delaware Press.
Marx, K. 1976. *Capital*. Translated by B. Fowler. 3 vols. London: Penguin.
——1993. *Grundrisse*. Translated by M. Nicolaus. London: Penguin.
McCaulay, R. 1953. *The Pleasure of Ruins*. London: Weidenfeld and Nicolson.
McFarland, T. 1981. *Romanticism and the Forms of Ruin: Wordsworth, Coleridge, and Modalities of Fragmentation*. Princeton: Princeton University Press.
McGann, J. 1983. *A Critique of Modern Textual Criticism*. Chicago: University of Chicago Press.
——1985. "The Monks and the Giants: Textual and Bibliographical Studies and the Interpretation of Literary Works." In *Textual Criticism and Literary Interpretation*, edited by J. McGann, 180–199. Chicago: University of Chicago Press.
McLaverty, J. 1991. "Issues of Identity and Utterance: An Intentionalist Response to 'Textual Instability.'" In *Devils and Angels: Textual Editing and Literary Theory*, edited by P. Cohen, 134–151. Charlottesville: University Press of Virginia.
McLuhan, M. 1962. *The Gutenberg Galaxy: The Making of Typographic Man*. Toronto: University of Toronto Press.
Momigliano, A. 1966. "Mabillon's Italian Disciples." In *Terzo contributo alla storia degli studi classici e del mondo antico*, 135–152. Rome: Edizioni di storia e letteratura.
Montfaucon, B. 1712. *The Travels of the Learned Father Montfaucon from Paris thro' Italy*. London: E. Curll, E. Sanger, R. Gosling, and W. Lewis.
——1721–1722. *Antiquity Explained and Represented in Sculpture*. Translated by D. Humphreys. London: Tonson and Watts.
——1970 (1708). *Palaeographia Graeca*. Farnborough: Gregg.
——n.d. 1702. *Diarium Italicum*. Rome: Bibliopola.
Morris, I. 2000. *Archaeology as Cultural History: Words and Things in Iron Age Greece*. Malden: Blackwell.
Mortier, R. 1974. *La poétique des ruines en France*. Geneva: Droz.
Musgrave, S. 1762. *Exercitationum in Euripidem*. Leiden: Dammeanus.
Nancy, J.-L. 1993. *The Experience of Freedom*. Translated by B. McDonald. Stanford: Stanford University Press.
——2000. *Being Singular Plural*. Translated by R. D. Richardson and A. E. O'Byrne. Stanford: Stanford University Press.
Nichols, F. M., ed. and trans. 1986. *The Marvels of Rome*. New York: Italica Press.
Nietzsche, F. 1974. *The Gay Science*. Translated by W. Kaufmann. New York: Vintage.
Nochlin, L. 2001. *The Body in Pieces: The Fragment as a Metaphor of Modernity*. New York: Thames and Hudson.
Page, D. 1934. *Actors' Interpolations in Greek Tragedy*. Oxford: Clarendon.
Pasquali, G. 1952. *Storia della tradizone e critica del testo*. Florence: Felice Le Monnier.
Patey, D. 1984. *Probability and Literary Form*. Cambridge: Cambridge University Press.

Pedrick, V., and N. S. Rabinowitz. 1986. "Introduction." *Arethusa* 19: 105–114.
Peyron, A., ed. 1827, 1829. *Papyri Graeci regii Taurinensis musei Aegypti.* Turin: Typograpia Regia.
Pfeiffer, R. 1968. *History of Classical Scholarship from the Beginnings to the End of the Hellenistic Age.* Oxford: Oxford University Press.
Plantinga, A. 1974. *The Nature of Necessity.* Oxford: Clarendon Press.
Poincaré, H. 1913. *The Foundations of Science.* Translated by G. B. Halsted. New York: The Science Press.
Porson, R. 1812. "Praelectio in Euripidem." In *Adversaria,* edited by J. H. Monk, 2–31. Cambridge: Joannes Smith.
Porter, J. I. 2000a. *Nietzsche and the Philology of the Future.* Stanford: Stanford University Press.
——2000b. "Review of Walter Ludwig, *Hellas in Deutschland* (Hamburg: Jungius-Geschellschaft der Wissenschaften, 1998)." *BMCR* 2000.09.05 (September 5). http://ccat.sas.upenn.edu/bmcr/2000/2000-09-05.html (accessed March 5, 2004).
——2003. "The Materiality of Classical Studies." *Parallax* 9(4): 64–74.
Prins, Y. 1999. *Victorian Sappho.* Princeton: Princeton University Press.
Purkiss, D. 1999. "Blood, Sacrifice, Marriage: Why Iphigenia and Miriam Have to Die." *Women's Writing* 6: 27–45.
Quentin, H. 1922. *Memoire sur l'établissement du texte de la Vulgate.* Paris: Gabalda.
——1926. *Essais de critique textuelle.* Paris: Picard.
Rabinowitz, P. 1986. "Shifting Stands, Shifting Standards. Reading, Interpretation and Literary Judgment." *Arethusa* 19: 115–134.
Rand, R. A., ed. 1992. *Logomachia: The Conflict of the Faculties.* Lincoln: University of Nebraska Press.
Readings, B. 1996. *The University in Ruins.* Cambridge: Harvard University Press.
Reneham, R. 1969. *Greek Textual Criticism: A Reader.* Cambridge: Harvard University Press.
Reuvens, C. J. C. 1830. *Lettres à M. Letronne sur les papyrus bilingues et grecs, et sur quelques autres monuments gréco-égyptiens du Musée d'antiquités de l'Université de Leide.* Leiden: Luchtmans.
Reynolds, L. D., and N. G. Wilson. 1991. *Scribes and Scholars: A Guide to the Transmission of Greek and Latin Literature.* Oxford: Clarendon Press.
Robortello, F. 1662. *De arte sive ratione corrigendi antiquorum libros disputatio.* Amsterdam: Pluymer.
Ronell, A. 2002. *Stupidity.* Urbana: University of Illinois Press.
Rorvik, D. M. 1971. *As Man Becomes Machine: The Evolution of the Cyborg.* New York: Doubleday.
Said, E. 1994. *Orientalism.* New York: Vintage.
Sandys, J. 1967. *History of Classical Scholarship.* New York: Hafner.
Sartre, J. P. 1947. *Théâtre I.* Paris: Gallimard.
Schelling, F. 1980. "Philosophical Letters on Dogmatism and Criticism." In *The Unconditional in Human Knowledge: Four Early Essays, 1794–1796.* Translated by F. Marti. Lewisburg: Bucknell University Press.
Schiller, F. 1967. *On the Aesthetic Education of Man.* Translated by E. M. Wilkinson and L. A. Willoughby. Oxford: Clarendon.
——1981. *On the Naïve and Sentimental in Literature.* Translated by H. Watanabe-O'Kelly. Manchester: Carcanet New Press.

Schlegel, F. 1991. *Philosophical Fragments.* Translated by P. Firchow. Minneapolis: University of Minnesota Press.

Schmidt, D. J. 2001. *On Germans and Other Greeks: Tragedy and Ethical Life.* Bloomington: Indiana University Press.

Schoppe, K. 1662a. *De arte critica.* Amsterdam: Pluymer.

—— 1662b. *Verisimilium libri quatuor.* Amsterdam: Pluymer.

Schottus, A. 1615. *Observationum humanarum lib. V.* Hanover: Wechelianis.

Schow, N., ed. 1788. *Charta papyracea Graece scripta musei Borgiani.* Rome: A. Fulgonium.

Seyhan, A. 1996. "Chaos and System in the Romantic Fragment." In *Beyond Representation: Philosophy and Poetic Imagination,* edited by R. Eldridge, 133–150. Cambridge: Cambridge University Press.

Shepard, W. 1930–1931. "Recent Theories of Textual Criticism." *Modern Philology* 28: 129–141.

Siegel, H. 1981. "Agamemnon in Euripides' *Iphigenia at Aulis.*" *Hermes* 109: 257–265.

Snell, B., ed. 1971. *Tragicorum Graecorum fragmenta.* Göttingen: Vandenhoeck & Ruprecht.

Stillinger, J. 1991. *Multiple Authorship and the Myth of Solitary Genius.* New York: Oxford University Press.

—— 1994. *Coleridge and Textual Instability: The Multiple Versions of the Major Poems.* New York: Oxford University Press.

—— 1999. *Reading "The Eve of St. Agnes:" The Multiples of Complex Literary Transaction.* New York: Oxford University Press.

Stinton, T. C. W. 1990. "Euripides and the Judgment of Paris." In *Collected Papers on Greek Tragedy,* 17–75. Oxford: Clarendon.

Stray, C. 1998. *Classics Transformed: Schools, Universities, and Society in England, 1830–1960.* Oxford: Clarendon.

Suidas (A. S. Adler, ed.). 1928. *Lexicon.* Leipzig: Teubner.

Šukys, J. 2004. "The Hypothetical Skeleton (A Letter to Tahar Djaout)." *Culture, Theory and Critique* 45: 63–76.

Swift, J. (A. J. Rivero, ed.). 2002. *Gulliver's Travels.* New York: Norton.

Szondi, P. 1986. *On Textual Understanding and Other Essays.* Translated by H. Mendelsohn. Minneapolis: University of Minnesota Press.

Taminiaux, J. 1993. *Poetics, Speculation, Judgment: The Shadow of the Work of Art from Kant to Phenomenology.* Translated by M. Gendre. Albany: SUNY Press.

Tanselle, G. T. 1990. *Textual Criticism and Scholarly Editing.* Charlottesville: University Press of Virginia.

Tarrant, R. J. 1991. "The Editing of Latin Literature." In *Scholarly Editing,* edited by D. Greetham, 96–148. New York: MLA.

Tuilier, A. 1968. *Recherches critiques sur la tradition du texte d' Euripide.* Paris: Klincksieck.

Turyn, A. 1957. *The Byzantine Manuscript Tradition of the Tragedies of Euripides.* Urbana: University of Illinois Press.

Valéry, P. 1972. *Collected Works of Paul Valéry.* 15 vols. Translated by M. Cowley and J. Lawler. Princeton: Princeton University Press.

Varia. 1567. *Tragoediae selectae Aeschyli, Sophoclis, Euripidis.* Geneva: Stephanus.

Verstraete, G. 1998. *Fragments of the Feminine Sublime in Friedrich Schlegel and James Joyce.* Albany: State University of New York Press.

Vitelli, G. 1877. *Intorno ad alcuni luoghi della "Ifigenia in Aulide" di Euripide.* Florence: Tipografia dei successori le Monnier.

Vretska, K. 1961. "Agamemnon in Euripides' *Iphigenia at Aulis.*" *Wiener Studien* 74: 18–39.

Walsh, G. 1974. "*Iphigenia at Aulis*: Third Stasimon." *Classical Philology* 69: 241–248.

Wellek, R., and A. Warren. 1954. *Theory of Literature.* London: Jonathan Cape.

West, M. L. 1973. *Textual Criticism and Editorial Technique Applicable to Greek and Latin Texts.* Stuttgart: Teubner.

—— 1981. "Tragica V." *Bulletin of the Institute of Classical Studies of the University of London* 28: 61–78.

Wharton, T. 1747. *The Pleasures of Melancholy.* London: Dodsley.

Wilamowitz-Moellendorff, U. 1907. *Einleitung in die griechische Tragödie.* Berlin: Weidmann.

—— 1982. *History of Classical Scholarship.* Translated by A. Harris. London: Duckworth.

Wilkins, J. 1985. "*Censura*: F. Jouan, ed. *Euripide t. VII: "Iphigénie à Aulis"* (Paris: Les belles lettres, 1983)." *Classical Review.* 35: 252–253.

Willink, C. W. 1971. "The Prologue of *Iphigenia at Aulis.*" *Classical Quarterly* 21: 342–364.

Winckelmann, J. J. 1872. *History of Ancient Art.* Translated by H. Lodge. Boston: Osgoode.

Wolf, F. A. 1795. *Prolegomena ad Homerum.* Hale de Saale: Orphanotrophei.

Wood, G. D. A. 2001. *The Shock of the Real: Romanticism and Visual Culture, 1760–1860.* New York: Palgrave.

Yeats, W. B. (A. Jeffares, ed.). 1989. *Yeats's Poems.* London: Macmillan.

Zeller, H. 1975. "A New Approach to the Critical Constitution of Literary Texts." *Studies in Bibliography* 28: 231–264.

—— 1995. "Record and Interpretation: Analysis and Documentation as Goal and Method of Editing." In *Contemporary German Editorial Theory,* edited by H. W. Gabler, 17–58. Ann Arbor: University of Michigan Press.

Zetzel, J. 1993. "Religion, Rhetoric, and Editorial Technique: Reconstructing the Classics." In *Palimpsest: Editorial Theory in the Humanities,* edited by G. Bornstein and R. G. Williams, 99–120. Ann Arbor: University of Michigan Press.

Zumthor, P. 1992. *Toward a Medieval Poetics.* Translated by P. Bennet. Minneapolis: University of Minnesota Press.

Zuntz, G. 1969. *An Inquiry into the Transmission of the Plays of Euripides.* Cambridge: Cambridge University Press.

Index